AUDITING THE MODERN HOSPITAL

B.J. Hall, CPA

Prentice-Hall, Inc., Englewood Cliffs, N.J.

Prentice-Hall International, Inc., *London*
Prentice-Hall of Australia, Pty. Ltd., *Sydney*
Prentice-Hall of Canada, Ltd., *Toronto*
Prentice-Hall of India Private Ltd., *New Delhi*
Prentice-Hall of Japan, Inc., *Tokyo*
Prentice-Hall of Southeast Asia Pte. Ltd., *Singapore*
Whitehall Books, Ltd., *Wellington, New Zealand*

"This publication is designed to provide accurate and authoritative information in regard to the subject matter covered. It is sold with the understanding that the publisher is not engaged in rendering legal, accounting, or other professional service. If legal advice or other expert assistance is required, the services of a competent professional person should be sought.

. . . From the Declaration of Principles jointly adopted by a Committee of the American Bar Association and a Committee of Publishers and Associations."

Library of Congress Cataloging in Publication Data

Hall, B. J.
Auditing the modern hospital.

Includes index.
1. Hospitals--Accounting. 2. Auditing.
3. Hospitals--Administration. I. Title.
HF5686.H7H27 657'.832 77-1762
ISBN 0-13-051672-4

Printed in the United States of America

To mother and daddy

About the Author

Mr. B.J. Hall is a certified public accountant and Fellow of the Hospital Financial Management Association. He began his accounting career with Ernst & Ernst in Louisville, Kentucky where he helped to develop an audit guide and internal control questionnaire used in performing Medicare audits.

In 1969 Mr. Hall left Ernst & Ernst to become the controller of St. Anthony Hospital in Louisville. There he installed that hospital's first budgeting system, computerized billing system, accounts receivable system, and property and general ledger systems with cost-finding capabilities. He also implemented the hospital's first cash flow statements and capital investment analysis. The cash generated exclusively from its operation financed the construction of the hospital's $2 million maintenance and power plant.

Mr. Hall was the first chairman of the Financial Steering Committee established by the Sisters of St. Francis Seraph of the Perpetual Adoration, Inc., and was chairman of the joint Kentucky Hospital Association and Kentucky Society of Certified Public Accountants Committee, which drafted the state's official comments on the A.I.C.P.A.'s Hospital Audit Guide.

Mr. Hall has been the financial management consultant to the Kentucky Hospital Association's committee investigating the financial problems of hospitals.

A graduate of Western Kentucky University, Mr. Hall has served as Vice President of the Kentucky Chapter of Hospital Financial Management. He has lectured to civic, educational and professional groups on the Economic Stabilization Program, maximizing third-party reimbursement, hospital management, accounts receivable management, cash management and employment opportunities in the health care field.

Mr. Hall is presently Assistant Administrator at Providence Hospital, a 360-bed "Friesen" concept institution in Cincinnati, Ohio. He is also a member of the American College of Hospital Administrators.

A Word from the Author

Hospitals did not occupy a prominent position in the public's eye prior to the 1960's, since, until then, the financing of a spell of illness was predominantly a private matter. The demand for reliable financial and statistical data was not present in most health care institutions. During the 1960's, with the advent of Medicare, demands were applied to hospitals for more accurate financial and statistical data. Demands reached new heights when, on August 15, 1971, wage and price controls went into effect.

Reacting to these stimuli, hospitals began implementing systems to gather data, contain cost, or increase revenue, without always giving proper consideration to internal control. Many times internal control was sacrificed because of a shortage of qualified personnel necessary to implement the desirable checks and balances.

Many hospital trustees then realized that a new approach was needed to safeguard the assets of the hospital. This new approach involved the employment of independent certified public accounting firms to render an opinion on the hospital's financial statements and to comment on the system of internal control.

The independent certified public accountant (CPA) is incidentally concerned with the detection and prevention of fraud, unless the statements are materially affected.

To further safeguard the hospital assets, hospital trustees and administrators are now seeking internal auditors who have the educational training in accounting (and, in many cases, certification) and a capacity for human understanding.

The hospital's internal auditor, a hospital employee, is primarily concerned with serving the needs of management. In performing his reviews to improve operations, he uses techniques that are more concerned with operating functions in lines of management responsibility.

The internal auditor will, necessarily, use some of the same methods and cover some of the same procedures as the independent CPA. Many of his tests will also be identical to those performed by the independent CPA.

It is recognized that the audit of hospitals presents unique problems in technique and the presentation of financial data. This uniqueness led to the issuing, in April 1972, by the American Institute of Certified Public Accountants (A.I.C.P.A.), of the "Hospital Audit Guide." The "Hospital Audit Guide," however, could not delve into sufficient detail to be a working manual for the independent and internal auditors.

The objective of this book is to go beyond the scope of the A.I.C.P.A.'s "Hospital Audit Guide" and present in a concise form questions that may be used to evaluate the adequacy of the internal control, related thoughts that will help you in developing recommendations for the management letter, and procedures particularly designed for use in auditing the records and controls of hospitals.

This book is not intended as a definitive discussion of the theory and practice of auditing. It is meant to be a working manual for the daily use of independent and internal auditors, that will facilitate the audit and help to avoid the omission of any essential auditing procedure.

It is assumed that the auditor is familiar with the following publications by the A.I.C.P.A.:

1) "Statement on Auditing Standards"
2) "Accounting Principles and Board Opinions"
3) "Hospital Audit Guide"
4) "Statements on Auditing Procedure"

Since these publications constitute the most authoritative guidelines available, reference will be made in the text to them.

Auditing is a practical function, and therefore the cost of an audit must be commensurate with its value to the hospital. It is a further objective of this book to outline efficient audit methods, suggest means of increasing the hospital's revenues, and offer some practical means of cost containment. Each chapter contains exhibits showing the type of information that should be included in the working papers. The internal auditor will also find useful the exhibits of the "model" employment application, conflict of interest statements, accurate method of computing the Medicare Contractual Allowance for interim financial statements, and other documents relating to the operations of the hospital.

Certainly no book can highlight all the potential for the commission of crimes in a business as well as provide procedures to reduce the likelihood of these commissions. This book will, however, help you identify those areas that need careful examination. Actual events that have taken place in hospitals will often be used as examples to point out weaknesses in internal control. Whenever an example has been given, a sample procedure, which will strengthen controls, will be included in the chapter. The procedure will indicate how the effect of the situation in the example can be minimized.

The last two chapters address the problems of control in the highly specialized areas of third-party reimbursement, cost finding, budgeting, and electronic data processing. These chapters contain detailed objective bases from which the auditor may develop the audit program for his employer or client. The included internal control questions, related thoughts for developing recommendations for improvement, and audit procedures will serve as invaluable aids in the audit of these specialized areas.

B.J. Hall

ACKNOWLEDGMENTS

I have been very fortunate in having the cooperation of many individuals in the development of this book, particularly that of Mr. Earl R. Gilreath, Administrator of Providence Hospital, for affording me the opportunity to make this contribution to my profession. In addition, special acknowledgment is given to Mr. David Willman, partner of Ernst & Ernst, for permitting the use of manuals, internal controls questionnaires, and other related material.

Although many persons have contributed material for the examples, procedures and internal control questionnaires, the author alone is responsible for the material presented.

Particular appreciation is expressed for the untiring efforts of Mrs. Jacqueline Davis, my secretary, in preparing this manuscript.

Table of Contents

AUDITING THE MODERN HOSPITAL

1

Starting the Audit of the Modern Hospital

KNOWING THE OBJECTIVES

Good auditing requires a clear understanding of the audit objectives. These objectives may be broad or narrow; i.e., a conventional opinion on the fair presentation of financial statements, or a specific, limited report on an engagement directed to a unique purpose. Next, the auditor must select the appropriate audit procedures to attain the objectives in the most efficient and effective manner. Finally, the audit procedures must be applied in compliance with generally accepted auditing standards.

The short form of the accountant's report recommended by the American Institute of Certified Public Accountants (A.I.C.P.A.) includes this sentence:

> Our examination was made in accordance with generally accepted auditing standards, and accordingly included such tests of the accounting records and such other auditing procedures as we considered necessary in the circumstances.

Throughout this book the words "examination" and "audit" will be used interchangeably as the context may dictate.

The short-term report refers to "auditing standards" and to "auditing procedures." These two terms cannot be used interchangeably, and the distinction between them is important.

The Institute Committee on Auditing Procedures explained the distinction in these words:

> Auditing standards may be said to be differentiated from auditing procedures in that the latter relate to acts to be performed, whereas the former deal with measures of the quality of the performance of those acts, and the objectives to be obtained in the employment of the procedures undertaken.[1]

1. Copyright 1972 by the American Institute of Certified Public Accountants, Inc.

The objective of the usual audit might be described, in very broad terms, as follows:

> To satisfy the auditor that the financial statements do or do not present fairly the financial position and results of operations in conforming with generally accepted accounting principles, applied or not applied on a consistent basis.

In addition to the objective that relates to the expression of an opinion on the financial statements, the following are important objectives for the internal auditors and should be considered secondary objectives for the independent auditor:

1) To detect defalcations and bookkeeping errors (see note below).
2) To determine opportunities for tax savings or maximization of third-party reimbursement, through application of the auditor's familiarity with laws and regulations to the conditions noted in the hospital's transactions during the audit.
3) To assist management in establishing effective, economical, recordkeeping procedures. These suggestions may result merely from conditions observed during the audit, or at other times the auditor may encounter situations where it will be helpful to suggest that management have further studies or surveys made by management services specialists.

NOTE: A.I.C.P.A. Statement on Auditing Standards #1, Section 110.05 states: "The responsibility of the independent auditor for failure to detect fraud (which differs as to clients and others) arises only when such failure clearly results from failure to comply with generally accepted auditing standards."

SATISFYING THE OBJECTIVES

In satisfying these objectives, the auditor must make five critical determinations, these generally being:

1) *Internal Control.* To what extent may the hospital's system of internal control and accounting procedures be relied upon in limiting audit procedures to testing as opposed to detail checking.
2) *Assets.* Are the assets in existence, or do they represent expenditures that will benefit future periods. Have the assets been properly stated, described, classified in the balance sheet, and are they free of any pledge or lien.
3) *Liabilities.* Are all significant liabilities stated, properly described, and classified in the balance sheet. Are reserves provided for unearned income and contingent liabilities properly disclosed.
4) *Income.* Has all income that should accrue to the hospital been recorded in proper amounts, properly described, and classified in the statement of revenue and expenses. The auditor must also determine that income has not been recorded in excess of amounts attributable to the period.
5) *Costs and Expenses.* Have all costs and expenses applicable to the period been recorded, properly described, and classified. Are significant costs and expenses applicable to future periods carried forward as inventory, prepaid expenses, deferred charges, or fixed assets.

The ideal audit will result in complete and perfect accomplishment of the auditor's objectives. If properly coordinated with the independent certified public accountants, it would result in a minimum fee being paid to these professionals for the rendering of their opinion, which can not be rendered by a corporate employee. Although the ideal is not often obtainable because of human imperfections and limitations of time and costs, planning for the audit should in every case include selections of the procedures that will most closely approach the ideal.

It must be remembered that every audit has an objective, and the auditor must not lose sight of the objective by becoming too engrossed in the procedures being followed to attain it.

This book is concerned primarily with auditing procedures and their application. It is assumed that the reader is familiar with the auditing standards. The audit program steps, checklists, internal control questionnaires, exhibits, etc., included in this text are not intended to be all inclusive, but rather are intended to provide the reader with a sample approach.

PLANNING THE PRE-AUDIT ACTIVITIES

The internal auditor should be responsible for the planning and performance of the majority of the departmental audits during the year, and therefore should be responsible for most of the pre-audit activities. All pre-audit activities should be coordinated with the independent certified public accountants. These pre-audit activities will consist of:

1) Development of the internal control questionnaire.
2) Development of the audit program.
3) Assignment of personnel.
4) Form and content of internal audit working papers to maximize effectiveness.

The internal auditor must develop and maintain a proper, professional rapport with the independent certified public accountants who will review all internal control questionnaires and audit programs, and who should initial their review and approval thereon.

The internal auditor should then strive toward developing procedure outlines and/or flow charts describing the procedures for every department or area audited. In those departments where procedural manuals have been developed by the department managers, the internal auditor should obtain copies of these manuals. Each time an examination is performed in a department, the procedures should be reviewed and updated where appropriate. An indication should be made in the working papers that the procedures have been reviewed and there has been no change in them, or that there have been changes which have been reflected in the procedural manuals.

DEVELOPING THE HOSPITAL AUDIT PROGRAM

The audit program is a written plan or outline of the various procedures to be followed in performing the audit. The exact form of the audit program is unimportant; however, the most efficient form will provide the following information:

1) Hospital name.
2) Period covered.
3) When and by whom the work was performed.
4) Estimated and actual hours required.
5) Working paper index.
6) When and by whom the work was reviewed.
7) Approval of executive responsible for engagement.

The purpose of the audit program is to insure that no essential audit procedure is omitted. The competent auditor will use the program as an outline and apply his knowledge and experience to see that no phase of his examination is omitted.

The design of the audit program should start, after discussion of the audit objectives, with the client hospital or Administration, depending upon your being an independent CPA or an internal auditor, respectively. While the purpose of the audit may not in any way change the basic auditing principles, the discussions will indicate certain phases that may require additional attention. Additional audit procedures will develop as you review the hospital's internal control.

Following is a basic format which may be useful in the development of an audit program.

AUDIT PROGRAM

(Each item must be completed. If not applicable, indicate by N/A. Be certain the audit program is approved by the executive responsible for the engagement.

HOSPITAL: ____________	OFFICIAL TO CONTACT: ____________
ADDRESS: ____________	TITLE: ____________
PERIOD COVERED: ____________	AUDITOR IN CHARGE: ____________
EXECUTIVE: ____________	REVIEWED BY: ____________

GENERAL

	WORK PERFORMED		HOURS	
	NAME/DATE	W/P Ref.	EST.	ACT.
1. Review minutes.				
2. Prepare internal control questionnaire.				

As a supplement to the audit program, a master time schedule should be prepared. A time schedule such as the following will prevent the overlooking of procedures that must be accomplished at a particular point in time.

MASTER TIME SCHEDULE

This schedule must be prepared for each audit prior to the start of the field work, and be approved by the executive responsible for the engagement.

HOSPITAL: ______________ AUDITOR IN CHARGE: ________________

PERIOD COVERED: ____________ EXECUTIVE: ___________________

AUDIT DATE (Balance Sheet Date): _________________________________

PRIOR TO AUDIT DATE

	Date Required	Date Completed	Estimated Hours	Actual Hours
1. Assignment letter (if required).				
2. Prepare internal control questionnaire.				
3. Arrange for accounts receivable confirmation request as of ________ .				
4. Review and approve client's instructions for physical count of inventory.				
5. Prepare audit program.				
6. Prepare bank confirmation request.				
7. Prepare accounts and notes payable requests.				
8. Prepare attorney and governmental confirmation request.				
9. Schedule preliminary work that can be scheduled prior to audit work. (List).				

AS OF AUDIT DATE

	Date Required	Date Completed	Estimated Hours	Actual Hours
1. Count cash.				
2. Count securities.				
3. Verify cutoff of cash receipts.				
4. Verify cutoff of cash disbursements.				
5. Verify cutoff of inventory issues.				
6. Verify cutoff of receiving.				
7. Observe inventory counts.				
8. Other special procedures. (List.)				

SUBSEQUENT TO AUDIT DATE

	Date Required	Date Completed	Estimated Hours	Actual Hours
1. Cash.				
2. Accounts receivable.				
a) confirmation follow-up.				
b) other.				

Additional audit procedures, which could be a part of each audit program, will be provided throughout the remaining chapters.

DEVELOPING AND USING AN INTERNAL CONTROL QUESTIONNAIRE

The second standard of field work states:

> There is to be a proper study and evaluation of the existing internal control as a basis for reliance thereon and for the determination of the resultant extent of the tests to which auditing procedures are to be restricted.[2]

This review can best be facilitated by using a questionnaire designed in the same form and content as the one presented here. The questionnaire used here provides for "Yes" or "No" answers to most questions. In subsequent chapters, the form of the questionnaire is not provided. In preparing for your audit you will want to use the applicable questions as well as develop other questions that will be unique to your setting.

Should your questionnaire format be like the one in this chapter, you would complete the questionnaire by placing a check mark in the appropriate column, or a reason for no answer; i.e., "Not applicable." In addition, provide space throughout the questionnaire for names of hospital personnel who perform various procedures. Also provide space for brief descriptions of individual controls.

Obtaining answers to questions on a questionnaire does not complete the review of internal control. The auditor must determine that the procedures indicated are actually practiced. Space therefore should be provided on the questionnaire to indicate those answers which are later substantiated through observation and/or tests. The audit working paper memoranda or analyses should generally provide evidence of those answers substantiated by tests.

The questions in this guide have been devised so that a "Yes" answer indicates a satisfactory control. In the case of "No" answers, the auditor should consider whether such answers ought to be amplified by supplemental statements. For example, a "No" answer might be coupled with a statement that the hospital's alternative procedure provides the same degree of control. In designing the questionnaire, space should be provided in the body or margin for such clarifying statements.

With the responsibilities of the internal auditor and independent certified public accountants properly defined beforehand, the audit work performed by both should be kept at a minimum. If working papers are properly documented so each will "stand on its own," the amount of fees paid to the independent certified public accountant will be further contained.

---

2. Copyright 1972 by the American Institute of Certified Public Accountants, Inc.

Questioning the General Accounting and Administrative Controls

	Answer Yes	Answer No	Answer Substantiated* During Audit: Observed	Answer Substantiated* During Audit: Test
Accounting–				
1) Is the general ledger posted . . .				
a) by a responsible person?	___	___	___	___
(Indicate who.)	___			
b) at least monthly?	___	___	___	___
c) from entries supported in books of original entry?	___	___	___	___
2) Are journal entries . . .				
a) approved by a responsible person?	___	___	___	___
b) standardized for recurring monthly entries?	___	___	___	___
c) satisfactorily explained and supported by underlying papers?	___	___	___	___
3) Is a chart of accounts used?	___	___	___	___
(Obtain copy and comment on adequacy.)	___			
4) Are accounting routines set forth in an accounting manual?	___	___	___	___
(Obtain copy and comment on adequacy.)	___			
5) Does the hospital have . . .				
a) a controller or equivalent?	___	___	___	___
b) an internal auditor?	___	___	___	___
6) If the hospital has an internal auditor, does he . . .				
a) write reports on results of examinations?	___	___	___	___
b) report to someone other than the chief accounting officer?	___	___	___	___
(Indicate who.)	___			
7) Is the accounting department separate from the . . .				
a) purchasing department?	___	___	___	___
b) cashiering department?	___	___	___	___
c) credit and collection department?	___	___	___	___
d) personnel department?	___	___	___	___

*Supported with proof or evidence.

	Answer Yes	Answer No	Answer Substantiated* During Audit: Observed	Answer Substantiated* During Audit: Test
8) Are employees who handle cash or other valuables . . .				
a) bonded?	___	___	______	______
b) required to take regular vacations?	___	___	______	______
9) Are periodic financial statements prepared?	___	___	______	______
(If yes, indicate frequency.)	____________________			
10) Does the hospital budget . . .				
a) revenues?	___	___	______	______
b) expenses?	___	___	______	______
c) cash receipts?	___	___	______	______
d) cash disbursements?	___	___	______	______
e) capital expenditures?	___	___	______	______
11) Are periodic budget-actual performance reports prepared?	___	___	______	______
(If yes, indicate frequency.)	____________________			
12) Are basic accounting records stored in a vault when not in use?	___	___	______	______
13) Are all bank accounts in the name of the hospital recorded on the books?	___	___	______	______
14) Is a calendar or follow-up file kept for due dates of tax returns, reimbursement reports, and deadlines for reimbursement program approvals and elections?	___	___	______	______
(If yes, indicate by whom.)	____________________			
Administrative–				
15) Is there an organization chart?	___	___	______	______
(Obtain a copy and comment on potential weaknesses.)	____________________			
	____________________			
	____________________			
16) Is the insurance protection reviewed . . .				
a) at least annually?	___	___	______	______
b) by a responsible person or committee	___	___	______	______
(Indicate who.)	____________________			
17) Does the insurance protection cover . . .				
a) current replacement cost of property?	___	___	______	______

*Supported with proof or evidence.

	Answer Yes	Answer No	Answer Substantiated* During Audit: Observed	Answer Substantiated* During Audit: Test
b) loss of accounts receivable records?				
c) inventory in storage areas and floor stock?				
18) Is there a long-range plan?				
a) If yes, does it delineate future health service programs?				
b) If yes, is it updated periodically?				
(If yes, indicate frequency.)				
19) Is the hospital . . .				
a) accredited by the Joint Commission on Accreditation of Hospitals?				
b) licensed by the state licensing authority?				
c) certified as participating in federal health programs?				
20) Are formal educational activities conducted?				
a) If yes, are they approved by licensing authorities?				
b) Describe programs and method of accounting for revenue and expense.				
21) Are research activities conducted?				
a) If yes, are they related to patient care?				
b) Describe method of accounting for expense.				
22) Is business transacted with any related organizations?				
(If yes, list organizations' names and business activities.)				
23) Are employees and Board of Trustee members prohibited from participating in enterprises doing business with the hospital?				
(If no, explain.)				

*Supported with proof or evidence.

	Answer Yes	Answer No	Answer Substantiated* During Audit: Observed	Answer Substantiated* During Audit: Test
24) a) List governing body members, office held, and primary employment or community responsibility:				

1) ______________ ______________
____
____
2) ______________ ______________
____
3) ______________ ______________
____
4) ______________ ______________
____
5) ______________ ______________
____
6) ______________ ______________
____
7) ______________ ______________
____
8) ______________ ______________
____
9) ______________ ______________
____
10) ______________ ______________
____
11) ______________ ______________
____
12) ______________ ______________
____
13) ______________ ______________
____
14) ______________ ______________
____

b) Designate Trustee committee assignments by line numbers in 24A:

Executive ______ Building & Grounds ______
Finance ______ Professional Affairs ______
Budget ______ Public Relations ______

*Supported with proof or evidence.

	Answer Yes	Answer No	Answer Substantiated* During Audit: Observed	Answer Substantiated* During Audit: Test
25) Are the following on file . . .				
a) Articles of Incorporation?	___	___	___	___
b) IRS Tax determination letters?	___	___	___	___
c) Provider Reimbursement agreements?	___	___	___	___

*Supported with proof or evidence.

PREPARING AUDIT WORKING PAPERS THAT "STAND ON THEIR OWN"

The third standard of field work states:

> Sufficient, competent, evidential matter is to be obtained through inspection, inquiries, and confirmations to afford a reasonable basis for an opinion regarding the financial statements under examination.[3]

The audit working papers must contain a complete record of the audit procedures followed in the performance of your examination. The working papers should be so clearly prepared that it would be possible, at any time, to determine from them the conditions found, the exact audit procedures employed, the data collected from analyses and from outside sources, and the conclusions reached. Primarily your working papers serve as the bases for your recommendations given to management, or the expression of an opinion if you are the independent certified public accountant. As such, they are subject to review, in some cases, years after your examination has been completed.

Mere copying of the general ledger accounts is not substantiation and in most cases should be avoided. The workpapers of preceding years should be challenged to see whether they may be prepared in an easier fashion or give more information. The auditor must be alert for changes in the hospital's procedures, organization, or other circumstances that may require substantial changes in the working papers from the preceding year. Following prior year working papers is no excuse for poor audit work.

For your benefit, you should take the time to write legibly and file all working papers in an orderly manner. This will facilitate their subsequent review and will indicate to outsiders the competence of the work.

Often the constraints of time lead to our taking shortcuts, usually in the form of failing to prepare proper headings on our working papers and to cross reference them. It is very important, however, to take time to prepare proper headings and cross-referencing. Why? Few things can be as embarrassing to an auditor as to have someone

3. Copyright 1972 by the American Institute of Certified Public Accountants, Inc.

review the working papers and not be able to locate all those relating to a particular audit procedure. This problem can be minimized through:

1) Using proper headings on working papers, showing the name of the hospital (using a rubber stamp for this saves time), the date of preparation, the initials or last name of the auditor, and the date of the balance sheet or period of time covered for the examination.
2) A descriptive title of the data contained in the working papers.
3) If the contents of the working paper have been reviewed or mathematically verified, a notation to that effect with the name or the initials of the individual performing this review and the date of such review.

If continuation sheets are used they should be appropriately identified, using the same headings as the first sheet of the working paper, and, in the lower right-hand column, the sheets should be numbered "1 of 2," "2 of 2," so that their order can be ascertained and the sheets bound in the proper order. In this way, if sheets become separated or misplaced the individuals performing a later review will know that there were additional audit steps performed, and perhaps can locate the missing working papers.

Standardize the type of key-in marks or symbols and indicate in the first part of your workpapers what these symbols mean. This will improve the efficiency of your audit since you will no longer waste time in recopying or making notations on working papers indicating that you have *computed* the amount of interest earned, *footed* the column of figures, etc.

Throughout this book the following standardized keys will be used, when applicable, on the exhibits of audit working papers:

F —Footed
C —Computed
CF—Crossfooted
T —Traced to general ledger
A —Agrees with supporting journal

Next, your working papers should contain memoranda of all important discussions with administrative personnel, department managers or other third parties, that relate to the various aspects of your examination.

Such memoranda should give the date of the conference, the persons present, a summary of the matters discussed, policies or changes in procedures that were agreed upon, and the conclusions reached.

Maintain copies of letters in which you have requested a third party to furnish certain information relating to the financial statements; i.e., confirmation of accounts receivable, confirmation of outstanding accounts payable, confirmation of the location and amount of assets in storage in areas outside the hospital. Generally the copy should be attached to the reply received and all information should be bound in the working paper folder under the heading of "Confirmations."

If you are preparing a trial balance or analysis that would extend for several sheets, each page should be footed and the page totals summarized on the last page of the related working papers.

Emphasis must always be placed on written comments to supplement the figures and analysis.

A summary of work performed, prepared in a neat and grammatically correct form, is a reflection of your professional abilities and should be prepared with great care. This summary should contain comments about the exact scope and extent of the clerical accuracy test applied to each category of the audit program. The memorandum must include a conclusion, in terms consistent with the audit objective, reached by the auditor.

TEN KEY ELEMENTS OF GOOD AUDIT WORKING PAPERS

In summary, audit working papers that can stand on their own possess the following elements:

1) Legibility and grammatical correctness.
2) Proper, complete headings showing the period of time covered for the examination, the date of preparation, identity of auditor, date of subsequent review, and identity of the person performing the review.
3) Proper cross-referencing.
4) Numbering of continuation sheets.
5) Standardized key-in marks or symbols.
6) Complete memoranda of all important discussions, including date of conference, persons present, topic, agreements reached, and conclusion.
7) Copies of all confirmations and indication of reply.
8) Page totals for analyses that extend for several pages and a summary of page totals on the last page.
9) Written comments to supplement the figures and analyses.
10) A written summary of audit work performed, indicating the exact scope and extent of the clerical accuracy test applied to each category of the audit program. The summary must include the conclusion reached by the auditor.

ARRANGEMENT OF THE WORKING PAPERS

Occasionally we may drop our professional guard and allow sloppiness to creep into our techniques. One area that may suffer first is the arrangement of the audit working papers. All working papers should be bound in folders and the contents of each folder noted on the cover or jacket.

Voluminous confirmations, statements and correspondence relating to receivables and payables need not be bound in the working papers, but should be retained for at least one year in a separate file. A summary of the work performed, appropriately cross referenced, and conclusions reached, should be included in the working paper folder.

Working papers should be bound in a folder and indexed in a logical order. For example:

a) Trial balance.
b) Adjustments.

c) Correspondence.
d) Pertinent memoranda relating to the audit.
e) Data relating to the review of internal control.
f) The audit program.
g) Assets and liabilities in balance sheet order.
h) Stockholder equity and excerpts of minutes.
i) Operations and tests of transactions.

With an understanding of our objectives, proper pre-audit arrangements, and an appreciation for the key elements of good audit working papers, let's consider the work to be performed within the hospital.

TOURING THE HOSPITAL—SELLING YOUR RESULTS

It is recommended that you tour the hospital from the basement to the penthouse before you begin the audit or series of departmental audits for the year. It doesn't matter how long you've been employed by the hospital, or how much you know about its operations. You'll see new things during this tour that will affect your audit.

Ask the department manager to conduct the tour of his areas of responsibility. Discard the cloak of secrecy and inform the manager of your purpose.

During your tour be alert for the following items and their effect upon your audit:

a) reallocation of space	– cost finding
b) remodeling of areas	– capitalization policy
c) new services	– third-party reimbursement
d) condition and adequacy of work areas	– need for long-range planning
e) addition of major items of equipment	– change in physicians' contracts
f) substantial changes in the contents of the bulkstores room	– goods on consignment
g) employee attitudes	– recommendations on improved security, policy, or management changes

As you make your observations, discuss them with the department manager. Keep him informed of your findings. Solicit his opinions. Make him a part of the "team." If, during your tour with him, you have stressed the advantages of a synergistic relationship, your recommendations for change will be better received. You will often find the managers extremely cooperative if they view you as an objective person who can get things accomplished through Administration.

If, however, during the tour you appear to be aloof and secretive, you will have a difficult time in making recommendations for change that will be received cooperatively. It can not be overemphasized that you should be extroverted, creative, and show a capacity for human understanding. These qualities, coupled with adaptability and understanding of hospital policies and procedures, will add to your value. Also remember that many good recommendations for your management letter can come from the departmental managers.

WRITING EFFECTIVE MANAGEMENT LETTERS

As an auditor you must negotiate the items included in your management letter. Before someone suggests that I have abdicated my professional responsibility, let's review the basis for this thought:

> Nothing could be simpler in definition or broader in scope than negotiation. Every desire that demands satisfaction—and every need that wants to be met—is at least potentially an occasion for people to initiate the negotiating process. Negotiation is an element of human behavior. Whenever people exchange ideas with the intention of changing relationships, whenever they confer for agreement, they are negotiating.[4]

Now review your job. Isn't it one of your specific responsibilities to recommend improvements in the hospital's system of internal control; i.e., change the existing relationships, or situation?

One of the attributes possessed by the successful auditor is diplomacy. This suggests the old adage that "the wheels of diplomacy often turn on the grease of ambiguity." The following of this adage leads to the writing of effective management letters.

Extreme care must be exercised in selecting the items upon which you will comment. Equally critical is the development of the wording in any particular item selected for comment. A good rule is to afford options for the hospital or department manager.

For example, if you discover inadequacies in the control and processing of charge tickets for patient services, avoid stating "Account for the numerical sequence of all charge tickets." Remember, unless you've done a complete system analysis, you have not had time to develop a way of accumulating and processing this information. A more diplomatic way of commenting upon this weakness would be to say ". . . accounting for the numerical sequence of charge tickets or otherwise controlling charge tickets." This, then, puts you in the position of negotiating with the department managers an acceptable method of strengthening this weakness.

Whenever possible, accent the positive and eliminate the negative in choosing your words for the management letter. Positive language emphasizes what can be done and leaves what cannot be done to implication.

> The disagreeable tone of "failed," "no," "can not" is negative and unpleasant. . . . However, if, the message to be conveyed is negative, it becomes more difficult to keep the tone positive. The use of limiting words such as "only" and the use of conditional words such as "if" and "would" can sometimes produce a positive effect from a negative situation.[5]

Much has been written on the subject of writing; however, if you are a positive person, writing positively will come naturally.

---

4. Reprinted by permission of Hawthorn Books, Inc., from *The Art of Negotiating*, Gerard I. Nierenberg. Copyright 1968 by Gerard I. Nierenberg.
5. *The Art of Writing Effective Letters*, Rosemary T. Fruchling and Sharon Bouchard. McGraw-Hill Company, 1972, page 44.

GUIDELINES FOR WRITING EFFECTIVE MANAGEMENT LETTERS

1) Keep a positive tone.
2) State briefly the present procedure.
3) State the deficiency in terms of the results obtained from the procedures presently followed.
4) Make a recommendation. The recommendation should be in general terms, as the department manager may find a more efficient method of performing the work.
5) Afford the department manager options.
6) With the department manager, review a draft of your management letter before submitting it to the Administration.
7) With the controller and administrator, review a draft of your management letter before submitting it to the Board of Trustees.

CHECKLIST OF POSSIBLE MANAGEMENT LETTER ITEMS

____ Are employees who handle cash bonded?
____ Are bank accounts reconciled monthly and reviewed by a responsible person?
____ Are invoices or statements cancelled so as to prevent their reuse?
____ Is there adequate segregation of duties in the accounting department?
____ Are accounts receivable details reconciled monthly to the general ledger control account?
____ Are accounts payable details reconciled monthly to the general ledger control account?
____ Are prepaid and accrued expenses properly recorded and classified?
____ Are physical inventories taken at least annually?
____ Are changes in the inventory unit of issue conveyed to accounting or data processing employees in order that inventory may be relieved by the proper values?
____ Is there adequate control over patient service charges; i.e., lost charges, improper departmentalization?
____ Is there a separate accounting for Medicare bad debts for deductibles and co-insurance?
____ Is there a capitalization policy approved by the Board of Trustees?
____ Are major movable equipment items properly departmentalized?
____ Are monthly statistics necessary for cost allocations properly gathered on a timely basis.
____ Have the personnel applications been reviewed by the hospital's legal counsel for compliance with Federal and State Labor laws?

HOW TO REVIEW THE HOSPITAL BOARD MINUTES

Auditors review the Board of Trustee minutes to gain an overall understanding of the relationship of the Board and the Administration, as well as to verify certain transactions. The independent certified public accountant would find it impossible to render an opinion without having read the minutes.

The internal auditor should review each month's minutes to see what new policies have been promulgated in order that he may properly follow up on their implementation. In addition, other items to be noted by the auditor from the minutes would be:

1) *Authorization for Loan Agreements.* Your audit will determine if the authorized limits have been exceeded. Furthermore, you should determine the effect upon reimbursement if the loan has been made by a related organization.
2) *Policy for Capitalization of Fixed Assets.* Your audit should verify that the policy is being adhered to and that proper accounting treatment is made for leased assets.
3) *The Purchase of Fixed Assets.* Ascertain that major additions to fixed assets have been properly authorized by the Board of Trustees. Later, determine the effect on third-party cost reimbursement if the asset was purchased from a related organization.
4) *Investments.* Verify, during the audit, that investments are made in accordance with Board policy. (See Figure 1.1.)
5) *Fringe Benefits.* Determine that the new benefit programs have been approved by the Board of Trustees.
6) *Approval of Expenditures.* The auditor should ascertain whether all major expenditures have been approved by the Board of Trustees. Examples of such expenditures would be consultant fees, contracts for group purchases, and other purchase service contracts for changes in data processing equipment.
7) *Approval of Wages, Salaries, and Professional Fees.* The auditor should ascertain that the increase in merit plans or wage scale adjustments were approved by the Board of Trustees prior to implementation.

   The auditor should ascertain that the salaries paid to officers have approval of the Board. The auditor should also ascertain that the Board has approved all hospital-based physician agreements.
8) *Related Organization Transactions.* The auditor should review the minutes for any indication of transactions with related organizations. The probable effect of such transactions upon third-party cost reimbursement should be disclosed in your management letter.
9) *Contingent Liabilities.* The auditor should be aware of any contingent liabilities that may have a future impact on reimbursable cost. Advance notice of such liabilities, and the use of creative accounting, could result in action that may benefit the hospital.
10) *Other Matters.* Have the members of the Board of Trustees submitted signed statements noting any potential areas for conflict of interest? (See Figure 1.2.)

    Has the Board of Trustees properly authorized the individuals signing checks on behalf of the hospital?

    If the hospital is tax exempt, has the Board of Trustees authorized any action or transaction that could jeopardize its tax exempt status?

PERFORMING THE REVIEW OF INTERNAL CONTROL

In practice, there is usually no distinct line between the review of internal control and the development of the audit procedures that are selected on the basis of the review.

Frequently they begin together, with procedures being adapted to findings of the methods in use.

If the internal controls are strong, the auditor may properly limit his test. If the controls are weak, additional auditing procedures and more testing are required. To avoid unnecessary emphasis on testing records whose reliability is adequately assured, and to avoid the risk of accepting records that have little basis for reliance, information must first be obtained as to the adequacy of the system of internal control.

Basically, the components of the review of internal control are:

1) Determination of what procedures and controls have been established by the hospital.
2) Determination by inquiry and tests of recorded transactions of the extent to which established procedures and controls are actually functioning.
3) Evaluation of the system of internal control and determination of the extent to which other auditing procedures must be expanded or curtailed.
4) Determination of what recommendations may be made for improvements in controls or procedures.

As the results of the review of internal control and accounting procedures are the bases for determining the scope of the audit, it is only logical that the survey of the controls and procedures should be the first step in carrying out any engagement.

TREASURER'S AUTHORITY TO
INVEST CORPORATE FUNDS

"BE IT RESOLVED that the Treasurer be and he is hereby authorized to invest any unrestricted corporate funds which may come into possession of the corporation pending their use, in any indebtedness of the Federal Government, or Federal Agency thereof, or in any Certificate of Deposit in any commercial bank secured or insured by the Federal Government or any Federal Agency, in any prime commercial paper, or in corporate securities rated AAA, all subject to maturity restrictions stated below. No investment shall exceed sixty (60) months from the date of purchase, and moreover, investment of funds in securities, as defined above, maturing in excess of twelve (12) months from the date of purchase shall not exceed $600,000 without the approval of the Finance Committee.

"BE IT FURTHER RESOLVED that with respect to legally Restricted Funds the Treasurer be and he is hereby authorized to either (1) invest such funds in accordance with any legal restrictions that may exist with respect to any such Restricted Fund, or (2) if no investment restrictions exist, invest in the same manner above authorized for unrestricted funds, except that in this instance the maximum permissible maturity is sixty (60) months from the date of purchase and the limitation of $600,000 for maturities in excess of twelve (12) months from the date of purchase does not apply."

FIGURE 1.1

______________ HOSPITAL

"TO: Governing Authority

"In accordance with a policy statement heretofore adopted by the governing authority, I, the undersigned, a member of the governing authority, do hereby declare and affirm that I am either an officer, member, owner, employee, agent of, or associated in some manner with the following business, businesses, or organizations:

. . . .

. . . .

. . . .

"This disclosure is made because the said hospital has, or might reasonably be expected in the future to have, a relationship, transaction, or business dealings with the said organization which might in some way constitute a conflict of interest with respect to the undersigned because of his membership on the governing authority and association with the above business organization.

"The undersigned agrees that if at any time any matter should come before the governing authority concerning the above organization or businesses, the undersigned shall make known the potential conflict and withdraw from the meeting so long as the matter shall continue under discussion and shall not either vote on the matter under discussion or attempt to influence a decision of the governing authority with respect to such matters, upon which there could possibly be a conflict of interest.

"The undersigned further agrees that in the event his relationship with the above businesses should change, or should he establish other relationships with other businesses which could give rise to a potential conflict of interest, he shall inform the governing authority and withdraw from participation in any decisions affecting such business or organizations.

This ______ day of ______________ , A.D. 19____

____
Governing Authority Member"[6]

FIGURE 1.2

6. Recommendations on Standards to the Joint Commission on Accreditation of Hospitals, American College of Hospital Administrators Task Force. Copyright 1974.

2

Auditing to Safeguard Cash Receipts and Disbursements

Certainly the area of cash offers the greatest opportunity for misappropriation of hospital assets. Those hospitals that have a good system of internal control for cash from the collection of patient accounts often overlook cash from the infrequent sale of property, plant and equipment items, rebates, donations, or transactions with the ladies' auxiliary. If proper controls are not being utilized, the opportunity to embezzle cash can start in the mail room and progress to the controller.

This chapter highlights the pitfalls of inadequate controls and offers suggested procedures to protect this hospital asset. Also provided is an internal control questionnaire, audit program, and sample working papers that will flag weaknesses in the hospital system of controls. Once these weaknesses have been identified, the appropriate steps can be taken to correct the inadequacies, thereby shutting the door on internal theft.

The Controller

One hospital had granted the controller the authority to transfer funds from the hospital general account to special transaction accounts, without written approval for such transactions being countersigned by someone from Administration. Soon the controller realized the potential for such authority and created a secret banking account, known only to him, to which selected rebates were deposited. The new account was with another bank, under the name of the hospital but with a post office box number not that of the hospital.

This situation continued for a number of years until the hiring of an agressive new purchasing agent who prepared an annual report that included a section on rebate income generated as a result of his contract negotiations with vendors. The chief financial officer compared this report with the rebate income, per the financial statements. He confronted the controller with this discrepancy and ultimately learned the truth.

Protective Procedure

This situation would never have occurred if the hospital had required two signatures for all transfers of funds.

Furthermore, the problem could have been avoided if the chief financial officer had maintained a list of companies who made rebates to the hospital and reviewed such rebates periodically. Such a list should be developed with the cooperation of the purchasing agent. Then, once a year, it would be beneficial to send letters to the largest vendors, particularly the pharmaceutical and hospital supply companies, requesting that they furnish an accounting of the rebates made to the hospital during a specified period of time.

Human Frailties

As an auditor, you should be aware of weaknesses involving the human element as well as weaknesses in internal control.

While performing an audit, an auditor noted that an elderly nun with a large black purse, and an elderly lay chauffeur who relied on a pacemaker, would stop by the accounting office, then the cashier's office, and then leave the building for about an hour. Upon their return, they would reverse this sequence by stopping first at the cashier's office, then the accounting office. The auditor made a few inquiries and learned that every morning the pair would stop by the accounting office to pick up their request for cash denominations, then go to the cashier to pick up the previous day's receipts for deposit. Upon their return, the pair would deliver the denominations as requested by these departments.

If you were the auditor, would you have noted this situation in your management letter?

It *should* be noted. If the chauffeur were to have a coronary while driving, the chances are great that he and the nun would be involved in a property damage accident in which an opportunity for someone to steal these funds would be provided. Sadly enough we must acknowledge that in today's society there are individuals who would not hesitate to rob a nun of a purse containing thousands of dollars.

Protective Procedure

The auditor mentioned his concern to the administrator. The administrator concurred with his observations, and one week later they began using an armored car service.

REVIEWING THE CONTROL OF CASH

To reiterate, the questions for reviewing internal control contained in this book have been specifically designed for hospitals. The items listed after each question are to stimulate your thinking of other applicable questions and to assist you in preparing comments for improvements that you will present in the management letter. The questions are not intended to be all inclusive.

Mail Receipts

Q. Is the mail opened by someone other than the cashier, accounts receivable bookkeeper, or credit and collections personnel?

- Who opens the mail when the primary person is unavailable for work.
- Could the chief financial officer's secretary perform this duty for a limited time.
- How are mail receipts controlled to prevent abstraction before entry in the cash receipts records.

Q. Does the person opening mail prepare a list of the cash receipts?

- Does someone other than the cashier compare the list with the bank deposits.
- Does the list show the payee and date as well as the amount.
- Shouldn't the comparison include checking agreement with the individual items.
- How are the discrepancies in the two totals reconciled.
- Is someone in the next level of management involved in reviewing these reconciliations.
- Does this individual review the actual items involved.

Q. How many persons handle the receipts before they are deposited?

- Should more than two people handle the receipts before they are deposited.
- What are the security precautions used during each transfer.

Counter Receipts

Q. Are counter receipts received by persons with no duties relating to the accounts receivable or bookkeeping function?

- If someone who maintains accounts receivable ledgers receives the cash, isn't there an opportunity for defalcation.
- Is the cashier familiar with insurance coverages so she can answer basic questions.
- Is it possible for the cashier to withhold a receipt and charge off a portion of a patient's account through the issuance of credit memoranda.

Q. Are receipts recorded by cash register or other mechanical devices, such as a pegboard?

- Are the cash receipt totals checked by the accounting department.
- Are manual receipt books used.
- Are the receipts prenumbered.
- Is the numerical sequence of the receipts used checked daily by the accounting department.
- Are the original receipts of all voided receipts attached to the copy for supervisory review.

- Are unused receipts books safeguarded and under lock.
- Are the receipts books assigned to specific cashiers.

Q. *Is the original record of receipts compared with the bank deposits?*

- Is this done by someone other than the cashier.
- Shouldn't the comparison include checking for the agreement of individual items.
- What steps are taken to see that the cash receipts record is not underfooted.

Q. *How many persons handle the receipts before deposit?*

- Is there any way you can reduce the number of persons handling the cash and not weaken the existing internal control.

The Deposit
(See Figure 2.1.)

Q. *Do the cashiers prepare the bank deposits each day?*

- Are such deposits made intact and without delay.
- If someone other than the cashier is preparing the bank deposits, what is his opportunity to gain access to patient accounts receivable ledgers.

Q. *Does someone other than a cashier take the deposits to the bank?*

- If armored car personnel obtain such deposits, what are the safeguards against these individuals being impersonated.
- If a hospital employee makes such deposits, what security precautions are taken.
- In the event of a robbery, do we have insurance to cover such losses.

Q. *Are checks cashed from cash receipts?*

- If yes, are they cashed only after approval of a responsible individual.
- Is this practice being abused by a select few.
- Is there a dollar maximum for which such checks can be cashed.
- Shouldn't this practice be discouraged.
- How can the day's receipts be verified by item.
- If the practice of cashing employees' checks must be maintained, shouldn't they be cashed from petty cash.

Q. *Are duplicate deposit slips kept by someone other than those who prepare the deposits?*

- Are any of the duplicate tickets marked void.
- Is the reason for such voiding apparent, or suspicious.
- Shouldn't the voided original deposit be attached to the copies for supervisory review.

Q. *Are N.S.F. checks delivered directly to a responsible person other than the cashier for investigation?*

- How thorough an investigation does the individual receiving the N.S.F. check perform.

- What are the safeguards against irregularities with this type of check.

The Cashiering Function
(See Figure 2.2.)

Q. Are the cashiers' duties entirely separated from the accounts receivable, credit collection, and general ledger posting duties?

- Who relieves for vacations and holidays.
- Should someone from data processing be allowed to relieve.
- Who relieves at mealtime and breaks.
- For those individuals who relieve the cashiers for meals and breaks, is there a check-out procedure that could fix responsibility in the event of a cash shortage or overage.

Q. Are cashiers denied access to accounts receivable ledgers and monthly statements for patient accounts receivable?

- Is it possible for the cashier to substitute fictitious accounts for cash received on accounts.

Q. Are cashiers prohibited from handling other cash funds; that is, other than cash receipts?

Q. Is cash being received at locations other than the central cashier's office; for example, the cafeteria, the outpatient clinic, school of nursing, home health agency, etc? (See Figure 2.3.)

- Has the custodian signed a statement accepting full responsibility for the fund. (See Figure 2.4.)
- What types of security measures are taken when the delivery of cash from these locations is made to the central cashier's office.

Q. How would the nonreceipt of rents, dividends, interest, donations, rebates, and similar revenues be noted and investigated?

- Shouldn't the responsibility for the review of these receipts be vested in one individual.
- Shouldn't this individual maintain a list of the recurring types of revenues to be received monthly.
- Shouldn't these revenues be budgeted, and, therefore, their nonreceipts appear as a budget variance.

Questions of a General Nature

Q. Are the physical facilities adequate to protect the cash and the cash transactions?

- Is the safe out of the public view; i.e., out of sight, out of mind.
- Should the hospital install a camera which could be activated by the cashiers in the event of a robbery.
- Does the hospital have a policy regarding the employees' expected behavior in the event of a robbery; i.e., give up the money without a fight.

Q. *How are hospital employees who have access to current assets and accounting records bonded?*

- If on an individual basis, is the list current.
- If covered by a blanket policy, have you examined the policy to see that the areas mentioned are adequate.

Q. *Are persons having custody of hospital's cash prohibited from having custody of non-hospital funds; that is, credit union and employee benefits association?*

How to Question the Cash Disbursement Function

Q. *Are all disbursements, except those from petty cash, made by check?*

- Are the checks prenumbered.
- Are the checks printed on protective paper.
- If the checks are prenumbered, is the check sequence accounted for at the time of the bank reconciliation.

Q. *Are the checks prepared from vouchers or check requisitions?*

- Who prepares the checks.
- Are the vouchers or check requisitions approved by a responsible individual.

Q. *Do the present procedures assure the payment of invoices within the discount periods?*

- In order not to lose a discount would the hospital release checks without having sufficient funds in the bank; i.e., playing the "float."
- Is such a practice against state law.

Q. *Is the practice of drawing checks to cash or "bearer" prohibited?*

- If not, are such checks limited to payroll and petty cash reimbursement.
- Shouldn't the practice be discontinued and checks made payable to the custodian or to the payroll bank account.

Q. *Are voided checks defaced and retained?*

Q. *Are blank checks safeguarded?*

- Are the blank checks, keys, and signature plates for the check-signing machine in two separate locations.
- If the hospital uses a shared computer system to prepare its payrolls, are the controls employed by the computer service bureau adequate.

Q. *Are the checks recorded simultaneously with their preparation?*

- If not, who records the checks.
- Is the delay between the time of preparation and the time of recording checks a reasonable delay.
- Is it possible that unentered deposits and unentered checks could be made with the subsequent destruction of the unentered cancelled check.

Q. *Are all checks countersigned?*

- Is the countersigning routine cumbersome.

- Could adequate controls be maintained if countersigning were limited to checks over a certain amount; i.e., \$5,000.

Q. Is the advance signing of checks prohibited?

- Is the advance countersigning prohibited.
- Are authorized signatures limited to persons who have no access to accounting records or cash, and who do not prepare checks.

Q. Do vouchers or other supporting documents accompany the checks when submitted for signature?

- Does the individual signing the checks review the supporting documentation, or has this review been prepared prior to their submission.
- Is the individual performing the review of supporting documentation able to determine that the supporting documents have not been paid previously; i.e., paid invoices so marked.
- Is the person performing the review of supporting documents sufficiently familiar with the hospital operations to detect the substitution of fraudulent invoices in support of cash disbursements.
- Does the review of supporting documents call for a review of receiving reports to determine that the goods are received before paid.
- Is this review of receiving reports thorough enough to prevent the payment of fictitious invoices without the receipt of goods.
- Are supporting documents marked in such a way that the reviewer can readily determine that the documents have been footed, extensions checked, proper chart of account number assigned for reporting purposes, and price agreed to purchase order. (See Figure 2.5, # 8.)
- Does the reviewer periodically foot supporting documents to see if the attached adding machine tape of invoices has been manipulated.
- Does the reviewer check to see that the name of the payee is synonymous with that of the creditor indicated on the invoice.

Q. Is a check-signing machine used?

- Is the operator someone other than the person who prepares the checks.
- Does the machine use a document counter.
- Is the machine total of checks processed, logged, and agreed to the number of checks submitted for signing.
- Are voided checks also logged or noted as voided.
- Have you reviewed the log for accuracy.
- Is the signature plate and/or keys locked when not in use.

Q. Are checks mailed without returning to the person who prepared the checks?

- Are they returned to the accounts payable bookkeeper. If so, this should be discontinued.
- After the checks have been prepared and signed, are the vouchers and invoices permanently marked paid, either with a stamp or by a mechanical device that perforates all supporting documents.
- Have you carefully reviewed any checks before they are mailed to see if the amounts have been raised after signature.

How to Question the Reconcilation of the Bank Accounts
(see Figure 2.6.)

Q. Are the bank statements, including cancelled checks, receipted deposit tickets, and bank advices, received directly by the accounting department?

Q. Are the duties for the preparation of checks and reconcilliations of the bank account assigned to separate employees?

Q. Is the reconciliation procedure thorough?

- Is the reconciliation made promptly.
- Does the reconciliation procedure include the comparison of checks with entries in the cash disbursement record on a random basis.
- Does the reconcilation procedure call for examining paid checks for date, name, cancellation, and endorsements.
- Does the reconciliation procedure call for the accounting of the numerical sequence of check numbers.
- Is there a comparison of dates and amounts of deposits with the dates and amounts of recorded receipts.
- Is a list of outstanding checks made at the time of the reconciliation and then followed up on a later date.
- Are the reconciliations approved by an accounting official of the hospital.
- Does the reconciliation procedure require that the date of fund transfers be noted on transfers made at the end of the period. This would highlight attempts at "kiting."
- Is the cash disbursement journal footed so that erroneous footings of the cash disbursement journal to cover the unrecording of checks will be detected.
- Is the cash receipt journal footed so that erroneous footings of the cash receipt journal to cover the withholding of cash receipts will be detected.

Q. Is the hospital complying with the State's Escheat laws in the handling of old outstanding checks? (See Figure 2.7.)

THE AUDIT OF CASH

The Audit Objective

The primary objective in the audit of cash is to determine that the cash is under proper control and that the established systems and written procedures are being followed. Furthermore, you must be concerned that the amount of cash is stated properly on the hospital's general ledger.

How to Audit Hospital Cash Transactions

As was noted in the Introduction, the study of internal control, design of the audit program, and the tests of transactions are interrelated functions of an audit. Information developed during any one of the functions may modify consideration of the other two. In other words, no function is static during the audit. Each is subject to continuing appraisal and adjustment as additional information is gathered.

After you have completed the testing of the hospital cash transactions, you should reevaluate the system of internal control and reconsider the adequacy of the audit program.

The following list is intended to show representative tests of transactions to determine the reliability of the accounting controls and procedures as they relate to hospital cash transactions. The actual procedures will depend upon your hospital's accounting procedures and internal control.

Cash Receipt Transactions

1) Compare recorded receipts with the individual deposits shown by the bank statements for the month under examination.
2) Compare remittance advices or other receipts details with entries in the cash receipt journal.
3) Compare composition of authenticated duplicate deposit slips with the recorded receipts.
4) Compare recorded receipts with independent records prepared before receipts are transmitted to cashier. Examples of such independent records would be the prelist prepared in the mail room, cash register tapes, or collectors' reports.
5) Check administrative adjustments and other noncash allowance or credits granted to patients to determine that such adjustments and allowances were properly authorized and recorded.
6) Scrutinize cash receipts records for unusual items and investigate any that are noted.
7) Foot and crossfoot cash receipts journal for the month under examination.
8) Trace cash receipt and adjustment totals for the month to general ledger postings.
9) Trace two days' detail receipts per the deposit slips to cash receipt records and to posting to the patient ledgers.

Cash Disbursement Transactions

1) Compare paid checks with cash disbursements records.
2) Examine paid checks to determine that:
   a) the names of the signers are the names of the persons authorized to sign,
   b) checks are drawn to, and are endorsed in the name of, the payee recorded in the disbursements records, and
   c) the check belongs in the period under review, as indicated by the bank cancellation date.
3) Account for all the numerical sequence of all checks issued between the first and last checks drawn on the bank for the month.
4) Review all spoiled or voided checks for the month under audit.
5) Foot and crossfoot the cash disbursements journal for the month under audit.
6) Trace totals for the month to the general ledger postings.
7) Scan the cash disbursement journal for the month under audit, noting and investigating unusual items.

8) Review all entries in the general ledger cash accounts from other than cash journals.
9) Check recorded disbursements by inspection of supporting documents, or otherwise:
   a) Inspect paid invoices, noting the following: purchase terms, receipts of goods, discounts taken, approvals for payments, and cancellation to prevent duplicate payment.
   b) Account for bank transfers by tracing to the receiving bank statement to be certain both disbursement and deposit are accounted for in the same period.
   c) Investigate checks made payable to officers or to cash. Trace postings to general and subsidiary ledgers.
   d) Prove totals of data supporting reimbursements to petty cash funds; inspect the data to see that the receipts for payment have been obtained, payments have been approved for propriety, and the supporting data has been cancelled to prevent reuse.

How to Audit the Cash on Hand

(See Figure 2.8.)

1) Count cash on hand, including undeposited receipts.
2) In counting the cash on hand, always follow these precautions to the extent practical:
   a) Make your counts in the presence of the fund custodian, and obtain his signature acknowledging that all items counted have been returned.
   b) Control should be maintained over undeposited receipts until they are deposited in the bank, mailed to the bank, or transferred to the armored truck service.
3) Summarize amounts counted and trace, or reconcile, to the general ledger balances. Trace amount of cash, per books, to custodian acknowledgment memo. (See Figure 2.4.)
4) Review the contents of the cash count and discuss significant undistributed disbursements, payroll advances, and old or postdated checks with the chief financial officer or the administrator.
5) Note the source of undeposited receipts and determine at a later date that they have been credited to the proper accounts.
6) Obtain a duplicate deposit ticket and have it authenticated by the bank.

NOTE: Your cash count should always be on a surprise basis. The auditor should avoid a pattern such as the 15th of each month, the 3rd Monday of each month, or any similar pattern.

Auditing Hospital Cash on Deposit

1) Subsequent to the audit date, request direct confirmation from each bank of the balance of the hospital's account, as of the audit date.
2) Prepare a four-column bank reconciliation or review the monthly bank reconciliation prepared by the accounting personnel (see Figure 2.6), and trace the balances per the reconciliation to the general ledger.
3) Attach a list of the outstanding checks.

4) Record on the list of outstanding checks the date and payee of checks for large amounts drawn payable to banks, other bank accounts, related organizations, cash, office employees, or checks that appear to be unusual.
5) Examine supportive data for these checks and determine that checks to other bank accounts and to related organizations have been recorded as cash receipts by the payee.
6) Review supporting data, such as bank memoranda, for reconciling items other than deposits in transit and outstanding checks.
7) Periodically, obtain directly from the bank a "cutoff" bank statement for a period ending at least ten business days after the end of the month.
8) Trace amounts shown on the reconciliation as deposits in transit to the deposits shown on the cutoff bank statement.
9) Show on the bank reconciliation the date of bank receipts. Consider comparing a random number of the individual items included in such deposits with the cash receipts record and with the detailed accounts receivable records.
10) Confirm the deposits in transit if the cutoff statements are not received directly from the bank.
11) Compare paid checks from the bank at the cutoff date with the outstanding check list at the balance sheet date.

NOTE: Be alert for the return of unrecorded checks.

12) Investigate large checks outstanding at the end of the month that remain outstanding at the cutoff date.
13) Obtain information about deposit items that have been charged back by the bank during the cutoff period.
14) Prepare a bank transfer schedule to cover a reasonable period prior and subsequent to the balance sheet date.
15) Show the date of each transfer check issued during the period and the date deposited as shown in the depositary bank statement.

NOTE: Transfer checks included in undeposited receipts, or in deposits in transit, at the balance sheet date must be traced to the outstanding check list of the bank on which they were drawn or otherwise accounted for.

16) Review bank statements for all inactive bank accounts to determine that such accounts were truly inactive.

WORKING PAPERS REQUIRED

Cash Counts

(See Figure 2.8.)

A working paper such as Figure 2.8 is necessary in the event a subsequent question is raised regarding the accounts.

Proof of Cash

(See Figure 2.6.)

A bank reconciliation should be made for each account as of the audit date and the cutoff date.

The reconciliation should note that the outstanding checks and deposits in transit were verified by reference to the returned paid check and subsequent bank statements, respectively.

Summary of Audit Work Performed

A memorandum should be prepared stating the test month selected, the extent of verification of cancelled checks to the cash disbursement journal, and the disposition of any discrepancies.

The memorandum should also state the extent of verification of cash receipts to the bank statement and cash receipts journal.

Include in this summary a brief statement of the amount of verification to prove footings, postings, and journal entries made in the cash accounts of the general ledger.

The last notation in this memorandum should be your opinion, or conclusion, of the fair presentation of the cash balances as shown on your cash summary. If the amount per cash summary does not agree with the hospital's records, an explanation of the variance should also be included in the memorandum.

Summary of Cash

A summary of the cash balances as of the audit date should be made and put as the first working paper in the section entitled "Cash." The summary should show the working paper reference of each schedule that has verified the cash balance.

FINANCIAL STATEMENT PRESENTATION

There are several acceptable captions used to present cash on the balance sheet; i.e., "Cash," "Cash on Hand and in Banks," etc. The exact caption used will depend upon the circumstances.

Cash is usually shown as the first item in the current asset section of the balance sheet since it represents the most liquid of the assets.

If there are any restrictions on the use of cash in banks, such as an agreement to retain a specified balance or a restriction for a specific use, it must be noted on the balance sheet itself either by footnote or separate classification in the case of restricted fund cash.

PROTECTIVE PROCEDURE

SUBJECT: Daily Cash Control

PURPOSE: To outline procedure for summarization and control of cash receipts.

RESPONSIBILITY	ACTION
Window Cashier, Mail Cashier, Outpatient, Emergency Room Counselor	1) Summarizes Cash Transaction Journal as to type of receipts (patient, cafeteria, etc.).
	2) Batches cash receipts slips (inpatient and outpatient separately).
	3) Completes Batch Control Ticket, one for inpatient, one for outpatient, except in the case of Blue Cross and Medicare payment listings which have one Batch Control Ticket for each sheet.
	4) Completes Daily Cash Receipts summary and agrees with total of Batch Control Tickets to A/R patients.
	5) Completes deposit envelope.
	6) Forwards all documents to Window Cashier for summary deposit.
Window Cashier	7) Summarizes the above and posts detail to Cash Receipts Journal.
	8) Submits Cash Receipts Batches to Accounts Receivable Reconciliation Control Clerk for final batching.
Accounts Receivable Reconciliation Control Clerk	9) Receives cash receipts batches, logs amounts collected on Accounts Receivable Cash Control sheet and forwards batches to Data Processing for keypunching.
Window Cashier	10) At month end summarizes Cash Receipts Journal for preparation of journal entry and forwards to the Accounting Supervisor.
Accounting Supervisor	11) Prepares journal entry from Cash Receipts Journal and submits it to Data Processing.

FIGURE 2.1

PROTECTIVE PROCEDURE

SUBJECT: End-of-Month Closing of Cash Receipts

PURPOSE: Outline the procedure for closing the cash receipts journal and the preparation of the necessary journal entry.

RESPONSIBILITY	ACTION
Accounts Receivable Reconciliation Control Clerk	1) Foots and crossfoots the log of Cash Control sheets.
	2) Agrees total of cash receipts and adjustments to the window cashier's summary of cash receipts.
	3) Submits Cash Reconciliation Report to Accounting Supervisor.
Window Cashier	4) Summarizes Cash Receipts Journal for preparation of monthly journal entry.
	5) Forwards summary of cash receipts to Accounting Supervisor.
Accounting Supervisor	6) Reviews window cashier's summary to Cash Reconciliation Report and prepares journal entry.

FIGURE 2.2

PROTECTIVE PROCEDURE

SUBJECT: Closing Cafeteria Cash Register

PURPOSE: Outlines the procedure and responsibilities for closing the cafeteria cash registers during the morning, afternoon, and evenings.

RESPONSIBILITY	ACTION
Responsible Window Cashier	1) Obtains Daily Cafeteria Register Reading Report.
	2) Obtains a "ZQ" key from the Business Office safe.
	3) Goes to the cafeteria and inquires from the cafeteria cashier which register is to be closed.
	4) Inserts the "ZQ" key in the top keyhole as far as possible.
	5) Rings up each key, reads and records the totals shown.

FIGURE 2.3

RESPONSIBILITY	ACTION
	6) Presses the sub-total key and the Employee key; presses the sub-total key and the employee key a second time.
	7) Removes the "ZQ" key from the machine.
Cafeteria Cashier	8) Counts funds in cash drawer, excluding the bank, and gives the money to the responsible window cashier.
Responsible Window Cashier	9) Recounts the funds, excluding the bank, reconciling any discrepancy that may exist with the first count.
Cafeteria Cashier	10) Gives the "excess over" banks funds to the window cashier.
Responsible Window Cashier	11) Counts and records amount on report.
Cafeteria Cashier	12) Recounts funds to assure proper amount is in the bank.
Responsible Window Cashier	13) Recounts funds to assure proper amount is recorded on report.
	14) Removes transaction tape from register and changes date, if ncecssary.
	15) Reinserts the "ZQ" key in the top keyhole of the register in accordance with paragraphs 5 and 6.
	16) Insures that the register is properly cleared and all readings are "O."
	17) Clears "Persons Served" counters by inserting key in lower right rear key hole. (Place it on # 4, which is indicated by flat side of key; drawer opens.)
	18) Pulls the handle to the left—all the way down, and all the way back up. (All counters should now read four zeros. If not, repeat the above operation.)
	19) Removes key from position four (4) and inserts in position one (1).
	20) Locks the register by closing the register drawer.
	21) Places a mark on the register printout tape to indicate "Finished Location."

FIGURE 2.3 ***(continued)***

RESPONSIBILITY	ACTION
	22) Returns to station and records the receipts on the Cash Control sheet as "Cafeteria Income and Taxes."
	23) Submits completed Daily Cafeteria Register Reading Report to the Accountant.
	24) Places register tape in office safe with previous tapes—for possible audit.

FIGURE 2.3 ***(continued)***

PETTY CASH CUSTODIAN STATEMENT OF RESPONSIBILITY

The undersigned hereby states that he/she is the Custodian of the $ __________ petty cash fund established for the ____________________ Department.

As Custodian of this fund, he/she is responsible for all the accounting and balancing of this fund and any shortage will be deducted from his/her paycheck.

As Custodian, I hereby authorize *(Name of hospital)* to make a payroll deduction for any shortage in this fund.

Signature ____________________

Date ____________________

Witness ____________________

Date ____________________

FIGURE 2.4

PROTECTIVE PROCEDURE

SUBJECT: Payment of Invoices

RESPONSIBILITY	ACTION
Invoice Clerk	1) Receives invoice from company and places in open file in Purchasing department.
	2) Receives packing slip or substitute and closed Purchase Order forms from Receiving department.
	3) Matches invoice and Purchase Order in open file with packing slip and closed Purchase Order forms.
	4) Verifies price and price extensions on invoices.
	5) Investigates any price difference on invoice, gaining assistance from buyers to justify price difference with vendor.
	6) Places one copy of Purchase Order in closed file in Purchasing department.
	7) Staples one copy of closed Purchase Order to invoice and packing slip (or substitute).
	8) Stamps invoice with hospital stamp, (Sample form of a stamp with necessary approval is shown below.) MATERIAL REC'D ________ PRICE O.K. ________ EXTENSION O.K. ________ ACCT. TO BE CHGD. ________ EQUIP. TAG NO. ________ O.K. FOR PAYMENT ________
	9) Records accounting classifications on invoice.
	10) Initials stamp on invoice, indicating the material has been received and that prices and extensions have been verified.
	11) Sends invoices to Accounting Supervisor.

FIGURE 2.5

RESPONSIBILITY	ACTION
Accounting Supervisor	12) Receives approved invoices from the Purchasing department. NOTE: Interjects at this point any approved invoices from Pharmacy or other department and patient refund slips.
	13) Checks invoices, patient refund slips, or other bills for proper accounting classification and initials in "O.K. for Payment" box on invoice.
	14) Forwards invoices to Accounts Payable Clerk.
Accounts Payable Clerk	15) Records due date on accounts payable voucher as follows: a) discounted invoices—10th of the month. b) A-K invoices—15th of the month. c) L-Z vendors—20th of the month. d) any voucher not previously released —25th of the month.
	16) Assigns vendor number to voucher. (See procedure #010 for assignment of vendor number.) NOTE: For one-time vendors, write check or voucher so that surname is printed prior to given name.
	17) Adds all invoice totals in a batch.
	18) Adds all voucher totals in a batch.
	19) Compares both totals, corrects any differences and writes correct total on transmittal.
	20) Forwards transmittal and vouchers to E.D.P.

FIGURE 2.5 ***(continued)***

______________ HOSPITAL

OPERATING ACCOUNT

BANK RECONCILIATION FOR ______________, 19___

	INITIALS	DATE
PREPARED BY	JLD	1-10-
APPROVED BY	BJ	1-15-

FORM P-554-2 (GREEN) P-554-B2 (BUFF) Post Rite SYSTEMS CELINA, OHIO DALLAS LOS ANGELES LITHO IN U.S.A.

		(1) BEGINNING BALANCE	(2) DEPOSITS	(3) DISBURSE-MENTS	(4) ENDING BALANCE
	PER BANK	64902439 4	143411690 F4	<170470695> C4	37843434 4 ✓
	DEPOSITS IN TRANSIT:	Per Bank		Per Book	
	Beginning 6/1	1506265 ✓E	<1506265>	5/31	
	Ending		63195	6/29	
			5660	6/29	
			69327	6/29	
			8947787	6/30	
			152551	6/30	
			7090	6/30	
			87994	6/30	
					9333604
	OUTSTANDING CHECKS:				
	Beginning	<44426799> ✓B		44426799	
	Ending			<28809483>	<28809483>
	PER BOOK	21981905	151239029	<154853379>	1867555
		T F	F A	F A	FT ✓
	OUTSTANDING CHECKS:		DATE ISSUED		
	33035	17627905	6/27		
	33341	10742548	6/27		
	33368	184620	6/28		
	33375	254410	6/28		
		28809483 F			
4	per bank statement ending ________ 19___				
✓	per prior months reconciliation				
E	examination receipted deposit ticket				
B	examined cancelled paid check				

FIGURE 2.6

ESCHEAT LAW

In defining "unclaimed funds" one state's law read in part, "Any sum payable as wages, salaries, . . . moneys owned under pension and profit sharing plans and all other credits, held or owed by any holder, unclaimed for five years from date payable or distribution. . . ."

This state's law then defines the proper reporting requirements as being, "Any holder of unclaimed funds . . . shall send notice to each owner of each item of unclaimed funds having a value of twenty-five dollars or more at the last known address of the owner as shown by the records of the holder before filing the annual report. . . ."

This state's law then provides for a civil penalty of five dollars per month not to exceed twenty-five months for failure to comply with reporting requirements.

NOTE: In some states, eleemosynary organizations such as non-profit hospitals are exempt from such filings.

FIGURE 2.7

______________ HOSPITAL
PETTY CASH COUNT
______________ 19___

	INITIALS	DATE
PREPARED BY	JLD	12/31
APPROVED BY	B	1-5-

FORM P-554-2 GREEN P-554-B2 BUFF — Fast-Rate SYSTEMS CELINA, OHIO DALLAS LOS ANGELES — LITHO IN U.S.A.

Date	Name	Account No. (1)	(2)	NO. (3)	TOTAL (4)
	CASH ON HAND:				
	Currency		$ 50	—	
			20	2	$ 40— C
			10	3	30— C
			5	1	5— C
			1	8	8— C
	Coin		.50	4	2— C
			.25	9	2.25 C
			.10	16	1.60 C
			.05	8	.40 C
			.01	31	.31 C
	TOTAL CASH ON HAND:				89.56 F
	PETTY CASH RECEIPTS FOR DISBURSEMENTS:				
12/22	R. Smith	416.26		$ 20.42	
12/22	W. Stevens	416.26		16.66	
12/22	S. Jones	416.26		25.27	
12/24	A. Vendor	500.89		9.29	
12/27	U.S. Postmaster	500.10		20.00	
12/29	H. & R. Office Supply	500.04		9.17	
12/30	B. Brooks	416.26		9.63	110.44
	TOTAL PETTY CASH FUND:				$ 200— TP

Received of ______________, auditor eighty-nine dollars and fifty-six cents ($89.56).

____
(Custodian)

P - Per signed petty cash custodian statement.

FIGURE 2.8

3

Auditing Petty Cash and Safeguarding Patient Valuables

Petty cash and the safeguarding of patient valuables warrant the same attention to audit and control as cash receipts and disbursements. Of course, much of this material could have been covered in the preceding chapter, but the problems relating to petty cash and patient valuables are different from those associated with patient receipts and deserve separate treatment. Figures that have been duplicated in this chapter are for the convenience of the reader.

This chapter will relate the most frequent type of weakness in the control of petty cash and patient valuables and offer procedures that will add the necessary control. Also included are an internal control questionnaire, audit program, sample working papers, and suggested forms that, when properly utilized, will reduce the likelihood of loss of petty cash or patient valuables.

Mileage Reimbursement Plus Gas and Oil

There is an amazing number of experienced and highly educated hospital employees who, having driven to a seminar, will innocently claim mileage reimbursement and also reimbursement for purchases of gasoline and oil. But what is unbelievable is the number of hospital managers who will approve such double reimbursement, probably because of too hasty a review of the employee's expense report.

Protective Procedure

A standardized expense report, such as presented in Figure 3.1, should be prepared by the department manager for any travel expenses incurred by either the manager or his departmental employees. The expense report should then be reviewed and approved by the appropriate administrative staff member and the controller before reimbursement is made to the employee. This will not only eliminate such errors as over-reimbursement for travel, but will strengthen the conscience of the employee who knows Administration will also be reviewing the expenses of his "seminar."

Unclaimed Patient Valuables

If your hospital is to maintain an exemplary image, it must not condone a particular hospital's past practice of allowing the head cashier to take unclaimed patient valuables home to her granddaughter. Although such a practice is relatively harmless, except from an employee relations standpoint, it should be discouraged because of its appearance to the public.

Protective Procedure

It would be more appropriate if, quarterly, a member of the hospital supervisory personnel, such as the chief of security, would review the list of patient valuables and verify their existence. Any unclaimed valuables that exceed the statute of limitations set forth in the state's *Innkeepers Law* should be disposed of as provided in the statutes. If there is no specific statutory instruction, the items should be donated to a tax-exempt organization that could make some productive use of them. The transmittal of such material should always be handled in a formal fashion in which the hospital maintains a written record of the items transmitted.

REVIEWING THE CONTROL OF PETTY CASH AND PATIENT VALUABLES

The following questions have been specifically designed for hospitals, but they are not intended to be all inclusive. The items listed after each question are to assist you in thinking of other questions and to guide you in developing your management letter comments for improvement.

Petty Cash

Q. Is the imprest system of maintaining petty cash used?

Q. Are the custody and responsibility for each fund vested in one person?

- Are the reimbursement checks for the petty cash fund payable to the order of the responsible custodian.
- Has the responsible custodian signed a statement acknowledging his responsibility. (See Figure 3.2.)
- Is the custodian an individual independent of the cashier or other employees handling remittances from patients or other cash receipts.
- Is an accurate list of the individual petty cash funds, amounts, and locations maintained in the accounting office.

Q. Is there a hospital policy prohibiting the cashing of personal checks from the fund?

- Are there exceptions to this policy.
- If so, does the deviation from this policy require the approval of an appropriate administrative staff personnel.
- If checks are cashed from the petty cash fund, are they immediately stamped for the "deposit to the hospital" account.
- Has the bank been instructed that all checks made or endorsed to the order of the hospital should be deposited in the hospital's general bank account and must never be recashed at the bank or deposited in a fund bank account.

Q. *Are employee advances from the petty cash fund prohibited by hospital policy?*

- Are there exceptions to this policy.
- If so, does the deviation from this policy require the approval of an appropriate administrative staff personnel.

Q. *Is there an administratively approved policy setting a maximum figure for individual payments from the fund?*

- Are payees required to sign vouchers for all disbursements.
- Is the amount of the voucher spelled out in words as well as written in numerals.

Q. *Is the petty cash fund small enough to require reimbursement at relatively short intervals; i.e., biweekly or at least monthly?*

- Would it be advisable to have all funds reimbursed on a scheduled basis.
- Are vouchers and supporting documents reviewed by a responsible person, independent of the custodian at the time of reimbursement.
- Does the person making the reimbursement count the unexpended fund balance before requesting a check for reimbursement.

Q. *After the reimbursing check has been drawn payable to the petty cash custodian, are the supporting vouchers mutilated, cancelled, or marked so as to prevent their subsequent reuse?*

Q. *Is there a separation of functions so that no one who is responsible for the disbursement of petty cash has access to other cash, securities, or funds not carried on the books of the hospital (i.e., employee credit union)?*

Questioning the Safety of Patient Valuables

Q. *Is a receipt system used for recording patient valuables?* (See Figure 3.3.)

- Is the receipt issued to the depositor when the valuables are given to an employee of the hospital; i.e., nursing service employee.
- Do both the depositor and hospital employee sign the receipt which shows a complete description of the patient valuable.

Q. *Are the patient valuables then sealed in an envelope?*

- Are the envelopes and receipts prenumbered.
- Do the appropriate receipt and envelopes bear the same number.
- Are the issued envelopes recorded in a log.
- If the envelopes are sequentially prenumbered, is the sequence accounted for.
- Does a responsible supervisory personnel periodically review the log.
- What record is there to prove such a review was made.

Q. *Is there an administrative policy stating that the receipt must be submitted to the patient valuables custodian before the hospital will release the patient valuable?*

- Must the person submitting the receipt first sign a log acknowledging receipt of the patient valuable.

- Is the signature on the log verified with the signature on the receipt.
- Does it require administrative approval before a patient valuable is released to someone other than the signed depositor.

Q. Are unclaimed valuables investigated by a responsible person?

- Is there a record of the action the hospital personnel took in trying to locate the owner of the patient valuables.
- Does the hospital maintain a record showing the disposition of unclaimed patient valuables.

THE AUDIT OF PETTY CASH

Now that we have "thought" our way through the Internal Control Questionnaire, we are ready to begin drafting an audit program to fit the needs of the hospital. The internal control questions can be presented in "cookbook" format, as these represent a logical approach to questioning the strengths and weaknesses of the hospital's internal control. Certainly there can be no "cookbook" approach to an audit program for hospitals. As each hospital is different due to the styles of management and constraints of manpower, so are the audit requirements.

There are, however, certain procedures that will usually be employed regardless of how strong the internal control of the hospital may be.

The Audit Objective

The primary objective in the audit of petty cash is to determine that such funds are under proper control and that the established systems and written procedures are being followed. In addition, you must determine that there are adequate safeguards and security precautions to insure the safekeeping of patient valuables.

Testing the Hospital Petty Cash Funds Transactions and Related Bank Balances

The following list can not technically be considered tests of "transactions," but the tests are interrelated with those found in the preceding chapter on cash. The actual audit procedures will depend upon your hospital's accounting procedures and internal control.

Once you have completed the testing of the hospital petty cash "transactions," you should reevaluate the system of internal control and reconsider the adequacy of the audit program.

Tests

1) Count petty cash and cash for deposit on a surprise basis.
2) Account for noncash items in funds.
3) Ascertain subsequently that cash for deposit has been recorded as cash received and is deposited.

4) Review the accounting office reconciliation of bank balances at the beginning and end of the test period.
5) Account for reconciling items appearing on reconciliations, such as undeposited receipts and unentered bank charges.

Audit Alerts

While performing these tests, were you alert to the following methods of concealing fraud? This list should be considered a reminder of the many methods that may be encountered. It is intended to stimulate the imagination of the auditor in relation to other possible methods that may be present in view of the existing system of internal control.

1) Overstating totals of vouchers in petty cash reimbursements.
2) Two entries for same voucher, one in petty cash and one in regular cash.
3) False vouchers for postage, supplies, and other expenditures.
4) Vouchers once properly reimbursed used to support a second reimbursement.

How to Audit the Petty Cash Funds

1) Count cash on hand, including undeposited receipts; i.e., cafeteria sales (see Figure 3.4) on a surprise basis.
2) In counting the cash on hand, always follow these precautions to the extent practical:
   a) Make your counts in the presence of the fund custodian, and obtain his signature acknowledging that all items counted have been returned.
   b) Maintain control over undeposited receipts until they are deposited in the bank or transferred to the cashier's office.
3) Summarize amounts counted and traced, or reconciled, to the general ledger balances. (See Figure 3.4.)
4) Trace amount of cash, per books, to custodian acknowledgment memo. (See Figure 3.2.)
5) Review the contents of the cash count and discuss significant undistributed disbursements, unusual receipts, or vouchers with the chief financial officer or the administrator of the hospital.

WORKING PAPERS REQUIRED

Cash Counts

A working paper such as shown in Figure 3.4 is necessary in the event a subsequent question is raised regarding the account.

Summary of Audit Work Performed

A memorandum should be prepared detailing the extent of your petty cash counts and your review of the safeguards of patient valuables. The memorandum should contain your opinion of the fair presentation of petty cash in the records of the hospital and the amount of any adjustment you may have had to make because of the hospital's failure to properly state the creation of any new or expended petty cash fund.

Summary of Petty Cash

A summary listing of petty cash funds amounts, location, and proper cross-referencing should be placed in the front of the audit working paper folder marked "Petty Cash and Patient Valuables."

FINANCIAL STATEMENT PRESENTATION

If the amount of "petty cash" is considered to be significant, it may be shown as a separate line item on the balance sheet. For example:

Cash in banks	$10,000	
Change funds (cash, on hand)	4,000	$14,000

If your examination of the "paid-out" vouchers reveals that they are a significant part of the balance, a journal entry should be made charging the paid-outs to the proper expense or asset account, and reducing cash. If the amount of the paid-outs is very small, it is usually ignored and the entire amount is shown as "Cash, on hand."

Since patient valuables are not assets of the hospital, they are not noted on the financial statements.

_____________ HOSPITAL

EXPENSE REPORT

Date ____________________

Employee ______________________________ Department ____________________

Activities ____

____

MONTH / DAY	/	/	/	/	/	/	/	/	/	/	ITEM TOTALS
Lodging*											
Meals: Breakfast											
Lunch											
Dinner											
Phone											
Parking & Tolls											
Taxi											
Mileage											
Public Transportation*											
Daily Totals											

DETAIL OF MILEAGE

Ending Mileage ________

Beginning Mileage ________

Total Miles ________ X 15 ¢ = ________

CASH SUMMARY

Cash Advanced $ ____________

Total Expended $ ____________

Cash Balance $ ____________

DETAILS OF PUBLIC TRANSPORTATION

From ____________________ To ____________ Cost ________

From ____________________ To ____________ Cost ________

* Attach Receipts

APPROVED BY: ____________________

Department Head

____

Assistant Administrator
Finance

FIGURE 3.1

PETTY CASH CUSTODIAN STATEMENT OF RESPONSIBILITY

The undersigned hereby states that he/she is the Custodian of the $ __________ petty cash fund established for the __________________ Department.

As Custodian of this fund, he/she is responsible for all the accounting and balancing of this fund and any shortage will be deducted from his/her paycheck.

As Custodian, I hereby authorize *(Name of hospital)* to make a payroll deduction for any shortage in this fund.

Signature ______________________________

Date ______________________________

Witness ______________________________

Date ______________________________

FIGURE 3.2

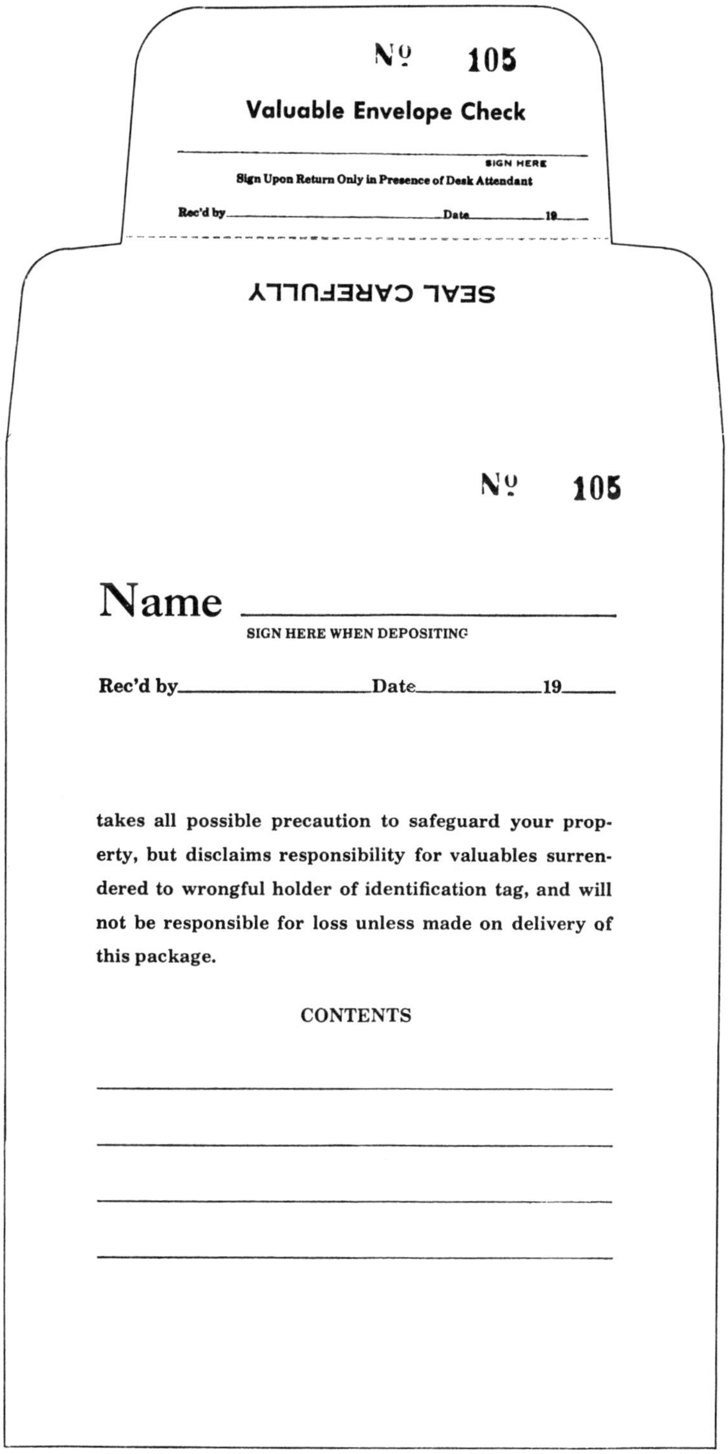

№ 105

Valuable Envelope Check

SIGN HERE

Sign Upon Return Only in Presence of Desk Attendant

Rec'd by__________ Date________ 19__

SEAL CAREFULLY

№ 105

Name ____________________

SIGN HERE WHEN DEPOSITING

Rec'd by__________ Date________ 19__

takes all possible precaution to safeguard your property, but disclaims responsibility for valuables surrendered to wrongful holder of identification tag, and will not be responsible for loss unless made on delivery of this package.

CONTENTS

____

____

____

____

FIGURE 3.3

HOSPITAL

PETTY CASH COUNT

______________ 19___

	INITIALS	DATE
PREPARED BY	JLD	12/31
APPROVED BY	Bj	1-5-

Date	Name	(1)	(2)	(3)	(4)
	CASH ON HAND:				
				NO.	TOTAL
	Currency		$ 50		
			20	2	$ 40 — C
			10	3	30 — C
			5	1	5 — C
			1	8	8 — C
	Coin		.50	4	2 — C
			.25	9	2 25 C
			.10	16	1 60 C
			.05	8	40 C
			.01	31	31 C
	TOTAL CASH ON HAND:				89 56 F
	PETTY CASH RECEIPTS FOR DISBURSEMENTS:				
Date	Name	Account No.			
12/22	R. Smith	416.26		$ 20 42	
12/22	W. Stevens	416.26		16 66	
12/22	S. Jones	416.26		25 27	
12/24	A. Vendor	500.89		9 29	
12/27	U.S. Postmaster	500.10		20 00	
12/29	H. & R. Office Supply	500.04		9 17	
12/30	B. Brooks	416.26		9 63	110 44
	TOTAL PETTY CASH FUND:				$ 200 — TP

Received of ____________________, auditor eighty-nine dollars and fifty-six cents ($89.56).

____

(Custodian)

P - Per signed petty cash custodian statement.

FIGURE 3.4

4

Auditing Receivables and Allowances for Uncollectible Accounts

Due to the complexity of third-party reimbursement formulae, the accounting for receivables and allowances for uncollectible accounts are often misunderstood by hospital trustees and administrators. The distinguishing characteristic of hospitals' accounts receivable is that full-rate charges to patients are usually settled for less than the full rate. The accuracy of a hospital's accounts receivable may not be known until challenged by an audit.

Case History No. 1

For example, while performing an audit for the Medicare Intermediary, it was noticed that this particular hospital had the lowest days' charges outstanding of any hospital previously audited. It was surprising, since the hospital business office appeared to be disorganized and the hospital was located in an economically depressed area.

Upon investigation, it was discovered that during the year the hospital had installed a new posting machine and redesigned patient ledgers. During the conversion to the new system, animosities developed and several office personnel were replaced.

The procedure for collecting an account was reviewed with the office manager. He told us the new machine allowed them to have all charges for the previous day posted by 4:00 a.m. When the patient was discharged, he was given the top copy of the four-part patient ledger. Two weeks later, the second copy was mailed to the patient with a sticker applied that politely asked for payment. Then 30 days after discharge, the third copy was mailed, and finally after 60 days from the date of the patient's discharge, the fourth copy was mailed. Apparently this was the first time the office manager had verbalized the procedure with anyone, for suddenly he exclaimed, "I'll be damned, we've been mailing our file copy." He was correct.

Protective Procedure

Whenever a new form is utilized or the duty of an existing form changed, insist upon a simple flow chart of the form. The flow chart does not have to be drawn by a systems engineer. There have been many excellent flow charts drawn by the representative of a forms company or a departmental manager who used a ruler and logic.

The small hospital without sophisticated electronic data processing equipment is not the only one that can have problems in the area of accounts receivable management.

Case History No. 2

During a conversion from a manual to a computerized accounts receivable system, the controller of a religious hospital threw away the computerized statements whenever the insurance billing clerks got behind in their work. This practice had escaped everyone's attention for over a year.

Why was the Sister performing in such an irrational manner? Because she thought the Order was wrong in going to a shared hospital computer system and she wasn't about to help make it work.

Protective Procedure

The statements of accounts receivable balances should have been mailed from the computer center. The hospital should receive only a duplicate copy of the information contained in the statement.

The above took place out of carelessness or spite; imagine what is happening where someone is using forethought and imagination! The following paragraphs will provide useful tools with which you may cut your way through the accounts receivable maze, recognize weaknesses in controls, develop improved procedures, and insure that your audit of this largest single "quick asset" is performed adequately and efficiently.

REVIEWING THE CONTROLS RELATING TO THE HOSPITAL'S ACCOUNTS RECEIVABLE

The Accounts Receivable Reconciliation

Hospitals often do not reconcile their accounts receivable, but merely stop when they find a figure that agrees with the general ledger.

If the hospital is not using a standardized form (see Figure 4.1) at month end for reconciling accounts receivable, implement such a form immediately. Through the use of this form, you will be able to determine that certain items, peculiar to your system, are consistently applied from month to month. In far too many instances the idiosyncrasies of a computer system are maneuvered to fit the maze of adding machine tape until two tapes total the same.

Utilizing the Computer

If the hospital uses electronic data processing for its accounts receivable, ask the data processing supervisor to provide you with the following reports, which are useful in evaluating the effectiveness of the hospital's credit and collection policies and procedures, and the patient accounts manager:

1) An aged trial balance by date of discharge.
2) An aged trial balance by date of last payment.
3) An aged trial balance (date of discharge) by area of responsibility; i.e., Blue Cross, Medicare, etc.
4) A report showing the number and dollar of accounts placed with collection agencies, and the number and dollar of accounts collected by the agencies.

By reviewing the "total balance matrix" (see Figure 4.2) of these reports, you can establish problem areas and trends and take corrective action.

The computer can also be utilized to request negative confirmation of the accounts receivable balances.

Analyzing the Accounts Receivable Trial Balance

In analyzing any listing of accounts receivable, always question any unusual symbols, letters, or markings that are not clearly defined in the hospital's procedural manual.

Many times you will learn that a symbol may mean that office personnel are not to mail statements or that the computer has been coded not to mail statements on these individual accounts. Naturally, if that is the case, the opportunity for manipulation is greater.

The auditor should issue positive confirmations to many of the accounts that have been so coded. This will often bring to light accounting or procedural irregularities.

If reasonable, ask that all accounts with credit balances be listed and totalled separately. If this is not possible, foot the credit balances. If these are a material portion of the receivables, consideration should be given to a separate classification of these balances on the balance sheet.

Unapplied Payments

In any hospital there will be a segment of the accounts receivable file called unapplied cash, credit balances, patient ledgers missing, or similar titles.

The easiest way to monitor these types of accounts is to request a separate listing of all accounts in this financial section. If the accounts do not already have a separate code, i.e., financial class, it is then recommended that such provision be made in your accounting process.

The responsibility of coding cash receipts should be vested in one individual. This individual should have the responsibility for locating and resolving all amounts that are coded as "unapplied cash." Through the use of the separate listing, management can monitor the individual's effectiveness.

From time to time you should audit the changes in two subsequent reports to determine that the amounts that have been eliminated from the unapplied cash report for the previous month have been applied to the proper patient's ledger. In making your examination, you should satisfy yourself that such amounts are not being applied to accounts that will result in credit balances and subsequent refunds made to these individuals. It could be that the individual receiving the refund is a relative or close friend of the employee coding the payments.

Equal Rights Amendment

In reviewing the application of the hospital's credit and collection policies, see that they are in compliance with the letter of the law. Many states have law suits pending against primary lending agencies for being discriminatory in their credit policies.

Also, with the passage of the equal rights amendment, women are now responsible for the debts of their deceased husbands. Review the collection file of applicable accounts to determine if the credit manager is taking advantage of this new opportunity.

Eighteen-Point Pre-Confirmation Checklist

Q. Are ledgers posted by persons with no access to cash receipts?

- Who relieves the cashier for sickness, vacation, and holidays.
- Is the system you are auditing today the same system used throughout the period under examination.
- Are corrections made to patient ledgers.
- Who approves such corrections.

Q. Are the ledgers balanced to the general ledger control account monthly?

- Is there a standard format completed that assures the consistent treatment of problem transactions.
- Is there an item on the reconciliation that could be considered a balancing item; i.e., amount of unlocated difference, misplaced charges, unapplied cash.
- Are recoveries of bad debts, collection of N.S.F. checks and third-party contractual allowances properly reported on the reconciliation.

Q. Is the accounts receivable reconciliation reviewed by a responsible person?

- What is the nature and extent of the review made by the responsible person.
- Is the reconciliation initialled and dated by the individual preparing the reconciliation, and initialled and dated by the individual making the review.
- What is the elapsed time between the end of the month and the date the reconciliation is completed and the date the reconciliation is reviewed.
- Is each step in the reconciliation process timely or does it appear that the accounting personnel are having trouble in preparing the reconciliation.

Q. Are statements sent out for all accounts on a monthly basis?

- If statements are not being mailed for all accounts, which accounts are not receiving statements and why.
- If there are balances owed by persons in the administrative suite, is the administrator or are the trustees aware of such amounts.
- If the balance owed by persons for whom statements are not being mailed is the result of a transaction not related specifically to the hospital activity, shouldn't such amounts be noted in the interim financial statements.

Q. Are statements mailed by a person who is independent of patient ledger posting?

- How is the process handled when the individual responsible for the mailing is sick, on vacation, or on holiday leave.
- Are the statements left in a public area that could be accessible to the individual who posts the ledgers.
- What is the disposition of statements that are returned by the postmaster.

Q. *Are monthly statements mailed by a person who has no access to cash?*

- How is the process handled when the individual responsible for the mailing is sick, on vacation, or on holiday leave.
- Are the statements left in a public area that could be accessible to the individual who handles cash.

Q. *Are cashiers denied access to ledgers?*

- Does the individual who handles the patient ledgers sometimes assist the cashiers.
- How closely are the activities of the office manager scrutinized. For example, does the office manager sometimes work or relieve the cashiers while they are on lunch break and then review and handle problem accounts receivable for the insurance clerks, and then approve the accounts receivable reconciliation.

Q. *Are reported exceptions to the accounts receivable balance mailed to patients reviewed by a responsible person?*

- If the responsible person is the office manager, is the chief financial officer aware, on a monthly basis, of the disposition of these exceptions.
- Is there a written record of exceptions received and reviewed by the office manager.
- Does the review of these exceptions indicate that there is a weakness or problem in the billing, cash receipts, or posting system and mechanism; i.e., are there problems of a recurring nature.

Q. *Does a responsible person approve accounts receivable journal entries?*

- Is the individual making this approval high enough in the organization "hierarchy" to make it more difficult for account manipulation.
- How thorough is the investigation or questioning made by the responsible individual of the journal entries before approval.
- What is the education or experience background of the individual approving journal entries to accounts receivable.

Q. *Are monthly aging schedules of the accounts receivable prepared?*

- If not monthly, is it frequent enough so that interim financial statements are fairly presented.
- Are the aging schedules reviewed for mathematical accuracy as well as the accuracy of the aging itself.
- Do the individuals preparing and making such a review date and initial these schedules.
- Are aging schedules reviewed by a responsible person.

Q. *Are overpayment refunds made after a responsible person's approval and under established policies and procedures?*

- Do the established policies and procedures minimize the chance of an individual's receiving a refund because of an incorrect posting to his account.
- Does the individual who is approving such refunds initiate the approval before refund checks are written.
- Are refund checks ever written without the initialled approval of the responsible person.

- Do refunds over a certain stated dollar amount require the written approval of the chief financial officer.

Q. Are credit and collection policies written?

- Did the Board of Trustees approve the policies.
- Are such policies in compliance with Federal and State guidelines, i.e., Hill-Burton charity regulations, requirements for the issuance of tax-exempt municipal bonds, and consistent with community practices.

Q. Are credit and collection procedures written?

- Have such procedures been written in a manner that is concise and clearly understandable.
- Have such procedures been approved by the chief financial officer.
- Do such procedures minimize the chance of accounts that could be collected by the hospital being turned over to a collection agency.

Q. Does the hospital, monthly, record bad debt write-offs, and other non-contractual write-offs?

Q. Are bad debt write-offs and non-contractual write-offs approved?

- Is the individual approving these write-offs in a position that would indicate that he has exercised good judgment in the past.
- Are write-offs consistent with established hospital policies.
- Is there adequate documentation relating to the description and classification of charity and bad debt accounts.
- Are policy discounts and administrative adjustments accounted for separately.

Q. Are bad debt ledgers governed by a control account?

- Are such amounts reflected in memorandum form in the interim financial statements.
- Are the written-off accounts kept on file in accordance with record retention guidelines as specified by the Hospital Financial Management Association.

Q. Are collection agency accounts, whether written off or not, governed by a control account?

- Are such amounts also reported to the trustees in the interim financial statements.
- Does it appear that the collection agency is "creaming" the accounts; i.e., making only the easy collections.
- Should two or more collection agencies be employed to generate competition between the agencies.
- Does the number of recoveries of uncollectible accounts indicate that the hospital policies are too weak and the accounts are being given to the collection agency without an adequate collection effort on the part of the hospital.

Q. Are third-party contractual adjustments cleared from patient ledgers monthly?

- Are such amounts adequately reflected in the interim financial statements so as not to result in an overstatement of accounts receivable.
- Are these amounts reviewed by a responsible person.

THE AUDIT OF THE HOSPITAL'S ACCOUNTS RECEIVABLE

The Audit Objective

The objective in performing an examination of accounts receivable is to determine the accuracy of the recorded amounts, their validity as claims against the recorded debtors, and their collectibility. You should also be concerned with the amount recorded as an allowance for uncollectible accounts to determine that the hospital is providing an adequate reserve for accounts that will be deemed uncollectible.

Pre-Confirmation Procedures

1) Obtain an aged trial balance of patient accounts receivable. This trial balance may be as of the balance sheet date or as of the date of confirmation, subsequent to the audit date.

a) Foot and crossfoot the trial balance (usually on a test basis) and reconcile the total, per the schedule, with the general ledger control account.
b) Test the accuracy and aging of amounts by reviewing some of the individual accounts.
c) In auditing the individual ledger accounts, watch for unusual debits, credits, or balances. On a separate piece of paper, note such items for further investigation.
d) Obtain information for segregation, if significant, of credit balances, receivables from trustees, members of the Administration, or employees.

2) Select certain patients and types of contractors, i.e., Blue Cross, Medicare, Medicaid, for confirmation. In the selection of confirmation methods, we should consider the following:

a) The positive type of confirmation request is preferable in cases where a limited number of individual balances are of relatively major importance, or where there is reason to believe that the possibility of disputes, inaccuracies, or irregularities in the accounts is greater than usual. (See Figure 4.3.)
b) The negative method of confirmation is acceptable in the majority of cases, but should not be used where there are clear indications that it is inadequate, as with receivables from the United States Government; i.e., Champus. (See Figure 4.4.)

Confirmation Procedures

Confirmation procedures may be carried out at appropriate times prior to the balance sheet date. If this is done, it is necessary to review intervening transactions in the receivable accounts from the confirmation date to the balance sheet date, and to consider the advisability of confirming large or unusual accounts again at a later date.

1) The accounts selected should be a representative sample. In addition, it may be desirable to request confirmation of accounts with large balances, past due accounts, and accounts of an unusual nature that do not fall within the selected sample. Consideration should be given to the use of statistical sampling in selecting accounts to be

confirmed. In selecting the sample, the auditor should be sure that the mass of accounts from which the sample is selected is whole; i.e., that he has free access to all accounts that might be selected.

2) The positive type of confirmation should include wording on the hospital's letterhead stationery, as shown in Figure 4.3.

3) For those accounts for which the negative method is used, the request may be rubber stamped on the hospital's regular statement to the patient, attached in the form of a sticker, or may be a special form or business reply card enclosed with the statement. Where the hospital uses electronic data processing, it is possible for messages to be printed on the statement by the computer. The message should be similar to that shown in Figure 4.4.

4) Requests or statements mailed must be compared with the ledger accounts which they are to represent, and continuous control must be exercised over the accounts and statements from the time the accounts have been selected for confirmation until the statements have been deposited in the mail. If it is necessary to have the confirmation procedure continued for more than one working day, make certain that you are the only individual with a key to the office in which such accounts are locked, or obtain a filing cabinet that can be locked and keep the key under your own control. In both cases, it would be advisable to seal the door or the file cabinet.

5) A rubber stamp stating "Return to the attention of the sender" should be used on the outside of the envelope.

6) To ensure that you will get a large number of responses for the positive confirmations, include with such confirmation a stamped, self-addressed envelope; however, it is preferable to use envelopes that have been franked with the hospital's postage permit number.

7) A record of the accounts selected for confirmation should be retained with the working papers. For positive requests, this may consist of copies of the request letters, notations on the aged trial balance, or a worksheet showing the patient's name, address, and account balance. For negative requests, a copy of the trial balance or adding machine tape of patient account balances is sufficient.

8) Amounts confirmed should be noted on the record retained. All exceptions reported, whether in reply to positive or negative requests, should be investigated. If the exceptions do not indicate serious weaknesses, or are not material in amount, they may be turned over to the hospital personnel for follow-up. Any differences that indicate the possibility of irregularities, particularly any claim that credit has not been given for a payment made prior to the statement date, should be followed up by the auditor.

9) In using the positive type of confirmation request, every practical effort must be made to obtain a reply. Second requests should be mailed to patients from whom replies have not been received after a reasonable time. In addition, alternative procedures, similar to those outlined in the following paragraphs, should be followed in respect to accounts of patients who did not reply to the positive request.

Alternative Procedures

Alternative procedures must be undertaken to substantiate accounts of patients not replying to positive requests. Such procedures may include, but are not limited to, the following:

1) Support collections subsequent to the confirmation date through the inspection of incoming checks, or remittance advices. Trace amounts collected to the patient's account and trace collected amounts to the record of cash receipts, and from there to the bank deposit.

2) Take such steps as are reasonable to establish the existence of the patient, if there is any question as to that fact; i.e., the examination of the patient's medical record.

3) Test the revenue cutoff by examining the admission register for several days prior to and subsequent to the balance sheet date, and tracing those patients' charge activities on the receivable records for the purpose of making sure that revenue is recorded in the proper accounting period. (See Figure 4.5.)

Determining the Collectibility of Accounts

1) Compare the current year aging with that of prior years for an appraisal or evaluation of the accounts in the aggregate.
2) Discuss the collectibility of the accounts with the credit manager or other responsible official of the hospital, and summarize his comments for the working papers. With respect to the past due accounts, indicate the collections since the balance sheet date and examine correspondence with the patients, collection agencies' reports, and other data in the patient's file.
3) Prepare an analysis of the allowance for doubtful accounts for the period, comparing the bad debt provisions and the experience with those of previous years.
4) Observe whether charge-offs, either to the allowance or directly to expense, have been properly authorized. Give consideration to sending some positive confirmation requests covering larger amounts charged off in the current and prior periods.
5) Determine that accounts considered uncollectible have been charged off and review the adequacy of the allowance for doubtful accounts.
6) Select a sample of patients incurring charges during the period, using random sampling with the population, including the following:
   a) Patients inhouse at the beginning of the test period. (Obtain from the accounts receivable detail.)
   b) Inpatients incurring charges and admitted during the test period. (Obtain from the patient register.)
   c) Outpatients incurring charges during the test period. (Obtain from the patient register.)

NOTE: If a numerical sequence is kept on all patients, consider testing a block of these patients instead of using steps a, b, and c above.

7) For the patients selected, trace the account balances to the billing statements.
8) Then trace the balances from the billing statements to the appropriate program patient logs.
9) For inhouse account balances, test check the calculation of routine service charges; examine charge tickets, on a random basis, for pricing and propriety.
10) Test foot patient account statements for clerical accuracy.

NOTE: The test of the accuracy of the revenue collection and recording system is covered in Chapter 10.

11) Review the cost reimbursement reports to determine that they were prepared in accordance wtih the third-party principles of reimbursement.

NOTE: The auditor must remember that the preparation of a cost report is the only accurate method of determining the contractual allowance and amount due to/due from the Program. Figures 4.6 and 4.7 are methods that could be utilized to arrive at a reasonable estimate of such amounts.

12) Review the hospital's provision for the differences between contractual interim billing rates and full rate charges. (See Figure 4.6.)
13) Review the hospital's calculation of the estimate due to/due from the Program provided for in the accounts. (See Figure 4.7.)

AUDITING NOTES RECEIVABLE

The Audit Objective

The objective in performing an examination of notes receivable is to determine that the balances recorded are collectible and accurate. The auditor must also be concerned with the amount recorded as an allowance for uncollectible notes to determine that the hospital is providing an adequate reserve for notes that will be deemed uncollectible.

Truth in Lending Act

Hospitals are beginning to adopt the practice of establishing notes receivable for those patients wishing to make payments on an installment basis. It should be noted that the "Truth in Lending Act" applies to hospitals as well as to commercial lenders. The "Truth in Lending Act" requires that the true interest rate be noted on the face of the note or in the material reviewed with the patient. If the hospital that is being audited uses such a collection procedure, the following auditing steps are necessary:

1) Obtain a list of notes, acceptances, and other instruments evidencing indebtness.

   a) Prove the footings of the list and reconcile the totals with the general ledger control accounts.
   b) Check the listing to individual accounts or other detailed records. Indicate past due or renewal on the list.

2) Account for notes or other instruments by inspection, by evidence of subsequent payment, or by confirmation, if the instruments are in the custody of others; i.e., banks. Any collateral should be inspected or otherwise accounted for. Notes and collateral preferably should be inspected concurrently with the counting of cash and the inspecting of securities.

3) Request confirmation from the makers of the notes, including notes discounted, or signed with recourse, or otherwise pledged. When positive confirmations are applied, alternate procedures must be applied to those notes whose makers do not reply.

4) To determine the collectibility of notes receivable:

a) Check the hospital aging of notes and secure summary for working papers.
b) Obtain information as to amounts maturing beyond one year from the balance sheet date.
c) Investigate generally the origin of notes and make inquiry regarding the hospital's practice for accepting notes for past due accounts and the policy as to note "renewals."
d) Discuss the collectibility of the notes with the chief financial officer of the hospital and review the credit files on large and past due notes.
e) Ascertain the collections since the balance sheet date on questionable items.
f) Determine that notes considered uncollectible have been charged off and provision has been made for loss on doubtful items.

5) Test the calculation of accrued interest or unearned interest.

6) If audit procedures are carried out at a date other than that of the balance sheet, review intervening transactions. In addition, review listings at the balance sheet date for possible reclassifications and for new large notes that possibly should be confirmed.

WORKING PAPERS REQUIRED

Accounts Receivable

1) A trial balance of accounts receivable as of the balance sheet date that has been footed, crossfooted, and reconciled to the general ledger. The trial balance should bear evidence of which accounts had been selected for positive and negative confirmation.
2) Returned positive confirmations and the alternative procedures noted on the copies of the positive confirmations not returned.
3) Memorandum of follow-up work performed on exceptions reported, whether in reply to positive or to negative requests.
4) A schedule showing the audit work performed in testing the revenue cutoff. Figure 4.6 is an example of a satisfactory workpaper.
5) A schedule comparing the current year aging of accounts receivable with that of the prior year. The schedule should contain a summary of the auditor's discussion regarding the collectibility of the accounts with the credit manager.
6) A schedule comparing the allowance for uncollectible accounts for the period with the bad debt provision and the experience of the previous year.
7) A memorandum summary of the audit work performed and conclusions reached regarding the reasonableness and proper disclosure of the accounts receivable and the related allowance.

Notes Receivable

1) A trial balance of notes receivable as of the balance sheet date. The trial balance should bear evidence that it was footed and reconciled to the general ledger.
2) A record of the notes selected for confirmation. This may consist of notations on the trial balance or copies of the request letters, or the negative request and adding machine tape of the patient account balances is sufficient.

3) Memorandum of follow-up work performed on the exceptions reported, or the alternative procedures followed to determine the collectibility of the notes.
4) A schedule comparing the allowance for uncollectible notes for the period with the bad debt provision and the experience of the previous year.
5) A memorandum stating the extent to which accrued interest calculations were calculated and indicating the hospital's compliance with the "Truth in Lending Act."
6) A memorandum summary of the audit work performed and conclusion reached regarding the reasonableness and proper disclosure of the notes receivable and the related allowance.
7) A summary of notes and accounts receivable with the appropriate allowances for uncollectibles. The summary should be footed, traced to the hospital's general ledger balances, and cross-referenced to the appropriate supporting working papers.

FINANCIAL STATEMENT PRESENTATION

Notes receivable, if material and bearing interest, should be shown after cash and before accounts receivable. Where third-party payor receivables are material, they may also be shown separately. It is generally acceptable, however, to combine all receivables in one amount.

The allowance for uncollectible accounts is usually shown as a deduction from the total accounts receivable.

Advances to employees or officers, amounts due from the sale of items not properly carried in inventory, or rental from non-operating property must be segregated on the financial statements as "Receivables—Other."

Notes receivable (net of $10,000 allowance)	$ 155,000
Patient accounts receivable (net of $345,000 allowance)	3,685,000
Receivable—Other	42,000

______ HOSPITAL

ACCOUNTS RECEIVABLE RECONCILIATION

______, 19___

Computer Balance (aged trial balance) discharge		$2,440,035.01	
Suspense File		49,000.00	
Inhouse Accounts		460,000.00	
Less:			$2,949,035.01
Cash Receipts Not Posted	$5,585.94		
Rejects (list)	821.50		
			(6,407.44)
Add:			
Deleted Accounts (list)	$4,742.33		
Unposted Medicare Adjustment for ___ mo.	2,022.00		
Unposted # 19200-5 Cr. to General Ledger	2,300.21		
Unposted 2250 Cr. to the Computer	(20.00)		
			9,044.54
Adjusted Computer Balance			$2,951,672.11
Balance per general ledger			2,951,672.00
Difference due to dollar rounding			$ 0.11

FIGURE 4.1

_______________ HOSPITAL

TOTAL DISCHARGED ACCOUNTS RECEIVABLE

________, 19____

FC	AGE 0–30	31–60	61–90	91–120	121–150	151–180	181–999	TOTAL	PREVIOUS MONTH
Blue Cross	312,000	66,000	34,000	45,000	9,000	5,000	22,000	493,000	394,000
Medicare	153,000	73,000	25,000	14,000	3,000	1,000	23,000	292,000	365,000
Medicaid	35,000	40,000	35,000	21,000	13,000	10,000	54,000	208,000	219,000
Comm.	179,000	107,000	40,000	27,000	13,000	14,000	49,000	429,000	379,000
Self-Pay	37,000	36,000	77,000	28,000	30,000	35,000	386,000	629,000	646,000
TOTAL	716,000	322,000	211,000	135,000	68,000	65,000	534,000	2,051,000	2,003,000
%	35.0	15.7	10.2	6.6	3.3	3.1	26.1	100.0	2.4+

NOTE: A review of this report reveals that a substantial increase has occurred in Blue Cross and Commercial Insurance accounts receivable. Explanations should be obtained, verified, and corrective action taken. The reports indicates that insufficient effort is being expended in the collecting of self-pay accounts. This could be attributable to several factors: (a) inadequate insurance information at the time of admission; (b) poorly organized collection department; (c) carrying accounts on the hospital records too long before placing with an outside agency.

FIGURE 4.2

Dear __________ :

Our auditors are conducting an examination of our financial records and wish to confirm, with you, the balance of your account with us at __________ (*Date*). Please sign on the space below and return. A stamped, self-addressed envelope is included for your convenience.

Account Balance $ __________ is the amount of my account with the hospital at

__________________ .
Date

______________________________   ______________________
(Signature)   *(Date)*

Exception, if any ____

____

____

____
(Signature)

FIGURE 4.3

Our auditors are making an examination of our financial statements. If the accompanying statement is not the correct balance of your account, please notify our auditors. A stamped, self-addressed envelope is enclosed for your convenience.

PLEASE DO NOT MAKE REMITTANCE TO THE AUDITORS.

FIGURE 4.4

________________ HOSPITAL

REVENUE CUT-OFF

____________, 19___

	INITIALS	DATE
PREPARED BY	JLD	2/5
APPROVED BY		

PATIENT NAME		ADMISSION DATE ч	ROOM CHARGE, DAY OF ADMISSION	
DONNA	H.	12/29	85.00 ✓	PRIVATE
FRANK	H.	29	75.50 ✓	SEMI
ALON	H.	30	75.50 ✓	SEMI
KEN	R.	30	75.50 ✓	SEMI
MARVIN	M.	31	120.00 ✓	ICU
ROBERT	O.	31	85.00 ✓	PRIVATE
RON	T.	1/1	97.50 ✓	PRIVATE
RODNEY	W.	1	85.00 ✓	SEMI
LINDA	O.	2	85.00 ✓	SEMI
WANDA	H.	2	85.00 ✓	SEMI
PAULA	O.	3	97.50 ✓	PRIVATE
LINDA	T.	3	140.00 ✓	ICU

ч - per admission log

✓ charge for day of admission as reflected on patient account - hospital implemented a rate increase on January 1, 19____.

NOTE: Routine laboratory tests required at admission were also noted to be charged on the day of admission. This also indicates that the hospital has made a proper cut-off of revenue at year-end.

FIGURE 4.5

HOSPITAL
MEDICARE & REVENUE EXPENSE

________________, 19__

	INITIALS	DATE
PREPARED BY	JLD	9-11
APPROVED BY		

LINE No.		(1) TOTAL REVENUE	(2) TOTAL INPATIENT REVENUE	(3) % INPATIENT REVENUE TO TOTAL REV.	(4) MEDICARE INPATIENT REVENUE	(5) % MEDICARE INPT. REV. TO INPT. REVENUE	(6) MEDICARE DAYS	(7) TOTAL INPATIENT DAYS	(8)	(9) TOTAL EXPENSE	(10) MEDICARE PER DIEM	(11) MEDICARE EXPENSE	(12)	(13)
1	Routine Service	5170172	5170172				26725	65017		5133116	7895	2109939		
3					2528910									
4	I.C.U.	180566	180566				586	1239		271894	21945	128598		
5	C.C.U.	651521	651521				1773	3812		409473	10742	190456		
6							29084	70068						
7	O.R. & R.R.	1040717	954655	9173	199225	2087				877484		167986		
9	Emergency Room	256050	31748	1240	12215	3847				326302		15566		
11–22		Total inpatient and outpatient Revenue per general ledger	Total inpatient revenue per general ledger	Column two divided by column one, except for room charges (see column 10)	Medicare inpatient revenue, discharge basis, per Medicare Log	Column four divided by column two, except for room charges	Medicare inpatient days per medical records; This figure includes inhouse & discharged patients	Total inpatient days per medical records		See figure 4.6(B) & figure 4.6 (C)	Room expense column nine divided by days in column seven	For allowable room expense multiply column ten by Medicare days in column six. For allowable ancillary expense, multiply column three(x) column five(x)column nine		
24	Total	12913530	11966221	9266	4853831	4056				10419031		3921098		
25	Room Difference	1.30 X APPLICABLE DAYS	26725		(34744)							140301	House Staff	
26					4819087	÷ 29084 =	$165.20					190560	Prof. Fees	
27													Nursing Diff *	
28												66011	2.47X 26,725	
29												4317970	÷ 29084 =	
30												$148.47	Allowable Cost Per Day	

Year-to-date
Amount due (to) from Intermediary

Allowable cost, per day	$	148.47
Interim per diem rate		140.00
		8.47
Allowable Medicare patient days		29,084
Year-to-date amount due from Intermediary	$	246,341.00

Year-to-date
Contractual Allowance

Covered charges, per day	$	165.70
Allowable cost, per day		148.47
		17.23
Allowable Medicare patient days		29,084
Total year-to-date contractual allowance	$	501,117.00

July Medicare Allowable Cost

per July "short factor"	$	4,317,970.00
per June "short factor"		3,654,472.00
July cost		663,498.00
divided by July Medicare Log		÷ 4,134
Medicare allowable cost, per patient day for month of July	$	160.50

* per prior years cost report

FIGURE 4.6

_____________ HOSPITAL
ALLOCATION OF EXPENSE PER
PREVIOUS YEARS COST REPORT - WORKSHEET B

	INITIALS	DATE
PREPARED BY	B.H	7-11-
APPROVED BY	JLD	7-11

FORM P-554-2 (GREEN) P-554-B2 (BUFF) Pearl Rite SYSTEMS CELINA, OHIO · DALLAS · LOS ANGELES LITHO IN U.S.A.

	(1) EXPENSE PER COLUMN 1	(2) EXPENSE PER COLUMN 23	(3) DIFFERENCE	(4) % OF COLUMN 3 TO TOTAL *
House staff	368687	451323	82636	1.048
I.C.U.	306997	469873	162876	2.066
C.C.U.	330506	644966	314460	3.988
Operating & recovery rooms	569814	1 291550	721736	9.154
Inpatient	3273224	7965871	4692647	59.517
Emergency room	305368	534661	229293	2.908
Home health agency	28239	37414	9175	.116
E.M.G.	2394	3722	1328	.017
Total	8898538	16783009	7884471	100.000

* Multiply each departmental percentage times the total indirect expense to arrive at the indirect expense allocation as shown in column two of figure 4.6. (C).

FIGURE 4.6 *(continued)*

______________ HOSPITAL

MEDICARE ADJUSTMENT

______________, 19____

	INITIALS	DATE
PREPARED BY	B.H.	7-11
APPROVED BY	JLD	7-16

FORM P-554-2 (GREEN) P-554-B2 (BUFF) Post-Rite SYSTEMS CELINA, OHIO · DALLAS · LOS ANGELES LITHO IN U.S.A.

%		(1) DIRECT EXPENSE	(2) INDIRECT EXPENSE ALLOCATED	(3) TO COLUMN 9 FIG. 4.6(A) TOTAL	(4)
1.048	Home staff	372324	50233	422557	To FIG. 4.6(D)
2.066	I.C.U.	172866	99028	271894	
3.988	C.C.U.	218319	191154	409473	
9.154	Operating & recovery room	438712	438772	877484	
59.517	Inpatient	2280335	2852781	5133116	
2.908	Emergency room	186915	139387	326302	
.116	Home health agency	19981	5560	25541	
.017	E.M.G.	233	815	1048	
100.000		6073906	4793223	10867129	10867129
	Controllable expenses	9704302	Less: home staff		<422557>
	Unassigned expenses	2160745		home health	<25541>
	Professional fees	<628772>			
	Other income	<362008>	Total to		
	T.V. maintenance	<53956>	figure 4.6(A)		
	Additional special cost	46818	Column nine (9)		10419031
		10867129			
	Less direct expense	<6073906>			
	Total indirect expense	4793223			

FIGURE 4.6 *(continued)*

______________ HOSPITAL

ALLOWABLE HOUSE STAFF EXPENSE

______________, 19____

	INITIALS	DATE
PREPARED BY	B.H.	7-11
APPROVED BY	JLD	7/11

FORM P-554-2 (GREEN) P-554-B2 (BUFF) Post-Rite SYSTEMS CELINA, OHIO - DALLAS - LOS ANGELES LITHO IN U.S.A.

(1) (2) (3) (4)

Total house staff expense $422557 (÷) TOTAL PATIENT DAYS (70,068) = $6.03

$6.03 (X) TOTAL MEDICARE DAYS (29,084) = $175377

$175377 (X) reimbursement percentage (80%) = $140301 *

* TO FIGURE 4.6 (A) COLUMN 11

FIGURE 4.6 *(continued)*

HOSPITAL

PROFESSIONAL FEES

, 19

	INITIALS	DATE
PREPARED BY	B.H.	7-11
APPROVED BY	JLD	9-11

FORM P-574 (GREEN) P-574-B (BUFF) Post-Rite SYSTEMS CELINA, OHIO · DALLAS · LOS ANGELES LITHO IN U.S.A.

LINE No.	DEPT		(1) MEDICARE Y.T.D. INPT. REVENUE	(2) DEPT. Y.T.D. INPT. REV.	(3) DEPT Y.T.D. TOTAL REV.	(4) PART A REIMB. (1 ÷ 2)%	(5) PART B REIMB. (1 ÷ 3)%
2		Radiology	187883	546263	876327	34.39	21.44
4		Pathology	611346	1327220	1413907	46.06	43.24
6		~~Nuclear Medicine~~	101212	229561	250020	44.09	40.48
9						REIMB.	
10			TOTAL		ALLOCATED	RATE PER	REIMB.
11			PROFESSIONAL EXP.		EXPENSE	ABOVE	FEE
13		Radiology	241866	(A) 10%	24187	34.39	8318
14				(B) 90%	217679	21.44	46670
16		Pathology	244051	(A) 80%	195241	46.06	89928
17				(B) 20%	48810	43.24	21105
19		Nuclear Medicine	60077	(A) 10%	6078	44.09	2680
20				(B) 90%	53999	40.48	21859
22			545994		545994 →		190560 *
28	*	TO FIGURE 4.6 (A)	COLUMN 11				

FIGURE 4.6 *(continued)*

_____________ HOSPITAL

MEDICARE AND MEDICAID ADJUSTMENT FOR ____, 19__

	MEDICARE REVENUE	MEDICARE EXPENSE	MEDICAID REVENUE	MEDICAID EXPENSE
Reimbursable Ratio		103.84%		66.87%
Revenue and Expense Per Financial Statements	750,000	651,000	750,000	651,000
Less Nursery—Actual Revenue & Estimated Cost	(5,000)	(12,000)		
A–5 Adjustments				
Cafeteria Sales		(5,000)		(5,000)
Vending Machine Sales		(400)		(400)
Cot Rental		(300)		(300)
Telephone Income		(1,000)		(1,000)
Medical Records Transcript Fee		(1,300)		(1,300)
Income from Oper-Fund Invest		(4,000)		(4,000)
Miscellaneous Income		(200)		(200)
T.V. Lease Payments		(3,800)		(3,800)
Prof. Fees		(5,200)		(5,200)
SUBTOTAL	745,000	617,800	750,000	629,800
Outpatient % to Apply to Expense Subtotal		3.06%		3.06%
Outpatient Revenue Per General Ledger and Applicable Expense	(22,000)	(18,900)	(22,000)	(19,300)
TOTAL INPATIENT REVENUE AND ALLOWABLE INPATIENT EXPENSE	723,000	598,900	728,000	610,500
Ratio of Cost to Charges		82.84%		83.86%
Reimbursable Ratio of Cost to Charges (82.84% x 103.84%)		86.02%		56.08%
Program Covered Charges		262,000		17,000
I. Reimbursable Cost (line above x 86.02 or 56.08)		225,400		9,500
Computation of 8½% Allowance				
Total Reimbursable Cost at End of Prior Fiscal Year (FY)		475,000		
8½% Due at End of Prior FY		4,000		
Percent of Total Reimbursable Cost		.84		

FIGURE 4.7

II. Estimated Reimbursable Cost	225,400	
8½% Reimbursement	1,900	
Computation of Reimbursable Equity Capital (use only if Proprietary Hospital)		
Equity Capital at End of Prior FY	38,000	5,000
Program Days for Prior FY	7,300	900
Equity Capital Per Program Day	5.20	5.56
Year-to-Date Program Days	3,000	200
III. Reimbursable Equity Capital	15,600	1,100
Other Reimbursable Cost		
TOTAL REIMBURSABLE COST (Total I, II, & III)	242,900	10,600
Less–		
Deductible & Coinsurance	17,000	
Amount Received	150,000	10,000
Total Deductibles, Coinsurance & Amount Received	167,000	10,000
Amount Due To (From) the Program	75,900	600
Less Prior Month's Year-to-Date Balance	65,100	(100)
Current Month Adjustment	10,800	500

NOTE:
The reimbursable ratio is computed by obtaining the following data from the previous year's Medicare/Medicaid Cost Reports and following these steps:

1) $\frac{\text{Total Inpatient Revenue}}{\text{Total Inpatient Allowable Cost}}$ Equals (A) %

2) $\frac{\text{Total Medicare Inpatient Revenue}}{\text{Total Medicare Inpatient Reimbursable Cost}}$ Equals (B) %

3) $\frac{\text{B \%}}{\text{A \%}}$ = Reimbursable Ratio

FIGURE 4.7 ***(continued)***

5

Inventories: Be Guided by What's Done, Not What's Said

Before you begin your audit of the hospital inventories, it is suggested that you consult the hospital Administration to determine their philosophy concerning pilferage.

Usually the Administration will give you positive assurance that they do not want pilferage. They will want inventories nailed down. "Should any employees be caught stealing, they will subject themselves to strict disciplinary action," Administration will say.

Before you get lost in this "smoke" give the Administration examples of "what if." That is to say, "what if" Max, in maintenance, has refinished his basement with materials that were "scrap" from other hospital projects, or "what if" Dorothy, the chief cook, and sole support of six children, has been taking "scraps" from the dietary department. You may be surprised to learn that, while Administration's intentions are good, their applications are seasoned by their opinion of right and wrong. It is not at all uncommon to find that Administration does have a lackadaisical attitude toward pilferage in certain areas by certain individuals.

It is well that you know this so that you may temper the content of your management letter. This does not mean that if you uncover pilferage you should ignore its existence because you know Administration is lenient. Instead, use good judgment in how you disclose its existence and in what you recommend to correct the situation.

Administrations come and go, and what one Administration may wink at, another one may strictly enforce. So be certain you cover all weaknesses in internal control in your management letter.

A cynical approach to auditing the hospital's inventory system is probably the best approach. Consider such things as:

1) Why do some departments purchase items direct without going through the Purchasing Department?
2) Why are salespersons permitted to enter the hospital without "signing in" at Administration or the Purchasing Department?

3) Why has Company "A" been the primary food vendor for an uninterrupted 20 years?
4) Why does the hospital permit the acceptance of gifts from vendors?

It will be interesting to learn what you do when you find that some "deals" have been made with administrative approval. After all—is it wrong for the administrators or purchasing managers to receive carpeting, household appliances, and automobiles, for their personal use, at dealer cost?

The Computerized Inventory System—Beauty or the Beast?

Several years ago a relatively new 350 bed hospital computerized its pharmacy inventory system and each year, for three consecutive years, made 50- to 60-thousand-dollar adjustments to this department's inventory. These adjustments occurred during a period of spiraling inflation and rising occupancy, which could account for, but not excuse, the failure of a national CPA firm to detect a serious deficiency in the inventory system. Each year when the Board of Trustees asked Administration and the independent auditors why such a material adjustment was made to the pharmacy inventory, the "explanation" given was rhetorical, involving patient mix, consumer price index, shortages by manufacturers, and improved pricing techniques.

The inventory system was relatively complex, involving the data recording of invoice cost, retail selling price, wholesale cost, and an industry index cost, all of which were coded as column numbers into reports. Between the period of system design and implementation and the first year-end inventory with the new system, the hospital lost its chief pharmacist and controller.

The new department managers for these two areas did not properly communicate, and therefore each month the accounting department would add to book inventory the purchases at invoice cost and deduct the pharmacy goods sold at the "industry index cost." The net effect of this error was to reduce the value of the inventory, per books, by 4 to 5 thousand dollars each month. At the end of each year the data processing manager gave the auditors and Administration an inventory stock status report that listed only quantity and last invoice cost, thereby properly stating the inventory, per books, at year end.

Protective Procedure

A new fiscal manager was hired who demanded that the accounting department receive the stock status report monthly. The accounting department then reviewed and reconciled, monthly, the difference between their previous method of calculating the inventory value and the value on hand per the stock status report. Once the accounting department involved the pharmacist and the data processing manager and learned the meaning of the coded columns they had been using, the differences quickly diminished. The next year there was only a $1,700 difference between inventory per count and inventory per book. An inquiring mind and improved communications solved this internal control problem.

New Management—New Philosophy—New Problems

Has a change in the hospital's financial management resulted in a new philosophy toward year-end inventories? For example, did the previous Administration consider items on the nursing floors to be expensed and therefore not to be inventoried, or items in the pharmacy night cabinet also expensed and not inventoried? If this was the case, and the present financial manager believes that all items not used or to be used within a 24-hour period should be properly inventoried, and as a result of the new fiscal management's inventory there appears to be only a small adjustment to the inventory system, don't write it off as "all's well that ends well."

Protective Procedure

Remember, items that were inventoried could very well cover up a large defalcation, or material adjustment, to the inventory. To more closely determine the accuracy of the inventory you should subtract the value of items that were not counted for the previous year to determine what the amount of the adjustment would have been under the previous Administration. This, then, should be the basis for your management comments.

Now before we begin our draft of the audit program, let us continue with some sample internal control questions and thoughts that will help you pinpoint weaknesses on which you should comment in the management letter.

REVIEWING THE CONTROL OF INVENTORY

Physical Controls

Q. *Are designated storekeepers held responsible for the custody of supply and repair parts?*

- Is the storekeeper, or his designate, usually in the storeroom.
- Are the storerooms locked when unattended.
- Are the storerooms locked at the end of each day.
- If an electronic lock, which is activated by a button, is used to open the storeroom doors, can the button be reached from the outside with a mop handle or other piece of equipment that an employee could possess without drawing suspicion.
- If there are double doors into the storeroom area, is it possible to pry these doors open after they are locked by pulling with equal pressure on both doors.

Q. *Who has the keys to the storerooms?*

- Shouldn't security officers be the only ones permitted in the storerooms after hours.
- Shouldn't a log be maintained of "after hours" entries.

Q. *Do the storekeepers notify the accounting department of all receipts by means of receiving reports?*

- Does the storekeeper's copy of the purchase order not show the quantity of items ordered, thereby making it necessary for items received to be counted and listed on his copy of the receiving report.

- Are there procedures for counting, inspecting, and reporting incoming materials, merchandise and supplies. (See Figure 5.1.)

Q. *Are storeroom issues made only from signed requisitions?*

- Can the storekeeper identify the appropriate approved signatures.
- Is there a dollar limit or quantity limit for which a supervisor's signature is not sufficient for requisitions, but for which a department manager must sign.
- Are standard storeroom items requested on a standard form indicating chart of account numbers, thereby eliminating coding errors for expense distribution purposes.

Q. *Are quantities physically counted at least once yearly?*

- Is there an inventory policy. (See Figure 5.2.)
- Are the physical inventories taken by employees other than the storekeepers and persons responsible for maintaining perpetual inventory records.
- Are the physical inventories taken by individuals who are familiar with the description and use of the items in inventory.
- Are there written procedures.
- Are the people making counts familiar with the procedures.
- Are listings checked for prices, extensions, footings, and summarization.
- Is someone in a position of responsibility and authority specifically designated for answering all questions regarding the counting of inventory items.
- Was the individual readily available.
- Was the procedure and system for identifying items counted adequate to insure that all items were counted and that items omitted could be readily determined by you.
- Were the individuals making the physical counts working in teams, thereby reducing the chance of errors.
- Were the inventory count sheets prenumbered and accounted for before the inventory teams were dismissed.
- Were tags, stickers, tab cards, or other means used to indicate which items were counted, and their location.
- Were all voided inventory sheets and other control mechanisms that were voided properly accounted for before the inventory teams were dismissed.

Q. *Are the inventories stored in an orderly and systematic manner to facilitate handling and counting of the items?*

Q. *Are the location and physical design of the storerooms such as to minimize the possibilities of pilferage by employees or others?*

Q. *Is a reasonable degree of control maintained over stationery and other supplies that are charged directly against operations?*

Q. *Are consignment-in goods physically segregated and under proper accounting control?*

INVENTORY ACCOUNTING AND PERPETUAL INVENTORY RECORDS CONTROL

Q. *Are general ledger accounts adjusted according to the physical counts?*

- Is there written approval by a responsible employee of adjustments of perpetual records to physical counts.
- Does a responsible and adequately trained individual review the inventory differences, by department, to determine that the inventory adjustment is not due to errors in the inventory relief system or inventory pricing.

Q. Are priced inventory sheets double checked as to invoice price, extensions, footings, and summarization?

Q. Are the inventory reports periodically reviewed for the purpose of determining which items are slow moving, obsolete, or overstocked?

Q. Are scrap, salvaged materials, and "no value" inventories under such accounting control as to assure the proper recording of the sale or reuse of such items?

Q. Are perpetual inventory records maintained?

- Maintained by quantities and costs.
- Maintained by persons other than the storekeeper.
- Governed by a general ledger control account.
- Verified at least annually by physical counts.
- Adjusted based on the physical counts.

Q. Have medical/surgical supply cost and/or pharmacy cost per patient day increased faster than the inflationary factors for these items?

- Is the purchasing department negotiating the best possible contracts.
- Has a long-term contract for high-volume items expired in the current year, resulting in substantial increases in cost.

Q. Are non-billable items used in patient care accounted for separately in the hospital's chart of accounts?

- Are the costs of such items reviewed periodically to see if the costs have increased significantly and should therefore be charged separately to the using patient.
- Does the change in practice require the prior approval of Administration.

AUDITING THE HOSPITAL'S INVENTORY

The Audit Objective

In auditing the hospital's inventory the auditor must determine:

1) that the inventory exists;
2) that the inventory is the property of the hospital;
3) that the inventory is usable and salable;
4) that the inventory has been priced in accordance with the hospital's established policies in a manner consistent with prior years; and
5) that free drugs, food, and other merchandise have been adequately controlled and appropriate recognition has been given the accounts.

There are several collateral objectives in the audit of inventory, such as:

a) Determining if there are adequate safeguarding methods employed by the hospital in maintaining the inventory.
b) Determining the care and accuracy with which the hospital employees took the inventory, the methods, basis followed in pricing the inventories, and the substantial correctness in the arithmetical computations.
c) Determining that management has taken adequate steps to identify obsolete and slow-moving inventories that should be either disposed of or returned to the vendor for credit.

Prior to Observation of Physical Inventory

1) Review the inventory procedures of the previous year. Determine the date or dates of the inventory and the extent to which the year-end inventory is based upon perpetual inventory records.

2) Determine the materiality of inventory in the possession of other hospitals; i.e., drugs loaned between hospitals, or medical/surgical supplies loaned between hospitals.

3) Determine whether any inventory is in the possession of warehousemen or other parties; i.e., salt used for snow removal which could be purchased by the hospital but maintained in the warehouse of a salt removal company; I.V. solutions or forms stored by the local manufacturer for "drop" delivery. Determine the approximate dollar value of inventory at each location.

4) Review the adequacy of the procedures for physical inventory taking. If the hospital relies on periodic test/checks of quantities, ascertain the frequency and extent of checks and nature and extent of adjustments.

5) Review and challenge Administration's inventory policies (see Figure 5.2) and the inventory count procedures (see Figure 5.3) to see if they cover the following matters:

a) The name of the persons drafting the instructions.
b) The dates and times of inventory taking.
c) The names of persons responsible for supervising the inventory taking.
d) Plans for prearranging and segregating stock in an orderly fashion; i.e., stock status alphabetic order or catalogue number order.
e) Provisions for control of receiving and issuing inventory during the inventory period and provisions for handling stock movements.
f) Detailed instructions for accurate description of items and for determination of quantities by count, weight, or other measurements.
g) Instructions for identifying obsolete and slow-moving items.
h) Instructions as to the use of inventory tags or sheets and their distribution, collections, and control.
i) Plans for determining quantities at outside locations (see 3 above).
j) Methods of transcribing the original counts to final inventory sheets, data processing tab runs, or summaries.
k) Methods followed in pricing the inventory quantities, including the extent of recheck or verification of prices.
l) Instructions for making extensions and footings to the extent of their recheck or verification.
m) Instructions for review and approval of inventory by department managers or other supervisory personnel who act as verifiers during the course of physical inventory taking. (See Figure 5.4.)

Auditing Inventory Quantities During the Physical Inventory at the Balance Sheet Date

1) Observe the methods of physical inventory for assurance that Administration's instructions were adequate and are being followed.
2) Visit all departments to observe and make notes regarding their following the established procedures.
3) Make counts of a selected number of representative items and list in the working papers. Identify the items selected for count by tag number, sheet number, part number (maintenance items), department, and storeroom aisle location, in addition to the description of the items counted. This will facilitate subsequent tracing to the final inventory sheets.
4) Be alert for possible double counts, empty containers, "hollow squares," or items or areas that may not have been counted.
5) Watch for and ask the person counting the inventory about items which, in your opinion, appear to be unusable, damaged, slow moving, or obsolete. Note these items and the counter's comments for further investigation.
6) Obtain the necessary cutoff information by visiting the receiving, processing, or distribution areas to make sure that a clear separation is made between items to be inventoried and those to be excluded from inventory. When prenumbered receiving or distribution tickets are used, note the last numbers and any unused prior numbers. When prenumbered tickets are not used, obtain information about several receipts immediately prior to the inventory date.

Auditing the Physical Inventory Taken at a Reasonable Time Prior or Subsequent to the Balance Sheet Date

Frequently management can not reasonably be expected to take a physical inventory at precisely the balance sheet date. This may be due to various physician or employee relations problems. When this occurs, the following additional steps must be taken:

1) Determine that the internal controls are adequate to permit a satisfactory accounting for the interim changes in the inventory accounts.
2) Follow the same procedures of observation and test counting as described earlier for a physical inventory taken at the balance sheet date.
3) Make appropriate review and test of the inventory accounts and records to support the interim changes.

Auditing the Physical Inventory When Counts Are Made of Individual Items from Time to Time, and the Detailed Perpetual Inventory Records Are Not Verified by a Complete Physical Inventory

As hospitals become larger and more complex, managers turn to electronic data processing for assistance. One method of assistance offered by electronic data processing is to furnish management with reports of inventory items below minimum and/or above maximum reorder quantities. Another useful electronic data processing report is a stock status report showing quantities on hand, monthly usage and year-to-date usage. Managers often successfully use these reports routinely to verify the inventory levels and thereby eliminate the requirement to disrupt operations annually by closing for physical inventory. Below are suggested audit procedures to be followed in this environment:

1) Be present while some of the counts are being made to observe the procedures being followed.
2) Make test counts and trace these test counts to the detailed perpetual inventory records.
3) Check a sufficient number of the employees' inventory counts and verification records to be assured of their dependability.
4) Test the listing of the inventory of the perpetual records to the inventory sheets that are used for verification purposes.
5) Review the departmental counts in support of quantity adjustments and investigate large differences with the Administration.
6) If the perpetual inventory records can not be relied upon, or the department manager has not made a satisfactory number of counts of the inventory during the year, consideration must be given to suggesting that Administration take a physical inventory at the balance sheet date. It is recommended that this matter be reviewed with the independent certified public accountants before making such a recommendation.

Useful Audit Procedures in Determining the Accuracy of Reported Inventory Quantities

1) Significant amounts of inventory in the possession of consignees, warehousemen, and other outside parties should be confirmed by direct communication with the custodian unless you are able to make test counts at their location. Where substantial amounts are held by any one party, you should check the existence and financial responsibility of the holder with the local banks or Dun & Bradstreet reports, or seek other such available independent verification of their fiscal responsibility.

2) Trace the test counts made at the time of inventory taken into the final inventory. If the tests counts included primarily all large quantity items, review the final inventory to identify the items of significant value not counted and consider the desirability of accounting for the existence of some of these items.

3) Test the transcribing of the department's original count to the inventory sheets, punched cards, or summaries.

4) Test the conversions such as weights into units, units into weights, or area into pounds or tons.

5) Check the data obtained at the time of the physical inventory relating to receiving and distribution cutoffs, and test purchase and receiving records and distribution records to determine that:

a) all materials received have been inventoried;
b) liabilities have been recorded for all materials included in the inventories;
c) liabilities have not been recorded for items that are not inventoried;
d) accounts receivable have been created for all chargeable items distributed to patients;

e) all material distributed has been excluded from the inventory; and
f) accounts receivables have not been charged for supply items included in the inventory.

Five Audit Procedures for Determining the Reasonableness of the Inventory Prices

1) Ascertain the methods of pricing; i.e., determine whether cost is first in, first out cost, last in, first out cost, standard cost, average cost, or other. If there has been any significant change in the pricing methods from the previous year, the effect of the change on the ending inventory should be determined and properly disclosed in the financial statements.
2) Test the prices of purchased items by comparison with the most recent vendors' invoices received prior to the inventory date covering the quantities in the inventory. Consideration must be given to the treatment of such items as freight, discounts, special rebates, storing, and handling charges.
3) Where cost is determined by the last in, first out (LIFO), method, test the LIFO computations and prepare the appropriate summaries and memoranda for review by the independent certified public accountants.
4) If the average cost is used, ascertain what method was employed and over what period the average was compiled. Test the calculations of the average prices.
5) Determine if the hospital needs to make a provision in the pricing or otherwise to cover losses that may be incurred upon the disposal of obsolete or slow-moving inventories.

Ten Quick and Effective Audit Tests to Determine the Clerical Accuracy or Pinpoint Potential Inventory Problems

1) Extensions and conversions may be sight tested; that is, scanned for misplaced decimal points, erroneous conversions, and failure to extend items.
2) Footings on the individual sheets may be proved to the nearest \$10, \$100, or more, depending upon the size, or test checks may be made of the page totals.
3) Page totals should be traced through the summaries and the summaries footed and compared with the general ledger account.
4) If the hospital takes an inventory at a date prior to the balance sheet date, it will be necessary to see that the proper adjustment has been booked as of the inventory date, and tests must be made of the inventory transactions in the intervening period.
5) Review the reasonableness of the entries in the inventory control accounts by reference to the purchase journals or other records.
6) Compare the gross profit margins with those of prior periods and obtain explanations for unusual variations.
7) Prepare a summary of the inventory, by department, and principal classification (i.e., dietary, bulk stores, I.V., and pharmacy) and compare with the preceding year. Investigate any unusual variations.

8) Summarize the adjustment between book and physical inventory, and obtain explanations of significant adjustments.
9) Compare the adjustments with those of the preceding year and determine if variances are reasonable.
10 Compute the inventory turnover and compare with those of prior years to determine if an unnecessary buildup of inventory is developing. Compare the turnover rates with area standards.

WORKING PAPERS THAT REDUCE AUDIT COST

Independent certified public accountants spend considerable time in reviewing inventories in order that they may express an audit opinion. An internal auditor can reduce the amount of time they spend and consequently reduce, or at least stabilize, their audit fee. To accomplish this, not only must the internal auditor perform an adequate review and testing of internal control, but also his working papers must indicate the extent of the work. The working papers should be so clearly prepared that it would be possible, at any time, to determine from them the conditions found, the exact audit procedures employed, the data collected, and the conclusions reached.

Working papers on inventory should include:

1) A copy of the hospital's policy on inventory and the appropriate inventory instructions.
2) An indication of the items counted and the method of tracing the counts to the final inventory records.
3) A statement as to the basis of pricing and the source of prices used in inventory price test.
   a) If the source is cost records, reference should be sufficiently identified to enable the independent auditors to readily locate the item.
   b) If the source is purchase invoices or vendors' quotations, reference should be adequate to enable subsequent location of the invoice or location. If the independent auditor will accept photostatic copies of these items, they should be included in the working papers.
   c) If the source is published market quotations, the reference should be specific.
4) The exact extent of work done with specific identification of the portions of the inventory checked for clerical accuracy, including working papers showing:
   a) The last receiving report so that it can be verified that all merchandise received by the audit date has been included in inventory and accounts payable.
   b) Method used to assure yourself that a proper cutoff was made of items used for patient care or consumed by the general service departments on the audit date.
   c) A worksheet showing in-transit items for which the hospital has been invoiced, or items received the afternoon of the physical inventory and not included in the physical count of the affected department.

d) Copies of the hospital's count sheets, noting on them the items checked, the method used, and the results; i.e., no errors, few errors, or many errors— "Hospital personnel instructed to re-count see worksheet ____ ."

e) A working paper for any inventory that is the property of the hospital, but that is stored off-site. The work paper should show the locations, names of warehousemen, total value of inventory and results of investigation of solvency of warehousemen.

f) Occasionally, the hospital may have material on hand that is on consignment from a vendor. A working paper should be prepared showing a description of each consignment, the consignor, memo billing reference numbers, and the value of total consignment goods.

5) An inventory summary (see Figure 5.5) showing the total value of inventory for each category and the percentage of the inventory value checked from the physical count. It is useful to include the preceding year's balances for comparison.

6) A statement of your conclusions as to the accuracy of the inventory.

FINANCIAL STATEMENT PRESENTATION

A hospital's inventories usually are not material in relation to its financial position, therefore inventories may be grouped in one total or listed by major classification; i.e., medical and surgical supplies, drugs, and so forth.

The basis of inventory valuation must be disclosed and if there has been a change in the method since the last audit date, a complete explanation must be made, noting the effect upon the hospital's Statement of Revenues and Expenses.

The inventory would be listed under the "Current Assets" section as follows:

Inventories (on a basis of first in, first out)	$525,620

In the "Supplemental Information" section of the report a detail comparative summary of the inventories should be made as follows:

	Year Ended December 31	
	19XX	19XY
Bulk Stores	$231,212	$238,149
S.P.D.	28,941	33,912
Pharmacy	62,300	61,532
Maintenance	94,788	112,560
Dietary	27,492	29,853
Operating Room	69,932	49,614
TOTAL	$514,665	$525,620

________________ HOSPITAL

PROTECTIVE PROCEDURE

SUBJECT: Receiving Storeroom Supplies

PURPOSE: Outlines the procedure to be followed in receiving Storeroom supplies from the vendor.

RESPONSIBILITY	ACTION
Receiving Clerk	1) Signs the truck driver's shipping papers after counting the cases, boxes, or packages and examining the outer packaging for possible damage.
	2) Removes the packing list from the carton and matches it with the Receiving Set in the open file.
	3) Posts date and quantities received on the Receiving Set, in white area of the first copy and in gray area of the second or third Back Order Received.
	4) Forwards first copy of the Receiving Set to the Inventory Control Clerk in daily batch.
	5) Attaches associated copies of the shipping papers to the remaining copies of the Receiving Set and returns them to the open file if the shipment is incomplete.
	6) Discards two (2) copies of the Receiving Set if the shipment is complete and places remaining copy with associated papers attached in closed file.
Inventory Control Clerk	7) Receives daily batch of Receipts from the Receiving Clerk and forwards to Data Processing.
Electronic Data Processing	8) Keypunches and verifies the receipts.
	9) Transmits data.
	10) Forwards updated report and receipts to the Inventory Control Clerk.
Inventory Control Clerk	11) Checks for any possible errors and resubmits to Data Processing in Daily batches with a batch control card.
	12) Forwards to Accounts Payable Clerk all processed receipts.

FIGURE 5.1

________________ HOSPITAL

PROTECTIVE PROCEDURE

SUBJECT: Inventory Policies

PURPOSE: Outlines the broad responsibilities and procedures to be followed by persons selected to accomplish the physical count and pricing of items to be inventoried. Also identifies those specific areas to be inventoried.

POLICY:

I. Physical inventory will be taken on ________________ .

II. Administration shall be notified not less than thirty (30) days prior to the scheduled inventory date.

III. Within five (5) working days after the notification of an inventory, the respective Administrative Staff members will designate the specific individual responsible for inventory to each area within his responsibility. This designation will be immediately communicated to the Controller.

IV. The annual inventory will include the following areas:

a) Bulk Stores, including exchange carts
b) Dietary Services
c) Emergency Room
d) Housekeeping
e) Maintenance
f) Pharmacy, including intravenous solutions (I.V.s)
g) Processed Stores, including exchange carts and nursing supply areas
h) Radiology
i) Receiving Dock
j) Surgery

V. Physical counting/recording will be accomplished by teams in all areas and will be recorded on the appropriate document as specified within the detailed procedure for each specific area.

a) The count/record teams will be appointed by the individual designated as responsible for each area, with the approval of the specific Administrative Staff member. The composition of these teams will be communicated to the Controller not less than five (5) working days preceding the actual inventory.

b) Emergency withdrawals from stock during the course of inventory will be recorded on Emergency Requisitions which will be forwarded to the Controller at the conclusion of the physical count with the count documents.

c) Receipts during the course of the inventory counting will be held within the Receiving Department and will be separately recorded on the appropriate document.

FIGURE 5.2

VI. Verification of physical count/recording will be accomplished by members of the Fiscal Division as designated by the Assistant Administrator. Verifiers will receive orientation to their area prior to inventory.

VII. Upon conclusion of the physical inventory, all count documents will be returned to the Controller by the individual responsible for the specific area, accompanied by the verifier responsible for that area.

a) Physical count/recording will be considered at a conclusion *only* upon release by the Controller, and count/record teams must not be dismissed until this release has been accomplished.

VIII. Pricing of non-computer inventories will be performed by members of the Purchasing Department unless specifically stated to the contrary.

IX. Extension/footing of non-computer inventories will be accomplished by members of the Accounting Department.

X. Reconciliation of the physical inventory to the general ledger inventory will be performed by the Controller and the appropriate reconciling accounting entries will be referred to his Assistant Administrator for review prior to transmission.

FIGURE 5.2 ***(continued)***

__________________ HOSPITAL

PROTECTIVE PROCEDURE

SUBJECT: Physical Inventory Count for Processed Stores

PURPOSE: Outlines the responsibilities and procedures to be followed by persons selected to take the inventory in Processed Stores.

COMMENTS:

I. Inventory will be taken in the above area in accordance with the basic Inventory Policies. Physical Inventory will be recorded on prepunched tab cards supplied by Electronic Data Processing Department.

II. Processed Stores may begin the inventory after all exchange carts are refilled on the last shift of the day preceding inventory. It is the responsibility of the Processed Stores supervisor to assure that an overstock condition does not exist in the nursing supply areas. Any excess inventory must be returned to the Processed Stores stock prior to the inventory.

III. All exchange carts must be stocked to the prescribed level prior to commencing of counting. It is the responsibility of Processed Stores supervisor to provide the Controller with a current exchange cart stock listing indicating the total number of such carts currently in use.

IV. In addition, Processed Stores must provide the Controller with a current nursing supply stock listing indicating the number of such units currently in use.

FIGURE 5.3

V. Inventory Documents:

a) Prepunched inventory tab cards.
b) Exchange carts stock listing.

PROCEDURE DETAIL:

Department Manager	1. Appoints sufficient number of inventory teams to take the physical count of items in Processed Stores.
	2. Conducts orientation of individual teams, outlining specific details and assigning areas of responsibilities.
	NOTE: Fiscal Service will participate upon request.
Electronic Data Processing	3. Prepares inventory tab cards, with a sequential control number.
Controller	4. Maintains inventory tab cards until inventory date.
Department Manager	5. Obtains inventory tab cards and stickers from Controller at 7:45 a.m., on ____________ .
	NOTE: Cart lists must be obtained, prepared, and given to the Controller within five (5) working days prior to physical count.
	6. Issues and logs inventory tab cards and issues bright-colored stickers by team.
Inventory Counter	7. Counts each item on shelf, bin, cart, pallet, floor, in assigned area—according to *unit of measure* shown on shelf label. (Includes items withdrawn by Emergency Requisition.)
	NOTE: Count only those quantities in unopened unit of issue containers.
	8. Calls out item to inventory recorder.
	9. Places brightly colored sticker, as issued by the Department Manager, on shelf, bin, cart, or pallet. This indicates to the auditors that the items have been counted.
Inventory Recorder	10. Writes the item count, as called, in the upper right corner of the inventory tab card.
	11. Verifies with the inventory caller the item description and count as recorded on the card.

FIGURE 5.3 ***(continued)***

Department Manager	12. Checks his area for completion and gathers all tab cards (using the inventory recorder).
	13. Verifies that all inventory tab cards issued have been returned.
	14. Delivers all inventory tab cards to the Controller for review.
	15. Releases inventory teams *after* review by the Controller.
Controller	16. Delivers inventory tab cards to Electronic Data Processing for machine sorting to finally verify that all cards issued have been returned.
Electronic Data Processing	17. Sorts tab cards for final verification.
	18. Keypunches quantity as recorded.
	19. Delivers, by courier, the inventory cards to the computer center for extension.
Computer Center	20. Runs all month-end and inventory reports as of______________ .
	21. Zeros the current units on hand in the inventory files.
	22. Loads the physical inventory counts referred to in Step 19.
	23. Prepares new inventory reports.
	24. Delivers, by courier, inventory reports to the Controller.

FIGURE 5.3 ***(continued)***

VERIFIER CERTIFICATION
PHYSICAL INVENTORY 19XX

I hereby certify that the______________department inventory has been tested by me for the following:

1) adherance to the inventory procedures,
2) accuracy of counts, and
3) positive mental attitude on the part of the employees taking the inventory.

In my opinion, the______________department inventory has been properly and accurately compiled.

______________________ ______________________
VERIFIER *DATE*

FIGURE 5.4

________ HOSPITAL			INITIALS	DATE
INVENTORY SUMMARY		PREPARED BY	JLD	1-15
________, 19___		APPROVED BY	B	1-18

FORM P-554-2 (GREEN) P-554-B2 (BUFF) Post-Rite SYSTEMS CELINA, OHIO - DALLAS - LOS ANGELES LITHO IN U.S.A.

ACT. NO.	DESCRIPTION	(1)	(2) PREVIOUS YEAR BALANCE	(3) BALANCE ______, 19___	(4)
113.01	BULK STORES				
	Per Computer Reports:		$ 226913	$ 233694	
	Less Manual Adjustments		<1906>	<277>	
	Plus Manual Inventories:				
	Housekeeping		1577	3228	
	Respiratory Therapy		775	941	
	Dietary Items		567	—	
	In-transit		3286	263	
	Balance at ________, 19___		231212 FT		$ 238149 TF
113.01	S.P.D. (process stores)				
	Per Computer Reports:				
	Exchange Carts		8524	11847	
	Crash Carts		596	526	
	Nurseservers		3406	4001	
	S.P.D. Floor Carts		8199	6288	
	Plus Manual Inventory:				
	X-Ray Carts		3154	2411	
	O.R. Carts		5062	8839	
	Balance at ________. 19___		28941 TF		33912 TF

NOTE:

detail working papers follow supporting 20% of bulk stores and 15% of process stores items checked by auditor.

FIGURE 5.5

6

Auditing Hospital Investments and Other Sundry Assets

Often, I've witnessed and heard many others make reference to the "new man" on the assignment doing the audit of investments and other sundry assets. The "new man" was usually a junior accountant just out of college. This is proper with direct supervision by the audit supervisor and with a thorough review made by the audit manager. Those employed by hospitals as internal auditors customarily have had several years of experience as independent auditors, but frequently have no one to turn to for an immediate and professional review of their internal audit working papers. Consequently the internal audit of items such as hospital investments and other sundry assets may not be as thorough as we might like to believe. Why?

A number of factors contribute to the conducting of a cursory review in lieu of a thorough audit. For example:

1) Few transactions in the account.
2) Transactions handled by individual of trust and authority.
3) Reliance upon verbal comments from person in authority rather than "testing" the system.
4) Fear of challenging authority because of "what they might think."
5) Boredom.

The circumstances surrounding hospital investment usually involve at least four of these five items.

The "Golden Opportunity" in Investments

It has been reported that the director of finance of a southern hospital purchased, with hospital funds, over $480,000 worth of gold coins. Then four days later, the director of finance and the 180 pounds of gold coins disappeared. How?

The director of finance, who had been employed by the hospital for less than two years, had gained the complete confidence of the local bank, the Board of Trustees, and the administrator. When a large investment had matured, the director of finance duped a 72-year-old trustee into signing a blank check drawn on the hospital's account. The director of finance then converted the check, made payable to the local bank, into two cashier's checks of $310,000 and $171,000, made payable to a northern coin company.

The director of finance omitted the word "coin" from the company name when requesting the cashier's checks and informed the banker that the checks were for the purchase of hospital equipment. The account the checks were drawn on was for this purpose and because of that, and with the maturing investment, the banker was not suspicious.

Protective Procedure

First, no written procedure will prevent people from being careless. The problem of a trustee signing a blank check can not be prevented by issuing procedures. The amount of the loss could have been substantially smaller if the Board of Trustees had properly bonded all employees who had access to cash or investments. In this case the director of finance was bonded for only $50,000.

Second, the need for cashier's checks by a hospital is questionable, and possibly their use should be excluded from administrative authority. Letters of credit issued by the bank could more properly be used in lieu of cashier's checks to vendors who will not accept the hospital's checks.

This chapter presents internal control questions, audit programs, and tests recommended in analyzing the strengths of the controls applicable to hospital investments and other sundry assets.

REVIEWING THE CONTROLS

Hospital Investments

Q. Are investments physically safeguarded to prevent unauthorized use, misplacement, theft, or other loss?

- Are investments kept in a bank safe deposit box.
- Does access to the bank safe deposit box require the signature of at least two persons acting together.
- Does the bank keep a record of the persons visiting the safe deposit box.
- If investments are not kept in a bank safe deposit box, are they kept by a broker or trustee.
- Do the broker and trustee have insurance to cover the loss of hospital investments held in their possession.

Q. Are investment transactions authorized by the Board of Trustees or an officer? (See Figure 6.1.)

- Are investment transactions recorded in a subsidiary record.
- Are the accounting records relating to investments kept by an individual who does not have access to the investments.
- Does the subsidiary record show the description, certificate numbers, and location of each investment.

- Does the subsidiary record call attention to unreceived investment income. (See Figure 6.2.)

Q. *Are all securities periodically inspected by independent persons?*

- Are the securities registered in the name of the hospital.
- Do the securities agree with the subsidiary accounting records.

Q. *Has the hospital received any donated investments?*

- Were the investments sold immediately.
- Were the investments held for a more opportune market.
- If so, who determined the selling date.
- Are written-off or fully reserved investments followed up for possible realization.

Q. *Are investments of two or more funds pooled?*

- Do the subsidiary records identify each fund's principal.
- Do the subsidiary records identify each fund's share of income, loss, or gain distribution.

Q. *Does someone other than the subsidiary record bookkeeper compare security income with published records or other sources?*

Sundry Questions to Determine the Control over Sundry Assets

Q. *Are subsidiary records maintained for such other assets as loans due from Administrative Staff members, officers, or Trustees; prepaid expenses, deferred charges, or other similar assets?*

Q. *Are the prepaid expenses and deferred charges reviewed by a responsible official to determine that they apply to future periods?*

Q. *Are these subsidiary records balanced monthly to the general ledger control account?*

Q. *Are write-offs of prepaid expenses and deferred charges recorded by standard journal entries?*

Q. *Are these standard journal entries approved by a responsible person?*

Now that we've "questioned" the system of internal control over investments and other sundry assets, we are ready to draft the audit program.

THE AUDIT

The Audit Objective

The auditor's objective in the examination of hospital investments is to satisfy himself that the securities owned are in the possession of the hospital. If not, the auditor should satisfy himself that the hospital investments are held by others for the account of the hospital. He must determine that the basis at which the securities or other hospital investments are recorded in the accounts conforms with generally accepted accounting principles applied on a consistent basis.

With respect to the other sundry assets, such as cash surrender value of life insurance, non-current receivables, prepaid expenses, deferred charges, etc., the auditor must be concerned with:

a) The authenticity, collectibility, and propriety of the amounts at which such assets are stated in the balance sheet.
b) The propriety of the future charges to operations.
c) The accordance of the amounts and allocation of costs and expenses with generally accepted accounting principles applied on a consistent basis.

Determining the Existence and Basis of Hospital Securities and Investments

1) Request the accounting department to prepare a list showing the securities at the beginning of the year, changes to date, and the securities owned at the balance sheet date. The list should contain the following details:

a) the exact name of the issuer and the security description,
b) certificate or bond number,
c) number of shares or total amount of principal,
d) cost, or carrying amount if other than cost,
e) per unit market price (noting source and basis),
f) total market price,
g) location of securities,
h) purchase date,
i) maturity date, and
j) interest rate.

If practical, income earned and gain or loss on disposal may also be shown on this schedule.

2) Prove the footings of the list and reconcile totals to the general ledger or subsidiary accounting records.

3) Examine brokers' advices or other independent evidence in support of purchases and sales during the year.

4) Check computation of gain or loss on sales. Note in working papers whether cost is determined by first in, first out (FIFO), specific certificate, or average cost method.

5) Inspect the securities on hand in the presence of the custodian.

6) Obtain, for the working papers, a signed receipt for the return of the securities to the custodian.

> NOTE: If the date of your inspection is other than the balance sheet date, account for all transactions in the intervening period. If the investments are in a bank safe deposit box, a letter from the bank attesting to non-entry during the interim period will eliminate the need to account for intervening transactions.

7) While inspecting the securities see that the stock certificates and registered bonds are issued in the name of the hospital, or that they are endorsed so as to be transferrable to the hospital, or are accompanied by powers of attorney. During this inspection, be alert for past-due coupons or for coupons clipped in advance of maturity dates.

8) Obtain confirmation of securities held by bank or custodian at the balance sheet date and as of the date of inspection of securities on hand. (See Figure 6.3.)

9) Determine the basis or carrying amounts of the securities.

10) Check market prices and indicate in the working papers the source or basis such as last sale price, bid price, etc.

11) Account for income from interest and dividends.

12) Verify recorded dividend income by reference to financial publications such as the *Wall Street Journal, Value Line,* etc.

13) Check computation of accrued interest.

14) Note if securities are properly appropriated for specific purposes such as construction, research, or funded reserves, or are restricted in any way.

15) Determine if an allowance for losses on investments is required. If such an account is already maintained by the hospital, obtain an analysis of the changes in the account, and consider the adequacy of the ending balance.

Determining the Authenticity, Collectibility and Propriety of Other Sundry Assets

A. Pledges Receivable

1) Obtain or prepare a detailed listing of pledges receivable.
2) Foot the detailed listing and trace the total to the general ledger or subsidiary accounting record.
3) Reconcile balance at beginning of year to balance at balance sheet date. Investigate any large or unusual items.
4) Using an acceptable method of statistical sampling, trace individual items on the listing to amounts on individual ledgers.
5) Foot receipts for test month and trace posting of appropriate debit and credit to general ledger.
6) Using an acceptable method of statistical sampling, trace individual receipts during test month to individual ledgers.
7) Mail confirmations to pledgers selected in step four (4) above.
8) Review confirmation replies and investigate differences.
9) Reveiw detailed listing for delinquent accounts; i.e., over ninety (90) days outstanding.
10) Determine whether pledges receivable have been discounted or otherwise pledged as security for any loans.
11) Determine if an allowance for uncollectible pledges is required. If such an account is already maintained by the hospital, consider the adequacy of the ending balance.

B. Other Accounts Receivable

1) Obtain a list of accounts from officers, directors, students, or others.
2) Confirm all large, non-current balances.
3) Analyze transactions in officers' and similar personnel accounts for the period. Investigate unusual items and have such an analysis reviewed by Administration.
4) Review significant entries in those accounts before and after the balance sheet date.
5) Determine that credits for salaries, bonuses, etc., have been entered properly.

C. Prepaid Insurance

(See Figure 6.4.)

1) Obtain a schedule of insurance policies showing coverage, premiums and unexpired premiums.

NOTE: If the hospital maintains an adequate insurance record, a list of policies need not be made, but a summary of the recorded coverage should be noted in your working papers.

2) Examine the policies.
3) Test computation of unexpired premiums.
4) Consider the adequacy of coverage as to both type and amount of insurance.
5) Inquire about workmen's compensation deposits and possible unrecorded liabilities.

D. Prepaid Rent, Interest, or Deferred Charges

1) Obtain schedules of the prepaid items.
2) Examine the leases, contracts, and other data in support of the prepaid items.
3) Check computation of the amount of the prepayment.
4) Confirm significant amounts.
5) Review the method and computation used in amortizing bond discount and expense.
6) If the hospital is a teaching institution and development, experimental, or other similar costs are deferred, challenge the propriety of deferment and amortization. If accounting practices are at variance with those followed for Medicare purposes, consider the effect of this deferment and see that this effect is noted in the financial statements.

E. Other Assets

1) Cash surrender value of life insurance:
   a) Request confirmation from the insuring companies, including information as to the beneficiary, who has the right to change the beneficiary, policy loans, assignments, or special conditions.
   b) Inspect the policies. (See Figure 6.5.)
2) Property that is not used in the operation of the hospital:
   a) Determine how acquired, basis of carrying amounts, depreciation, contemplated disposition, etc.

3) Review all items in this general category as to possible losses in realization and the adequacy of allowances provided.

WORKING PAPERS REQUIRED

Investments

The working papers should contain a copy or excerpt of the Board of Trustees' resolution relating to investments. The working papers should note that the Board policy has not been exceeded during the period of your examination.

A working paper similar to that shown in Figure 6.2 will be satisfactory in substantiating the ownership, basis, and value of the hospital investments.

A worksheet will also be needed to show the calculation of income earned and gain or loss on the disposal of investments.

When the auditor has inspected the securities held by the hospital, the working papers should contain a signed receipt for the return of the securities to the custodian.

Where securities are held by a bank or other independent custodian, the working papers must contain a confirmation of the securities at the balance sheet date.

If the hospital maintains an allowance for losses on investments, a schedule should be included in the working papers that explains the changes in the account and a notation of the adequacy of the ending balance.

A summary of audit work performed and the auditor's conclusion as to existence, basis, value, and conformity with generally accepted accounting principles should be included with the working papers.

Pledges Receivable

The working papers should include a detailed listing of the pledges receivable and notations as to the individual items tested for collectibility.

Returned confirmations, alternative procedures used, and memorandum of the results of your investigation of differences should be a part of the working papers.

A summary of audit work performed, and the auditor's conclusion regarding the pledges receivable, and the related allowance for uncollectible pledges should also be included in the working papers.

Other Accounts Receivable

A worksheet should be prepared that shows the amounts due from officers, directors, students, and others at the balance sheet date.

The worksheet should indicate the extent and results of confirmations and the auditor's opinion regarding the reasonableness and collectibility of such accounts.

Prepaid Insurance

Figure 6.4 is a satisfactory form of the working paper required for verifying the amount of the unexpired premiums.

The going business concept is used when reviewing the insurance unexpired premium. Therefore, the premium is usually computed on a pro-rata basis rather than on a short-term cancellation basis, unless it is known that the policy will be cancelled by the hospital.

The auditor should not be too concerned with minor differences in the calculated amount of the unexpired or prepaid insurance, and should not adjust for such differences unless they are significant.

Prepaid Expenses

A working paper should be prepared for each such general ledger account showing the date paid, amounts debited to the account, amounts written off during the current year, method of amortization, and source of entries.

Cash Surrender Value of Life Insurance

A working paper should be prepared showing the policy numbers, insurer, insured, beneficiaries, annual premium, and cash surrender value at the audit date.

Other

A working paper should be prepared for any other asset account not detailed above, showing for each the nature of the account and analysis of all transactions during the year.

FINANCIAL STATEMENT PRESENTATION

Under the caption "Investments and Other Assets" may be included such items as securities of a non-current nature, advances of a non-current nature, real estate (if held for investment purposes), cash value of life insurance, and other holdings if the intent of the hospital was to make or acquire an investment.

Where the aggregate of investments is relatively small as compared with the total amount of the assets classified in this group, the caption should simply be "Other Assets." The "Other Assets" classification may be presented as the final classification on the asset side of the balance sheet, if the nature of the items so classified makes that appropriate.

Prepaid expenses are preferably classified as current assets. Important unusual items should be set forth separately, but in the usual hospital balance sheet the prepaid expense category is relatively unimportant and adequate disclosure may well be afforded by a single caption such as "Prepaid Expenses," or "Prepaid Insurance and Other Expenses," with no descriptive subcaption.

The presentation of these items would be:

Current Assets:		
XXX		$ XXX
Prepaid Expenses	70,000	
TOTAL CURRENT ASSETS		4,000,000
INVESTMENTS AND OTHER ASSETS:		
Investments (at cost)	250,000	
XXX XXX	32,000	282,000

__________ HOSPITAL

TREASURER'S AUTHORITY TO INVEST CORPORATE FUNDS

"BE IT RESOLVED that the Treasurer be and he is hereby authorized to invest any unrestricted corporate funds which may come into possession of the corporation pending their use, in any indebtedness of the Federal Government, or Federal Agency thereof, or in any Certificate of Deposit in any commercial bank secured or insured by the Federal Government or any Federal Agency, in any prime commercial paper, or in corporate securities rated AAA, all subject to maturity restrictions stated below. No investment shall exceed sixty (60) months from the date of purchase, and moreover, investment of funds in securities, as defined above, maturing in excess of twelve (12) months from the date of purchase shall not exceed $600,000 without the approval of the Finance Committee.

"BE IT FURTHER RESOLVED that with respect to legally Restricted Funds the Treasurer be and he is hereby authorized to either (1) invest such funds in accordance with any legal restrictions that may exist with respect to any such Restricted Fund, or (2) if no investment restrictions exist, invest in the same manner above authorized for Unrestricted Funds, except that in this instance the maximum permissible maturity is sixty (60) months from the date of purchase and the limitation of $600,000 for maturities in excess of twelve (12) months from the date of purchase does not apply."

FIGURE 6.1

______________ HOSPITAL

INVESTMENTS

DECEMBER 31, 19__

	INITIALS	DATE
PREPARED BY	JLD	1-15
APPROVED BY	BH	1-20

FORM P-574 (GREEN) P-574-B (BUFF) — SYSTEMS CELINA, OHIO · DALLAS · LOS ANGELES — LITHO IN U.S.A.

LINE No.		DESCRIPTION	(1) CERTIFICATE NUMBER	(2) DATE ACQUIRED	(3) PAR OR FACE VALUE	(4) BEGINNING BALANCE	(5) COST ADDITIONS
2	ABC	Com. paper 7½%	4686	8/5/xx	100000 Ⓧ	-0-	
4	XYZ	Com. paper 7¾%	4773	10/4/xx	100000 Ⓧ	-0-	
6	ABC	Com. paper 7½%	4340	12/4/xx	100000 Ⓧ	-0-	
13	M	These are short term (90 days or less) securities.					
14		Market value exceeds cost.					
16	Ⓧ	Traced authority for purchase or sale to					
17		Board of Trustee minutes.					
19	E	Confirmed balance with bank safekeeping					
21	Ⓑ	Examined bank credit advice					

FIGURE 6.2

(6) OR SALES AND DATE	(7) BASIS TRADES AMOUNT	(8) ENDING BALANCE	(9) CURRENT MARKET VALUE	(10) INTEREST OR DIVIDENDS BEGINNING ACCRUAL	(11) EARNED INCOME	(12) CASH RECEIVED	(13) ENDING ACCRUAL	LINE No.
								1
9/31/XX	100000			-0-	61644	61644 Ⓑ		2
								3
11/3/XX	100000			-0-	63698	63698 Ⓑ		4
								5
1/2/XY		100000 E	M	-0-	55479		55479 C	6
								7
		100000			180821 cf	125342	55479	8

6	7	8	9	10	11	12	13

January____, 19____

ABC Bank
Financial Avenue
________________, Ohio

ATTENTION: Security Department

Gentlemen:

According to our records, you held the following securities in our name at December 31, 19___:

	RATE	MATURITY DATE	AMOUNT
Federal Home Loan Banks	9.20%	02/05/___	$150,000.00
Federal Land Bank	9.55%	11/26/___	100,000.00
General Motors Corp.	5.402%	01/06/___	100,000.00
	5.289%	01/21/___	50,000.00
U.S. Treasury Notes	8%	03/31/___	100,000.00
	8.75%	06/30/___	100,000.00

If the preceding information is correct, please sign in the space below. If the preceding information is incorrect, please explain any differences on the back of this sheet. In either case, please return this letter directly to our auditors, X, Y, and Z, 100 East Fourth Street, Hometown, State. A self-addressed envelope has been provided for your convenience.

Sincerely,

________________ Hospital

By: ________________
Administrator

The above is correct.

____
Signature

FIGURE 6.3

	INITIALS	DATE				
PREPARED BY	RD	2-5				
APPROVED BY	B.H.	2/8				

______ HOSPITAL

PREPAID INSURANCE

______, 19

COMPREHENSIVE BUSINESS POLICY AND POLICY NUMBER	PREMIUM PERIOD FROM	PREMIUM PERIOD TO	BEGINNING BAL. AS OF 01/01/	PREMIUM PAYMENTS	CHARGED TO EXPENSE	ENDING BAL. AS OF 12/31/
General Liability "Premises & Professional Liabilities" #12345	MONTHLY		26540	202539	229079	-0-
Umbrella Liabilities & Excess. Liabilities #AB 100	7-1	6-30	1249	257610	130054	128805
Fire/Casualty Pkg. "Property Coverage Building & Contents, Bus. Int. & Boiler" #XY 404	7-1	6-30	7028	18117	17167	7978
Misc. Floater All Risk "Building & Contents Accts. Rec." #6289	7-1	6-30	1400	3159	2979	1580
			36217	481425	379279	138363

FIGURE 6.4

January_____, 19_____

Life Insurance Company
Anyplace, U.S.A.

ATTENTION: PRESIDENT

Dear Sir:

In connection with our regular audit, please confirm directly to our auditors, X,Y, and Z, 100 East Fourth Street, Hometown, State, the following information with regard to each of the subject policies as of December 31, 19_____.

1) Beneficiary
2) Amount of insurance
3) Cash surrender value
4) Date to which premiums have been paid
5) Assignment, if any, of proceeds and/or cash values.

Subject policies:

1234 – John Doe, Insured
5678 – John Smith, Insured

A stamped, self-addressed envelope is enclosed for your convenience.

Sincerely,

____________________ Hospital

By: ____________________
Administrator

FIGURE 6.5

7

Auditing the Hospital's Property, Plant and Equipment

Prior to 1966 most hospitals did not maintain adequate records of their property, plant, and equipment. This is attributed to the fact that reimbursement for hospital services was not based on cost, and therefore the incentives for maintaining accurate records were missing. Just as a man inexperienced in playing a string instrument can not keep it properly tuned, so it was with many hospitals, who, inexperienced in maintaining records of property, plant, and equipment, failed to keep such records tuned.

Too Much Temptation

A 500+ bed hospital, located in the Midwest, found that over one million dollars worth of equipment and supplies had been stolen by their director of plant operations and his assistant during a ten-year period. How could this happen? The hospital was undergoing extensive remodeling and construction in an ongoing situation. The project coordinator would order equipment and supplies directly from the vendors, bypassing the purchasing department. The director of plant operations would then approve the purchase orders and subsequent invoices.

Then the white-collar thieves had the building supplies and appliances, such as refrigerators and window air conditioners, delivered to an off-site location for "storage." From this site they sold a portion of the equipment and supplies to cohorts involved in the building trade industry.

Protective Procedure

Proper segregation of duties, i.e., having the purchasing department make all purchases, would have considerably burdened this duo in perpetrating their crime.

Too Much Trust

Just as too much authority can be vested in one individual, so can too much trust. For example, the administrator of a respected rural religious-affiliated hospital was embarrassed to learn that she had been purchasing window air conditioners from a theft ring operating from a major city.

The purchasing of stolen goods can happen to anyone. The embarrassment occurred when the public learned that the hospital administrator was buying air conditioners with a retail cost of $400 for $100. Really now, should anyone be that trusting!

Protective Procedure

Yes, I can believe that the administrator, with her background, would continue to believe a vendor with whom she'd been dealing for years. A phone call, however, to the metropolitan supplier to "confirm" the vendor's story regarding the deal on air conditioners, would have been a simple audit technique the administrator could have utilized—and it would have saved her considerable embarrassment.

Appraisals—and Their Usefulness

In the absence of adequate property records, historical-cost-based appraisals may be used by the hospital. The auditor must satisfy himself as to the propriety of such appraisals before accepting their results for financial statement presentation.

In cases where a catastrophe has resulted in the destruction of property detail (invoices, etc.), the auditor may suggest an appraisal to support the amount shown as property, plant, and equipment.

Capitalization Policies and Assignment of Useful Life

The minimum acceptable capitalization policy would be the policy required by Medicare. This policy, which has changed since the beginning of Medicare, can be found in H.I.M.-15, Chapter 1.

The auditor should be aware that the rapid pace of technology in the health care field makes obsolescence a critical factor in considering the useful life assigned to hospital major movable equipment. In evaluating the hospital's depreciation policy, the auditor will find useful the 1973 edition of the American Hospital Association's *Chart of Accounts for Hospitals* and the *Estimated Useful Lives of Depreciable Hospital Assets*, published by the Hospital Financial Management Association.

Capital Budgets and the Games Administrators Play

All hospitals who participate in the Medicare Program prepare a capital expenditure budget for the current year and two subsequent years. Yet many such budgets are merely window dressing for regulatory purposes.

During the course of a year, the Administration may make substitutions to the Trustees' approved capital expenditure budget. Slight attention is paid to the fact that the purchases made against such a budget are usually reported on a "cash" basis. The only time someone notices is when the hospital encounters cash flow problems and is hit with a backlog of capital commitments; i.e., purchase order completed. What has happened?

Protective Procedure

The administrator made the substitutions, knowing the Trustees infrequently look at the details of the capital expenditures budget and look only at the total expenditures versus budget. Then, with the push to complete and review next year's budget, large commitments to purchase capital items are made and never reflected in any year's budget. The report isn't made for the last month, and they do not show on next year's budget.

An exhibit and procedure, such as shown in Figure 7.1., will eliminate the possibility of the Trustees being caught short of cash due to commitments made to purchase capital items that do not reflect on the hospital's financial statements. This schedule, prepared on a quarterly basis, will also assist the Trustees in auditing capital purchases made that were not a part of the Board-approved capital expenditures budget.

Tagging Equipment—Is It Worth It?

The pendulum has swung from hospitals having virtually no records and little control over property to elaborate plans now being used by some hospitals to tag every piece of equipment costing in excess of ninety-nine dollars and having a life of three years or more. Somewhere between these two extremes lies a reasonable approach.

Unless the hospital is willing to expend substantial sums of money to computerize its property records and employ the manpower to constantly survey the movement of equipment, don't bother to tag the hospital's equipment. It isn't worth a damn to know that each piece of equipment is tagged at the receiving dock.

In examining the major reasons for property records, we are reminded that:

1) Accurate property records are needed to claim the proper amount of cost reimbursement from third parties.
2) Accurate property records are needed to assure management that the hospital has adequate insurance on its investment. What is needed is not just property records, but "accurate" property records.

How, then, do we develop and maintain such records?

Protective Procedure

First, have a reputable appraisal company, familiar with hospital equipment and the related problems of idenity and obsolescence, give you a detailed appraisal of your property, plant, and equipment.

Next, utilize a request for a capital expenditure form, such as the one in Figure 7.2, which is forwarded to accounting for record purposes. By utilizing this form and working with the purchasing department, you can make sure that all capital expenditures subsequent to the appraisal will be charged to the proper department.

Then, utilize a system whereby no equipment is transferred from one area to another without the signed approval of the transferring-out and transferring-in departmental managers. A copy of such approvals should go to the accounting department, which would prepare an annual report of capital acquisitions and transfers for the department manager's review and approval. This report will stress the importance of accurate departmental property records and will cause the manager to "feel" like a manager.

If the hospital employs conscientious security personnel and requires the use of a property pass, such as the one shown in Figure 7.3, it can be reasonably certain that the property records are accurate. This system is less costly than a well-developed tagging system, which often causes departmental managers to feel the Administration doesn't trust them. The system also creates an awareness of property throughout the various levels of management, not just in the accounting department.

An often overlooked method of testing the accuracy of a major portion of the property records is to have a responsible person compare the property records to the engineering department's prevention maintenance schedule. If the equipment no longer exists, it won't be on the maintenance schedule.

Leases

As the hospital's economic resources continue to shrink, hospitals are forced to utilize leasing as a means of acquiring the capital equipment needed to provide patient care services.

The auditor should be familiar with the American Institute of Certified Public Accountants' publication: "Reporting of Leases in Financial Statements of Lessee," opinions of the Accounting Principles Board, #5.

REVIEWING THE CONTROL OF HOSPITAL PROPERTY, PLANT AND EQUIPMENT

Questioning the Hospital's Policies and Procedures Relating to Capital Expenditures

Q. Does the hospital have a systematic plan for the acquisition and financing of capital expenditures?

- Is a cash budget prepared and utilized for planning purposes.
- Is a capital expenditure report prepared and reviewed periodically by the Board of Trustees. (See Figure 7.1.)
- Are deviations from the plan explained by the Administration and approved by the Board of Trustees.
- Does the Administration prepare a current year capital expenditures budget, and a two-year prospective capital budget.
- Do the capital budgets contain leased equipment that must be capitalized for financial reporting purposes.
- Have the lease expenses and financing charges been properly treated in the operating budget.
- Are the capital expenditures budgets approved by the Board of Trustees in order to comply with Medicare Regulations.
- Does the Board of Trustees, in approving the capital budget, actually approve

the detailed items or are they, in fact, approving a dollar amount the Administration may spend for capital expenditures during the year.

- If the Board of Trustees actually approves the detailed items, is the reporting mechanism such that additions to property, other than those from the Board-approved Budget, are identified.

Q. *Is there a written policy, approved by the Board of Trustees, which differentiates between capital expenditures and repair items?*

- Does this policy comply with current Medicare regulations.
- Do new asset estimated useful lives approximate those recommended by the American Hospital Association or other authoritative source, such as Internal Revenue Service or manufacturers' guide.

Q. *Has Administration selected the best accounting techniques to maximize third-party reimbursement?*

- Is the depreciation method for book purposes the same as for third-party reimbursement purposes.
- If not, is a deferred liability account shown on the balance sheet.
- Is the accounting for minor equipment in accordance with one of the prescribed methods for Medicare reimbursement purposes.
- Is the accounting in accordance with the election the hospital made when the hospital chose its elections for Medicare purposes.
- Should the hospital apply for a change in elections chosen for any options relating to the accounting of property, plant, and equipment.

Q. *Are there adequate safeguards for the removal and accounting of major movable equipment sold or retired from the hospital?* (See Figure 7.3.)

- Is there an adequate system for the inspection of the condition of capital items, especially major movable equipment.
- Does the hospital have an adequate system of preventive maintenance.

Q. *Is there adequate accounting for physically retired property?*

- Are such retirements approved by a responsible person.
- Are retirements recorded in the detailed property records.
- Are sale and salvage proceeds properly and consistently recorded in the accounting records.

Q. *Are interdepartmental transfers approved by a responsible person?* (See Figure 7.4.)

- Is there a record maintained in the detailed property records of such transfers.
- Is there adequate control in making these transfers to properly safeguard the assets.

Q. *Is a work order system in use for capital additions and repair projects?*

- Are the salaries attributed to capital projects in progress also properly capitalized.

- Are these expense transfers budgeted for by the requesting department.

Q. *Is depreciation funded?*

- Is it maintained in a separate bank account or commingled with other funds.
- If depreciation is funded, does it require Board of Trustees' approval for additions and withdrawals from the funded depreciation account.
- If depreciation funds are borrowed for working capital purposes, is a reasonable amount of interest expense charged in order to make such expenses allowable for Medicare purposes.

Questioning the Adequacy of the Detailed Property Records

Q. *Are detailed records maintained to support the general ledger accounts?*

- Are they prepared and/or maintained by an independent service bureau or appraisal company.
- If they are maintained by the hospital, what is the frequency of their update.

Q. *Are the detailed records supporting the general ledger accounts balances adequate?*

- Are they based on historical cost or, if applicable, fair market value at the donated items' acquisition date.
- Are the detailed records balanced at least annually to general ledger control accounts.
- Are the detailed items classified by departments.
- Is the description, brand and serial number or other, adequate to identify the individual items.
- Are the individual items periodically checked by an inventory of the items and compared to the detailed record of assets by department.
- Are the detailed records the same as those used for third-party cost reimbursement purposes.

Q. *Is there a proper segregation of the detailed records supporting the general ledger account balances?*

- Do they employ at least the following classification system of:

  a) land improvements
  b) buildings
  c) building service equipment
  d) other fixed equipment
  e) major movable equipment
  f) minor equipment

- Do they include fully depreciated assets.
- Are assets owned by others properly identified.
- Are replacement values for evaluating insurance property protection calculated.

- Is the basis for calculating replacement values one that is generally recognized by appraisal firms.

With a complete understanding of the controls for property, plant, and equipment, you are ready to prepare the audit program for this important section of the balance sheet.

THE AUDIT

The Audit Objective

The auditor's primary objective is to determine that the accounting principles and practices of the hospital with respect to property accounting are in conformity with generally accepted accounting principles and that they have been consistently applied. The auditor must also satisfy himself as to the existence and ownership of the assets, determine whether they are subject to liens, and investigate evidence indicating idleness, abandonment, or loss of useful value.

In the area of property, plant, and equipment, the auditor has a secondary responsibility to see that estimated useful lives are realistic. In addition to the above, the internal auditor must determine if the estimated useful lives result in the maximization of third-party reimbursement.

Medicare Regulations provide for two primary alternatives in recording minor equipment items. The first alternative enables the hospital to recognize the existence of a fixed amount of minor equipment, and all subsequent replacements of minor equipment would be expensed in the period in which they are acquired. The second alternative permits the hospital to depreciate the minor equipment asset over a three-year period, and consequently all additions to this account are likewise depreciated over a three-year period.

The auditor should verify that the hospital is properly following the election they chose in the treatment of minor equipment.

If the internal auditor is unable to verify the existence of a substantial amount of the property, plant, and equipment items, he should recommend to the Administration that an independent appraisal company be employed. Furthermore, he should suggest that at least two reputable appraisal firms be asked to bid.

The Audit Program

1) Obtain an analysis of the asset and allowance accounts that show additions, deductions, and transfers for the period. (See Figure 7.5.)

2) Examine support for significant additions to the property accounts by reference to purchase invoices, contracts, authorizations, appropriations, and data evidencing charges for material, labor, and overhead for work done by the hospital's maintenance department.

3) Examine deeds or other evidence of title and closing documents pertaining to major acquisitions of land and buildings.

4) Where additions represent replacements, inquire as to how the corresponding retirements were handled in the hospital's records.

5) Review charges to maintenance, repairs, and similar accounts to determine that no significant items of a capital nature have been charged to expense.

6) Review procedures regarding sales, trade-ins, abandonment, or other retirements of property, and obtain a schedule of gains or losses on disposal.

7) Ascertain the amount and accounting treatment of fully depreciated assets.

8) The depreciation and amortization provisions for the period should be tested for arithmetical accuracy and consistency. Reconcile additions to the allowance accounts with charges to expense.

9) Determine how leasehold improvements are being amortized and consider propriety of amortization period in relation to leases and renewal options as well as to estimated useful life for the improvements.

10) Review lease agreements to determine if they are operating or capital leases, and that the hospital is properly accounting for such leases.

11) Prepare reconcilement of differences between book, income tax, or third-party reimbursement basis of assets, allowances, provisions for the period, and gains or losses. Consider the necessity of providing for a deferred asset or liability by reason of such differences.

12) During other parts of the examination, such as the inspection of the premises, rent receipts, insurance policies, and other documents, be alert to any indication of properties not on the books, unrecorded property disposal, retirements, or evidence that title to any part of the property does not rest with the hospital.

Auditing the Hospital's Construction in Progress

1) Obtain an analysis of the activity in the account for the period.
2) Analyze all major transactions in the account by:
    a) inspecting work orders and reviewing for proper grouping into major categories,
    b) ascertaining that all payments and changes in the specifications have been properly authorized, and
    c) testing or making transfer of accumulated cost to the appropriate asset accounts upon completion of project.
3) Obtain copies of bond contracts.
4) Confirm liability for purchase of land with seller.
5) Determine that the accounting for interest expense during the period of construction maximizes third-party reimbursement.
6) Examine all remaining contracts.
7) Reconcile charges to asset accounts with amounts specified in the contracts.
8) Prepare a schedule, if applicable, for the deferred financing fee, compute the amount of amortization, and trace the computed amount to the hospital's expense account.

WORKING PAPERS THAT SAVE TIME

Permanent File

1) Land:

Time can be saved, and your files more complete, if copies are made of the actual instruments indicating evidence of ownership; i.e., deeds, attorneys' opinions, escrow statements, and title insurance. Then prepare a summary of cost and place this summary in front of the copies. As subsequent land acquisitions are made, the summary should be updated.

2) Buildings:

All contracts, subcontracts, labor, and material furnished by the hospital, and other costs, must be detailed. Since this material is quite voluminous, it is not usually practical to keep complete copies in the auditor's files; therefore, summaries of such detail should be in the file.

Current Audit Files

1) A working paper should be prepared by the hospital for each general ledger account of property, plant, and equipment, including construction in progress. The schedule should show the balance at the beginning of the year (must agree with the previous year-closing balance), detail of each addition showing vendor, date of purchase and installation, cost, and journal reference. Retirements should be listed in a similar manner. The schedule should be footed and proved with the general ledger balance. (See Figure 7.5.)

> NOTE: Where the number of additions and retirements is relatively small, you may prefer to transfer the prior year's working papers from the file and show the current year's transactions as a progression. This procedure has the advantage of avoiding the unnecessary preparation of new working papers each year as well as verifying the opening balances.

2) A summary of property, plant, and equipment additions and transfers should be prepared from the detail working papers. This summary should then be typed and made a part of the audited financial statements. (See Figure 7.6.)

3) A working paper should be prepared by the hospital for each general ledger account for allowance for depreciation. These schedules should show the opening balance, retirements, and the provision for the current year's depreciation.

> NOTE: Usually the current year's provision will consist of twelve equal monthly entries which can be totalled, and one entry can be made on the working paper.

4) From the detail working papers for the allowance for depreciation, summary data will be prepared for the financial statements. (See Figure 7.6.)

5) Working papers should be prepared that show the extent of your testing of the charges to the repair and maintenance accounts for items of a capital nature.

NOTE: A fast and effective method is to photocopy the general ledger account and use this as your working paper. Care should be taken to adequately explain all keys.

6) A reconciliation of the provision for depreciation for book purposes and for income tax, or third-party reimbursement purposes, should also be a part of the current year's working papers.

7) Where applicable, a schedule should be included of the deferred financing fees and the related annual amount of amortization.

FINANCIAL STATEMENT PRESENTATION

A descriptive heading such as "Property, Plant, and Equipment" should be used in the financial statements. The basis on which the assets are stated should be described in the balance sheet or in a note.

Facilities which have been idle for an extended period, particularly if the facilities are awaiting sale or are definitely in a standby category, should be shown separately under "Property, Plant, and Equipment."

Real estate that is not a part of the operating plant should be reported separately in the balance sheet, preferably under "Investments and Other Assets." Examples of such real estate would be real estate received as a gift and real estate investments of endowment funds.

The deduction from gross property accounts for estimated depreciation may be described in a number of ways, such as, but not limited to:

Allowances for depreciation
Accumulated provisions for depreciation.
Estimated depreciation.

The following is an example of how Property, Plant, and Equipment should be reported in the financial statements.

PROPERTY, PLANT, AND EQUIPMENT— on the basis of cost.

Used in operations:	
Land	$ 621,000
Land Improvements	124,000
Buildings	5,225,000
Fixed equipment	2,949,000
Movable equipment	2,194,000
Less: allowance for depreciation	(2,901,000)
	8,212,000
Not used in operations:	
Land ($81,000) and buildings	118,000
	$8,330,000

In the Supplemental Information section of the report, a summary such as the one in Figure 7.6 should be furnished.

______________ HOSPITAL
CAPITAL EXPENDITURE REPORT
FOR THE PERIOD ENDED

	Authorized by Trustees	Approved by Administration
Prior period's commitments not booked at beginning of period (previous year's outstanding purchase orders)	$ 57,708 S	$ 57,708 S
Capital Expenditures approved (authorized by Trustees/and approved during current period)	545,691 S	541,557 (NOTE)
TOTAL Authorized/and Committed	$603,399 F	$599,265 F
Less Capital Expenditures booked against foregoing authorization	389,556 T	389,556 T
Authorized but not booked to date	213,843	209,709 F
Less portion of commitments not booked to date	209,709 P	209,709 P
Authorized but uncommitted for remainder of period	$ 4,134 F	$ -0- F

NOTE: This figure shows the total capital items booked and committed; i..e, purchase orders not issued. It must always be the net of the total authorized by the Trustees less the amount authorized, but uncommitted.

S—Same as last report; T—Traced to financial statements: F—Footed; P—Balance of outstanding purchase orders for the current year.

FIGURE 7.1

CAPITAL EQUIPMENT REQUEST[1]

DEPARTMENT ____________________ DATE ____________________

QUANTITY	BUDGET CODE	ITEM DESCRIPTION	COST[2]

REASON FOR CAPITAL ADDITION
(If not an original Capital Budget as approved by Board)

____

____

____

____

____

BID PRICES

VENDOR'S NAME	BID PRICE
1.	$
2.	
3.	

______________________________ DEPARTMENT HEAD SIGNATURE

______________________________ ASSISTANT ADMINISTRATOR SIGNATURE

DO NOT WRITE BELOW THIS LINE

( ) URGENT ( ) ESSENTIAL ( ) ECONOMICALLY DESIRABLE ( ) GENERALLY DESIRABLE ( ) NOT BUDGET

BUDGET DIRECTOR	ASSISTANT ADMINISTRATOR	ADMINISTRATOR
( ) APPROVED ( ) DISAPPROVED	( ) APPROVED ( ) DISAPPROVED	( ) APPROVED ( ) DISAPPROVED
DATE _/_/_	DATE _/_/_	DATE _/_/_
COST PER BUDGET $ ______	COMMENTS: ______	COMMENTS: ______
COST PER REQUEST $ ______		
COST VARIANCE $ ______		
SIGNATURE	SIGNATURE	SIGNATURE

(1) This form must be used when requesting any durable item having a life of three years or more and costing $150 or more or any group of items costing $300 or more.
(2) If item cost is not the lowest bid price attach memorandum explaining why you have requested a more costly item.

FIGURE 7.2

______ HOSPITAL

PERSONAL PROPERTY PASS*

______
(Date)

Security Officer:

It has been approved for ______ (Name) to remove the following personal property from the hospital. This property was/was not purchased from the hospital:

______
______
______
______
______

______ (Supervisor) ______ (Administration)

*IF THE PERSONAL PROPERTY IS THE RESULT OF A PURCHASE FROM THE HOSPITAL, THEN THE EMPLOYEE MUST ALSO PRESENT A PROPERLY COMPLETED AND DATED CASH RECEIPT FORM.

______
(Inspecting officer)

White Copy	- Kept by Employee
Pink Copy	- Security officer forwards to controller

FIGURE 7.3

______ HOSPITAL

EQUIPMENT MOVE NOTICE

DESCRIPTION OF ITEM ______

MODEL NUMBER ______

SERIAL NUMBER ______

DISPOSITION ______ TRANSFER ______ Disposed

TRANSFERRING DEPARTMENT ______

By: ______
Signature (Manager)

______
Administrative Staff Member

RECIPIENT DEPARTMENT ______

By: ______
Signature (Manager)

ACCOUNTING ACKNOWLEDGMENT ______

FIGURE 7.4

______________ HOSPITAL

RADIOLOGY EQUIPMENT A/C #115.50

________________, 19____

	INITIALS	DATE
PREPARED BY	B.H.	2-15-
APPROVED BY	JLD	2/18

FORM P-534 (GREEN) P-534-B (BUFF) Post-Rite SYSTEMS CELINA, OHIO - DALLAS - LOS ANGELES LITHO IN U.S.A.

	(1)	(2)	(3)	(4)
BALANCE, January 1, 19____				$ 572422 P
ADDITIONS:				
1 Xeroxradiographic Mammographic System			$ 30355 ⊗	
1 AMX-110 Suto Mobile X-Ray unit with battery pack, collimator, and extension cylinder			19437 ⊗	49792 F
DISPOSALS:				
3 Typewriters - Serial # 01367A			420 D	
97328X			420 D	
85327R			420 D	< 1260 > F
				$ 620954 F

F -
P - per working paper balance at 12/31/XX
⊗ - examined supporting invoice
D - examined properly signed property disposal slip

FIGURE 7.5

______ HOSPITAL

PROPERTY LAPSE SUMMARY

	Assets				Accumulated depreciation				
	Balance, December 31, 19XX	Additions	Retirements	Balance, December 31, 19XY	Balance, December 31, 19XX	Depreciation	Retirements	Balance, December 31, 19XY	Net, December 31, 19XY
Building:									
Building, all wings	$ 5,122,180	$ 45,352		$ 5,167,532	$ 910,525	$ 110,717		$ 1,021,242	$ 4,146,290
Day Care Center		1,267		1,267		32		32	1,235
Convent		56,293		56,293		704		704	55,589
	5,122,180	102,912		5,225,092	910,525	111,453		1,021,978	4,203,114
Building equipment	2,896,082	52,607		2,948,689	759,785	140,755		900,540	2,048,149
Departmental equipment	2,084,213	120,272	$ 10,266	2,194,219	776,785	155,548	$ 5,815	926,518	1,267,701
Land improvement	114,957	8,779		123,736	47,042	5,257		52,299	71,437
	10,217,432	284,570	10,266	10,491,736	2,494,137	413,013	5,815	2,901,335	7,590,401
Dwellings	108,919	36,651	77,815	67,755					67,755
Land	539,634	81,648		621,282					621,282
	$10,865,985	$ 402,869	$ 88,081	$11,180,773	$ 2,494,137	$ 413,013	$ 5,815	$ 2,901,335	$ 8,279,438

FIGURE 7.6

8

Auditing and Strengthening the Purchasing and Payables Functions

Small and medium-sized hospitals usually follow one of two procedures in accounting for trade accounts payable. The most common method is a detail ledger with an account for each vendor. The ledger is posted for invoices received and payments made, with a controlling account in the general ledger.

The second method utilizes a voucher register in which is listed all of the invoices as they are received. Most such registers have columnar space for recording the check number and the date of the check, which is entered in the register to show that payment has been made. Accordingly, therefore, the open items represent unpaid accounts. At the end of each month the open items are listed, totalled, and agreed with the general ledger controlling account.

Unfortunately, most small hospitals do not have a separate receiving department; therefore, receiving records are seldom available for verification and tracing to vendors' invoices. In such a situation, it is easy for an invoice to be omitted inadvertently or deliberately.

Protective Procedure

The auditor should compare the list of accounts payable from the previous year to the list for the current year. Omission of a creditor usually appearing in the previous year's list should be the subject of further investigation.

It is recommended that requests for confirmation of accounts payable be sent to creditors usually having open accounts, even if the hospital books show no liability at the audit date.

Requests for confirmation, which may include a request for statement of account, should be mailed a few days prior to the audit date. This will permit the vendor to mail the usual monthly statement direct to the auditor rather than to the hospital. In addition, accounts payable confirmations should be mailed sufficiently early so that adequate follow-up can be made on those requests which are not answered.

Purchasing—Centralized or Decentralized

Administrators wrestle with the problem of permitting such specialized departments as laboratory, dietary, and maintenance to act as their own purchasing agent or insist that the buying for these areas be handled by the purchasing department.

Let's review some case histories that help explain why some department managers may fight so hard against centralized purchasing.

THE LABORATORY

In many hospitals it is not uncommon for the pathologist to be employed by the hospital and also have a competing independent laboratory. This usually occurs where the Board of Trustees, for political purposes, gives in to a vocal minority of physicians. Why would other physicians be willing to strongly support the pathologist having his own independent lab? The pathologist is responsible for reviewing the "failures" of the other members of the medical profession. He therefore is the keeper of the key to the proverbial closet with the skeleton.

The fact that the pathologist has his own laboratory is not always distasteful; often the fee for his services rendered to outpatients will be less than the hospital's fee for similar services. Greed, however, often sets in and the pathologist, acting as the hospital's purchasing agent, will begin buying test tubes, reagents, slides, and other supplies for his independent lab. If he is patient, in a few years the majority of his supplies will be bought and paid for by the hospital.

A good materials manager or purchasing manager would note these increases by comparing current year usage to prior year usage and relating this data to the volume of hospital activity.

THE FOOD SERVICE DEPARTMENT

Usually, this will be one of the first departments to "fall" when the Administration decides to begin centralizing the purchasing function, and it should be. In all food service departments there will be a degree of petty theft—from eating free meals to "lifting" steaks and liquor.

The opportunity for material defalcations, however, occurs when the food service manager is also the purchasing agent for this department. The variations of the same theme will go from kickbacks for buying with friends and relatives to having the home freezer supplied and included in the bill to the hospital.

THE MAINTENANCE DEPARTMENT

As in the food service department, many of the items used by the maintenance department can readily be used at home. Chapter 7 on Property, Plant, and Equipment illustrated the problems that can be experienced when the director of plant operations acts as the hospital's purchasing agent. The auditor should examine such capital additions as refrigerators, panelling, small tools, and other such items.

In this chapter the purchasing and payables functions will be examined jointly, in order to present an efficient audit program for the auditor.

In performing the audit on purchases and payables, the auditor should remember that liabilities are more likely to be understated than overstated. While verification of the amounts recorded is important, the auditor must search to disclose those liabilities that have not been recorded.

As in previous chapters, questions and related thoughts are being offered for the auditor to consider while reviewing the hospital's system of internal control as they relate to these functions. The included audit program can be utilized to help the auditor discover weaknesses in the purchasing and payables functions which encompass notes payable and other liabilities.

Also presented are sample management reports, exhibits, and procedures that, properly adapted to your hospital, will strengthen the purchasing and payables functions.

REVIEWING THE INTERNAL CONTROL

How to Test the Strength of the Hospital Purchasing System

Q. *Has a purchasing policy been developed and approved by the Board of Trustees?*

- Does the policy specifically endorse the prudent buyer concept.
- Does the policy establish a purchasing department, separate from the receiving function, through which all purchases are to be routed.

Q. *Are all purchases of equipment, materials, and supplies made only on the basis of signed requisitions from authorized personnel?*

- Is a copy of the requisition retained by the requesting department for their follow-up.
- Do the requisitions show a general description of the specifications the item must meet before it can be utilized by the department.

Q. *Are prenumbered purchase orders prepared for all purchases?*

- Are all purchase orders approved by an appropriate responsible person.
- Is the numerical sequence of the purchase orders accounted for periodically.
- Are the terms of purchase clearly defined on the purchase order. (See Figure 8.1.)

Q. *Are employee purchases prohibited?*

- If no, are they cleared in a regular manner through the receiving, purchasing, and accounting departments.
- If the hospital is tax exempt, are the appropriate taxes collected on employee purchases so that the hospital's tax-exempt status is not jeopardized.

Q. *Does the accounting department, or the internal auditor, periodically review the prices paid for items to determine that such prices are not in excess of current market prices?*

- Are all special requisitions in excess of $150 subject to competitive bidding.

- Would the documentation satisfy a "prudent buyer"; i.e., proper consideration of delivery times, frequency of repairs, availability of parts and qualified servicemen.
- If the least cost item is not purchased, is there adequate documentation supporting the decision.
- Are recurrent purchases subject to at least annual bids and guaranteed price schedules.
- How are emergency needs of such areas as maintenance, respiratory therapy, or pharmacy handled.
- Are there associated problems with "phone-in" purchase order numbers.
- May only the purchasing manager phone in a purchase order number. If no, how are such purchase orders controlled.

Q. *Does the hospital participate in group purchasing?*

- Does the purchasing manager actively participate in buying through group-negotiated contracts or does he use the group contract to negotiate better prices with certain vendors; for example, I.V. solutions, oxygen, and office machine vendors.
- Is Administration aware of such maverick practices, which are detrimental to the group of participating hospitals.
- Is an accounting of rebates and discounts, obtained through group purchasing, made to each participating hospital.
- Do representatives of Administration, as well as purchasing managers, carefully review group-negotiated contracts before they are signed by the Manager of Group Purchasing.

Q. *Are the quantity, specifications, and quality of incoming goods determined by someone independent of the purchasing department?*

- How are weekend deliveries handled.
- Does the clinical engineer examine and test all equipment before it is accepted by the hospital and before the invoice is approved for payment.

Q. *Are prenumbered receiving reports prepared for all incoming goods by a person who does not have access to inventories or perform any duties in connection with ordering or vouchering?*

- Are the prenumbered receiving reports safeguarded against misuse.
- Is there a periodic independent accounting for the sequence of numbers.
- Is a copy of the receiving report filed in the receiving department.
- Are copies of the receiving report furnished to both the accounting and the purchasing departments.
- Is the accounting department *promptly* notified of goods returned to vendors.

Q. *Are unmatched purchase orders and receiving reports periodically investigated?*

- Is there a reporting system that readily identifies outstanding purchase orders, the date the purchase order was issued, and other related data. (See Figure 8.2.)

- Is Fiscal Services Administration notified, at least monthly, of outstanding receiving reports for which vendor invoices have not been received.
- Is there a proper investigation of such items to ensure there is no breakdown in the system of internal controls.

Q. Are partial shipments recorded and checked? (See Figure 8.3.)

Reviewing the Accounts Payable System
(See Figure 8.4.)

Q. Is a voucher system used for the processing of vendor invoices?

- Are vendor invoices registered immediately upon receipt to safeguard against loss or alteration prior to entry in the voucher register.
- Is the vendor's invoice delivered to the purchasing department for checking against the purchase order and receiving report.
- Is the receiving report carefully examined to assure that all items received agree with those ordered and invoiced by the vendor.
- Are exceptions subsequently accounted for.

Q. Are vendors' invoices verified independently for clerical accuracy prior to their payment?

- Are prices and terms verified by reference to purchase orders or their equivalent.
- Are extensions, footings, and freight charges tested.
- Are non-goods invoices (e.g., for fees, rentals, utilities) approved by responsible persons before payment.

Q. Does a designated individual record the general ledger account distribution on invoices or vouchers?

- Are the account distributions checked against those indicated on the purchase requisition, as approved by the department manager.
- Is a thorough review of the departmental monthly expense distribution reports versus the monthly budgets made by someone in the accounting department.
- Are the coding errors discovered as a result of this review discussed with the department managers and accounts payable coding clerk.

Q. Are invoices and vouchers reviewed and approved by a responsible person before payment?

- Are the supporting documents attached to and filed with the vouchers.
- Are processed vouchers and supporting documents properly cancelled to prevent their reuse.
- Are duplicate copies of invoices received from vendors clearly stamped "duplicate" or destroyed to prevent duplicate payment.
- Are returned purchases, claims for adjustments, and other charges against vendors recorded for follow-up.

Q. *Does the accounting department compare vendors' statements with individual vendors' invoices?*

- Do adjustments result from this comparison.
- Are accounts payable adjustments approved by a responsible person in the accounting department.

Q. *Are the unpaid vouchers, or accounts payable detail, balanced monthly to the general ledger control account?*

- Does someone other than the accounts payable clerk review and approve the monthly reconciliations.
- Are accounts payable adjustments approved by a responsible person.

Examining the Controls Over Other Liabilities, Including Long-Term Debt

Q. *Are subsidiary records maintained for other liabilities, including deferred income?*

- On a monthly basis, are the subsidiary records balanced to the general ledger.
- Are the journal entries and working papers, establishing the other liabilities or deferred income, properly reviewed and initialled by a responsible individual.
- Are pension plan contributions and the related liability calculated by an actuary.

Q. *Does a responsible person review interfund receivable-payable accounts?*

- Do the accounts balance between funds.
- Do the transactions agree with hospital policy.
- Do the transactions require Board of Trustee approval.

Q. *Is a notes payable register maintained?*

- Is the person maintaining the register someone other than the person authorized to sign checks or notes.
- Are paid notes cancelled and retained.

Q. *Does the Board of Trustees authorize all borrowings?*

- Are the banks from which funds may be borrowed specifically indicated in the minutes.
- Are the officers authorized to borrow specifically named in the minutes.
- Are two or more signatures required on the notes.
- Are there adequate accounting controls regarding the pledged assets and meeting the payment dates.

Q. *Does the hospital have any long-term debt outstanding?*

- Are the debt obligations in writing.
- Are the debt obligations executed in the hospital's name.
- Does the hospital use an independent trustee.
- Are redeemed notes, bonds, and interest coupons mutilated.

- Is the related interest expense properly recorded in the hospital's general ledger.
- Are there restrictions as to the amount of leased assets the hospital may have according to the terms of the debt agreement.
- Has the hospital exceeded this limit.
- Is there a requirement for the retention of compensating cash balances with the lending institutions.
- Is a requirement for minimum working capital specified in the debt agreement.
- Is the hospital maintaining adequate working capital.

THE AUDIT

The Audit Objective

The audit of the purchasing and payables functions is designed to establish, as far as possible, that all significant liabilities are included in the financial statements. In performing the audit, it must be remembered that liabilities are more likely to be understated than overstated.

In addition to verifying the amounts recorded, the auditor must also:

1) Determine that the established purchasing policies are being properly applied.
2) Identify liabilities on which assets have been pledged as collateral.
3) Determine that liabilities are properly described and classified in the financial statements.
4) Determine the amount of contingent liabilities and commitments, and ascertain that they are properly disclosed or provided for, where appropriate.

Determining the Amount of Short-Term Notes Payable and Compliance with Terms

1) Review the minutes of the Board of Trustees to determine if short-term borrowings have been approved.
2) Prepare a schedule showing dates of notes, maturity dates, payees, amounts, interest rates, collateral, endorsers or guarantors, if any, and accrued or prepaid interest.
3) Obtain written confirmation of principal amount, maturity dates, date to which interest is paid, collateral security, and other pertinent details of each liability directly from the creditor or Trustee (where applicable), and request any information as to noncompliance with the loan agreement.
4) Mail confirmation requests (see Figure 8.5) to all lenders from whom the hospital borrowed money during the period under examination.
5) Compare all direct liabilities reported in confirmations received to the appropriate liability accounts.
6) Obtain and review signed copies of note or loan agreements.
7) Investigate compliance with any restrictive provisions affecting the financial statements, such as requirements as to working capital or sinking funds, prepayments contingent on income, and similar matters.

8) Test the computation of accrued or prepaid interest.
9) Bring to the attention of Administration any significant unrecorded liabilities that were discovered.

Auditing Trade Accounts Payable for Unrecorded Liabilities

1) Obtain a detail trial balance, or listing of accounts payable at the balance sheet date.
2) Foot the schedule and reconcile the total to the general ledger control account.
3) a) Using an accepted method of statistical sampling, select vendors from the listing of accounts payable and compare the balance per the list to the vendors' statement.
   b) Request statements from vendors selected (see Figure 8.6), using either the hospital's stationery or your preprinted form, with the name of the hospital rubber-stamped on the form.
   c) Compare vendors' statements on file with those received as a result of your confirmation for correctness of the individual amounts shown in the trial balance.
   d) Have the purchasing department prepare reconciliations between vendors' statements received by you and the individual accounts shown on the trial balance.
   e) Test the larger reconciling items by reference to cash payments, receipt of merchandise in transit, credit memoranda received, etc.
   f) Request additional confirmation from vendor if an important account appears to be improperly stated or is in dispute. In some instances, the condition of the records or other reasons may make extensive communication with vendors advisable.
4) a) Request statements from principal suppliers when such statements are not on file, whether or not a liability to the supplier appears in the accounts.
   b) Compare vendors' statements received for correctness of the individual amounts shown on the trial balance.
   c) Repeat audit steps 3-d through 3-f, if applicable.
5) In searching for unrecorded liabilities, perform the following reviews:
   a) receiving records and unmatched receiving reports;
   b) voucher records, cash records, and journal entries subsequent to the balance sheet date;
   c) debit and credit memos issued subsequent to the balance sheet date;
   d) unentered invoices received subsequent to the balance sheet date;
   e) receiving cutoff records, if an inventory is taken at month end; and
   f) inquiries of purchasing and accounting personnel.
6) Review the trial balance of accounts payable for possible reclassification of accounts with affiliates, amounts due to officers or directors, payrolls, taxes, or any other significant amounts not representing usual trade accounts payable.

7) a) Investigate the nature of debit balances and determine their collectibility.
   b) Consider confirmation and reclassification of significant debit balances.
8) Investigate past due amounts of importance.
9) Prepare a schedule of unrecorded trade accounts payable showing source, vendor, nature, date of invoice, date goods or services were received, amount, and account to be charged.
10) Review this schedule with the chief financial officer and note proper disposition.

Determining the Extent of Other Liabilities

1) Employee Compensation:
   a) Determine dates on which salaries, wages, and other forms of compensation have been paid.
   b) Compute or test all unpaid balances by reference to subsequent payrolls.
   c) Review employee vacation and holiday pay policy and test the accrual for unpaid vacation and holiday pay.
   d) Ascertain the possibility of retroactive wage increases under union contracts.
2) Taxes (other than income taxes):
   a) Prepare an analysis of the accounts for the period under review.
   b) Reconcile additions to the accrual with charges to expense accounts or with collection of taxes as agent.
   c) Inspect cancelled checks or tax receipts to support the payment of taxes. The payments should clearly indicate their nature and the period covered.
   d) Test account balances at the end of the period by reference to tax statements, payroll tax returns, sales and use tax returns, or other applicable data, including calculations.
3) Other:
   a) Correspond with all attorneys with whom the hospital has dealt during the period under review to obtain the details of legal expenses not recorded and judgments against the hospital.
   b) 1) Correspond with the Medicare/Medicaid Intermediaries to verify the important details of amounts due to (or from) the intermediaries for prior periods.
      2) Determine if material amounts under appeal have been adequately disclosed in the financial statements.
   c) Determine the current year amount due to or due from third-party payors. (See Chapters 4 and 13.)
   d) Test the accuracy of the accrued liability for medical specialists' fees:
      1) Obtain and read a copy of the latest applicable contract.
      2) Note proper signatures and trace acceptance of contract to Board of Trustees' minutes.
      3) Review the method of compensation.
      4) Compute liability.
      5) Note subsequent payment of fees.

6) Review the copy of professional component rationale filed with the Medicare Intermediary.

e) 1) Proprietary hospitals, especially chain organizations, present several unique problems to the auditor. One such problem is the determination of income tax liability. To perform this audit, first prepare an analysis of changes in the reported income tax liability accounts during the period under review.
2) Reconcile additions to the accrual with appropriate expense account.
3) Inspect cancelled checks or other evidence of payment to support the payment of taxes. The payment should clearly indicate its nature and the period covered.
4) Obtain and test the necessary data for the allocation of income to various states, possessions, or foreign countries.
5) Investigate the possibility of a liability for income or similar taxes for which returns have not been filed.
6) Check the computation of the provision for income taxes.
7) Determine the status of prior years' tax returns and to what extent they have been examined by taxing authorities.
8) Obtain information on changes made by the taxing authorities and the effect of any unsettled matters.
9) Consider questionable items that may be present in returns filed that have not been examined and their effect on future years.

Auditing the Hospital's Compliance with Long-Term Liability Agreements

1) Obtain, from the accounting office, a schedule showing dates of notes, maturity dates, payees, amounts, interest rates, accrued interest, and collateral, if any.
2) Mail confirmation request (see Figure 8.5) to the creditor (or trustee) requesting confirmation of principal amount, maturity dates, date to which interest is paid, collateral security, and other pertinent details. Also request information as to any known noncompliance with the terms of the loan agreement.
3) Obtain copies of and read the bond indentures or other agreements covering the indebtedness, noting the principal provisions affecting the financial statements, such as:
   a) sinking fund or redemption requirements;
   b) requirements for current ratio or other asset amounts or ratios;
   c) surplus restrictions;
   d) pledge of assets;
   e) insurance requirements; and
   f) restrictions on amount of leased equipment.
4) Determine that such requirements have been met and that no restriction has been exceeded.
5) Inspect bonds redeemed, retired, or surrendered during the period. Obtain

confirmation of bonds retired or held by trustee in sinking or other funds during the period under review.

6) Ascertain amount of long-term debt maturing in one year. Also determine what amount, if any, is required to be paid into sinking or other funds within one year. Then note that such amounts are properly reflected in the financial statements.
7) Test the computation of accrued interest.
8) Examine, in detail, all changes in the long-term liability accounts during the period under review. Obtain and note the particulars of all transactions.

Auditing the Hospital Records to Locate Deferred Income, Commitments, or Contingent Liabilities

1) Deferred Income:
   a) Review the third-party reimbursement elections made by the hospital to determine if a portion of the reimbursement should be deferred; i.e., the use of accelerated depreciation for Medicare.
   b) Review all recorded classes of income to determine if there is any class of income that should be deferred.
2) Commitments:
   a) Obtain, from Administration and accounting, information on long-term lease commitments. Record the description, date of lease, renewal options, basic annual rent, and nature of any contingent additional rent. Review interim financial statements and note proper accounting treatment.
   b) Obtain copies of pension plans and note essential provisions. Obtain copy of actuarial estimate of annual cost of the plan and amount of unfunded past service liability, if any. Note proper accounting treatment.
   c) Inquire of the purchasing manager, engineer, and medical specialist for any unrecorded contracts payable.
   d) Review minutes of the Board of Trustees and Administrative Council for any unrecorded liabilities.
   e) Send confirmation to the hospital's independent architect for information regarding outstanding architectural fees, general contractor fees, or commitments.
   f) Secure information about, or copies of, any other significant contracts; i.e., employment contracts, union contracts, or third-party reimbursement contracts, in particular Blue Cross Provider contracts.

WORKING PAPERS REQUIRED

Notes Payable

The permanent file should contain:

1) Reference to by-laws and code of regulations of the hospital that set forth the approval required for the pledging of assets and for borrowing money.

2) Reference to the Board of Trustee minutes that indicate approval for each borrowing.
3) Copy of mortgage, if any.
4) Copies of bond indentures, loan agreements, etc.

The current working paper files should contain:

1) A schedule showing the dates of notes, maturity, payees, amounts, interest rates, collateral, guarantors, and accrued or prepaid interest.

NOTE: The schedule should also indicate the amount due within one year.

2) Confirmation request, replies, and any information as to noncompliance with the loan agreement.

Trade Accounts Payable

The current year working paper files should contain a detail trial balance of trade accounts payable at the balance sheet date. The schedule should be keyed in such a fashion as to indicate which vendors were selected for comparison to account balances per statements mailed to the hospital, and which were confirmed directly to the auditor.

A schedule should be prepared listing the principal vendors to whom confirmations were mailed, even though there was no liability indicated at the balance sheet date.

Copies of returned confirmations that indicated a difference in the amount due per vendor records versus the hospital's records and the final disposition of such differences should also be kept in the file.

A schedule of unrecorded trade accounts payable should be prepared, and notation made of the account to be charged and the hospital journal entry subsequently recording these liabilities.

A summary of audit work performed and conclusions reached should be prepared and placed in the front of the liabilities work paper files.

Other Liabilities

The current year working papers should consist of at least the following applicable schedules and memoranda:

1) Calculation of accrued salaries, wages, and bonuses.
2) Calculation of accrued vacation and holiday pay.
3) A schedule for each payroll tax and each payroll showing the beginning accrual, the taxes actually paid during the year (by quarter), the ending accrual, and the expense for the year.
4) Correspondence with hospital attorneys and architects.
5) Correspondence with third-party payors.
6) Calculation of specialists' fees for the year, including the accrued liability for such fees.

NOTE: The permanent file should include copies of the applicable contracts with reference to Board of Trustees' approval.

7) Analysis of changes in the reported tax liability accounts during the year, showing a reconciliation to the appropriate expense accounts.
8) Analysis of third-party reimbursement elections to determine the amount of deferred reimbursement that should be reported.
9) The permanent files should contain copies of all employment contracts, union contracts, pension plans, and third-party reimbursement agreements.

FINANCIAL STATEMENT PRESENTATION

Notes Payable

In the balance sheet, notes and trade acceptances payable generally should be segregated into their natural classifications. The following illustrates the principal types of notes payable found in hospitals:

TO banks
TO banks (marketable securities pledged as collateral)
TO finance companies (accounts receivable assigned as security)
TO trade creditors

The current portion of long-term debt is usually shown as the final item in the current liability section.

Accounts Payable and Accrued Expenses

A reporting problem often difficult to explain to the satisfaction of management is that of bank overdrafts. The overdraft need not be disclosed if the total cash position is adequate, or if the overdraft is a result of a delay in making a deposit or bank transfer. In such cases, the overdraft may be combined with accounts payable. If disclosure is required, the following presentation is suggested:

Bank checks outstanding	$65,000
Less cash on deposit, per bank	5,000
	$60,000

As noted in the chapter on Accounts Receivable, credit balances in patient accounts, where the aggregate amount is immaterial, need not be segregated from accounts receivable. If such items are material, they should be included with trade accounts payable.

Liabilities for social security tax and income taxes withheld from employee compensation may be combined and reported as "Payroll Taxes and Taxes Withheld from Employee Compensation."

The liability for the aforementioned taxes may also be combined with the payroll liability. In such cases, the suggested caption would be "Employee Compensation."

It is generally acceptable to combine all unpaid income taxes, including the unused provisions for prior years, into a single amount entitled "Federal and State Income Taxes." If taxes for prior periods are material the captions should be:

Federal and State Income Taxes:

For the year ending December 31, 19____	$xx.xx
For prior years	xx.xx

Deferred Income

Timing differences to which interperiod Medicare or other third-party cost allocations apply give rise to balance sheet accounts that are carried forward until the reverse timing difference occurs. The accounts should be classified as current to the extent that the related assets or liabilities are classified as current. The balance sheet accounts therefore should be classified into two categories, one for the net current amount and the second for the net non-current amount.

A suitable caption would be "Deferred Third-party Reimbursement," classified as either an asset account or a liability account. In addition, consideration should be given to disclosing the nature of the item giving rise to the deferral in a footnote. The footnote might be stated as follows:

> NOTE 1. The hospital uses accelerated depreciation in determining reimbursable cost under certain third-party reimbursement agreements, whereas depreciation is recorded on the straight-line basis for financial reporting purposes. Revenue (cost reimbursement) in the amount of $64,000 resulting from such difference in the current year is deferred and will be taken into income in future years.

Long-Term Debt

Where long-term debt consists of a single mortgage note or bond issue, it is permissible to use the name of the issue as the balance sheet caption.

When more than one issue is outstanding, it is preferred practice to use the caption "Long-Term Debt," and to list the issues below it. The title of the issue should be exactly as shown by the indenture or other government issue. The interest rate, maturity, etc., should also be reported whether or not they are a part of the title. As mentioned earlier, the portion of long-term debt maturing within one year from the balance sheet date should usually be classified as a current liability.

If default exists, whether as to principal payments, interest, or other specific covenants, the circumstances should be brought out in the balance sheet or a footnote.

Leases

When leases are capitalized in accordance with generally accepted accounting principles, the following may be suitable captions:

Capitalized Lease Obligation
Lease-Purchase Obligation

Additional disclosures relative to terms of payment, significant provisions, etc., of the capitalized leases should be made in a note to the financial statements. Rental payments due within one year should be classified as current liabilities.

G 14782

ABOVE NUMBER MUST APPEAR ON ALL CORRESPONDENCE AND INVOICES

VENDOR

TERMS:

1. SHIPMENTS ACCEPTED BETWEEN 8:30 A.M. AND 4:00 P.M. EXCEPT SATURDAY, SUNDAY AND HOLIDAYS.
2. ALL SHIPMENTS SUBJECT TO INSPECTION; INFERIOR OR DAMAGED GOODS RETURNED AT VENDER'S EXPENSE.
3. NOT RESPONSIBLE FOR MERCHANDISE DELIVERED UNLESS SPECIFIED BY A P.O. SIGNED BY DIR. OF PURCHASING
4. ALL SHIPPING CHARGES MUST BE PREPAID UNLESS OTHERWISE INDICATED.
5. PACKING SLIPS MUST ACCOMPANY ALL SHIPMENTS.
6. INVOICES MUST BE CLEARLY ITEMIZED INCLUDING TIME AND RATE FOR ALL LABOR WHEN APPLICABLE.

DATE OF ORDER	SHIP VIA	F.O.B.	TERMS	DATE REQUIRED

QUANTITY	DESCRIPTION		DEPT. NUMBER	SUB CODE	UNIT COST AS PURCHASED	TOTAL COST
		1				
		2				
		3				
		4				
		5				
		6				
		7				
		8				
		9				
		10				
		11				
		12				
		TOTAL				

ADDRESS ALL INQUIRIES TO:
DIRECTOR OF PURCHASING
SEND ALL INVOICES TO:
ACCOUNTING DEPT.

VENDOR

MANAGER OF PURCHASING

SPECIFICATIONS AND REQUIREMENTS
CHECK LIST

IN ORDER FOR PAYMENT TO BE RELEASED FOR THE ITEM (S) SPECIFIED ON THIS PURCHASE ORDER, THE ITEM (S) MUST MEET THE SPECIFICATIONS AND REQUIREMENTS CORRESPONDING TO THE NUMBERS CIRCLED IN THE BOX TO THE RIGHT. THE SPECIFICATIONS ARE IDENTIFIED ON THE BACK OF THE PURCHASE ORDER. REQUESTS FOR DEVIATIONS SHALL BE SUBMITTED IN WRITING TO THE UNDERSIGNED PURCHASING MANAGER.

1a	2b	5b	7b	10a	10f	11b
1b	3a	5c	7c	10b	10g	12
1c	4a	5d	7d	10c	10h	13
1d	4b	6	8	10d	10i	
2a	5a	7a	9	10e	11a	

1720 CO8

FIGURE 8.1

SPECIFICATIONS AND REQUIREMENTS

1. **Power Cords**
   a. All power cords shall have a 3-conductor (black, white, green) configuration and be of SJ, SJO or better quality. All conductors shall be at least No. 18 AWG wire. The current rating of the conductor shall be adequate for the rating of the device(s). A strain relief mechanism shall be provided on the chassis at the point where the power cord enters.
   b. The power cord shall terminate with a UL listed "Hospital Grade" attachment plug. In attaching the cord to the plug, the black and white conductors shall be cut at least 3/8 inches shorter than the green conductor.
   c. Resistance between any electrically conductive point on the chassis and the ground pin of the attachment plug shall be less than 0.15 ohms.
   d. A safe retainer for the storage of the power cord shall be provided on a portable device.
2. **Power Switches and Circuit Breakers**
   a. The main power supply switch shall be double-pole, arranged to "make/break" both conductors (hot and neutral).
   b. An operational overcurrent protective mechanism (i.e. fuse or circuit breaker) shall be installed only in the incoming power supply (black conductor) circuit. It shall be rated at the lowest value capable of safely and continuously carrying the device's rated current. It shall be physically placed in an easily accessible location with its ampere rating clearly displayed.
3. **Physical Protection**
   a. The device chassis shall be so designed that internal components shall be protected against humidity, gases (i.e. oxygen, helium and anesthetics), spilled liquids, dust and mechanical abuse.
4. **Labels and Markings**
   a. Abbreviated operating instructions shall be permanently affixed to the device(s) and shall be clearly referenced to the controls and readily visible to the operator.
   b. Clearly legible markings shall be affixed to the device(s) indicating the manufacturer's name, model of device, catalog and serial numbers, operating voltage, amperage and frequency, input watts (or volt-amperes), output voltage and current.
5. **Leakage Currents**
   Leakage currents through a 1,000 ohm resistance in all wiring modes (see NFPA 76B-T "Safe Use of Electricity in Patient Care Facilities," November, 1974) shall not exceed:
   a. 100 microamperes (AC, RMS) from any point on the chassis to ground
   b. Ten microamperes (AC, RMS) from patient leads to ground and 10 microamperes (AC, RMS) between any combination
   c. 50 microamperes (AC, RMS) from patient leads to ground and 50 microamperes (AC, RMS) between any combination of patient leads
   d. 500 microamperes (AC, RMS) from any point on the chassis to ground
6. Vendor shall supply warranty agreement with expiration date.

FIGURE 8.1 ***(continued)***

7. Statement by manufacturer (or vendor) of possible adverse effects resulting from:
    a. Improper gounding
    b. Lack of specific maintenance routine
    c. Improper control settings
    d. Potentially hazardous interactions with other types of equipment
8. Vendor agrees to supply adequate in-service training for all personnel involved in operation or maintenance of device.
9. Vendor shall supply name of (nearest) qualified maintenance service organization.
10. Vendor shall supply minimum of three (3) complete user manuals including:
    a. Operating instructions
    b. Performance specifications
    c. Complete schematic diagrams and circuit descriptions
    d. Complete replacement parts list
    e. Complete service and maintenance requirements and procedures
    f. Recommended "on hand" parts list
    g. Complete instruction for testing and/or calibration of device (including a list of equipment required to perform tests)
    h. Limitations of device
    i. Warnings of potential hazards, fault conditions and possible corrective measures (i.e., trouble-shooting procedures)
11. **Installation**
    a. Vendor shall provide qualified supervision of installation
    b. Vendor shall provide all labor and material required for installation
12. Equipment must be U.L. listed.
13. Additional information per addendum sheet attached to the purchase order.

FIGURE 8.1 ***(continued)***

__________ HOSPITAL

HOSPITAL INVENTORY ITEMS AT/OR BELOW MINIMUM 08/03/ RPT INVDO34 PAGE 2

ITEM NUMBER	DESCRIPTION	AVG. COST PER UNIT	MIN	MAX	ON HAND	ON ORDER	BACK ORDERED	LEAD DAYS MIN	LEAD DAYS MAX	AVG		
11331709	BANDAGE-KERLIX ROLL-4½ x 6P	.563	54	766	22	700	0	00	00	00	ORDERED	07/23/
11474301	GAUZE ½ PLAIN PACKING	.960	4	61	4	0	0	00	00	00		
11536281	PADS 0.B MODESS	.936	39	138	19	0	0	00	00	00		
11743879	SPONGE-4X4 12-PLY STERILE 1	3.774	107	368	91	0	0	05	08	07		
11753308	SPONGE LAP-RAYTEC 4 X 4-16 P	16.733	8	93	5	0	0	00	00	00		
11908308	STRIP-STERI ½ X 4	30.219	3	12	1	0	0	02	04	03		
12347688	GLOVE-SURG SZ 7 ½ STER DIS	71.000	5	11	2	0	0	01	04	03		
12412896	GLOVES, SURGICAL - PERRY SIZ	10.950	4	31	3	0	0	00	00	00		
12413001	GLOVE SURG SZ-6 ½ STER-DIS	10.950	7	46	4	36	0	00	00	00	ORDERED	08/03/
12413043	GLOVE SURG SZ-7 STER-DISPOSA	10.950	10	61	3	48	0	01	01	01	ORDERED	08/03/
12413126	GLOVE SURG SZ-8 STER-DISPOSA	10.950	8	50	4	36	0	02	02	02	ORDERED	08/03/
12521928	GLOVE EXAM STERILE MEDIUM	10.400	17	76	9	0	0	04	04	04		
13788617	NEEDLES, HYPO.-DISP. 19-1 1/	3.805	9	64	1	50	0	10	10	10	ORDERED	08/03/
13804893	NEEDLES HYPO DISPO 21 X 1	3.655	11	76	2	50	0	00	00	00	ORDERED	08/03/
13813001	NEEDLE 21 X 1½ HYPO MONOJ	3.805	7	54	4	40	0	00	00	00	ORDERED	08/03/
13829262	NEEDLES-DISPO-23 X 1	3.800	4	33	4	0	0	06	06	06		
13837398	NEEDLES, HYPO.-DISP. 25-5/8-M	3.804	6	45	1	30	0	00	00	00	ORDERED	08/03/
13837455	NEEDLE DISPO 25 X 2	6.260	2	18	1	5	0	00	00	00	ORDERED	08/03/
14329353	0.9 SODIUM CHLORIDE IRRIGATI	10.500	24	55	0	55	0	01	02	02	ORDERED	08/03/
14329957	0.9 SODIUM CHLORIDE IRRIGATI	14.820	31	60	5	95	0	01	02	02	ORDERED	08/03/
14457006	BUTTERFLY 23 GA X ¾	10.585	3	19	3	0	0	00	00	00		
15997158	SUTURE ETHICON 8682G	19.746	2	3	0	0	0	01	01	01		
16578601	SYRINGE-DISPO 30CC-NO NEEDLE	.206	10	296	10	0	0	00	00	00		
17053406	TRAY BONE MARROW ASPIRATING	8.100	10	38	4	50	0	00	00	00	ORDERED	08/03/
18102343	TUBES, CONNECTING	.549	235	1,467	179	0	0	00	00	00		

FIGURE 8.2

________________ HOSPITAL

PROTECTIVE PROCEDURE
RECEIPT OF PARTIAL SHIPMENT

RESPONSIBILITY	ACTION
Receiving Clerk:	1. Receives partial shipment of order together with packing slip from vendor.
	2. Pulls one copy of Purchase Order from the open file in the Receiving office, indicating on the Purchase Order which items have been received.
	3. Records date received and initials copy of Purchase Order.
	4. Forwards Purchase Order and packing slip to the Purchasing Department.
	a. For non-stock item, immediately sends copy of completed Purchase Order form and packing slip to Purchasing office.
	b. For stock items, gives copy of Purchase Order to Inventory Control Clerk who forwards the Purchase Order to E.D.P. When the copy is returned, the Inventory Control Clerk checks Purchase Order against the inventory status and forwards copy with packing slip to the Purchasing office.
Invoice Clerk:	5. Receives invoice from company billing for items of partial shipment.
	6. Receives packing slip and Purchase Order from the Purchasing Department.
	7. Processes invoice of partial shipment in usual procedure.

FIGURE 8.3

____________________ HOSPITAL

PROTECTIVE PROCEDURE

SUBJECT: Payment of Invoices

RESPONSIBILITY	ACTION
Invoice Clerk	1) Receives invoice from company and places in open file in Purchasing department.
	2) Receives packing slip or substitute and closed Purchase Order forms from Receiving department.
	3) Matches invoice and Purchase Order in open file with packing slip and closed Purchase Order forms.
	4) Verifies price and price extensions on invoices.
	5) Investigates any price difference on invoice, gaining assistance from buyers to justify price difference with vendor.
	6) Places one copy of Purchase Order in closed file in Purchasing department.
	7) Staples one copy of closed Purchase Order to invoice and packing slip (or substitute).
	8) Stamps invoice with hospital stamp. (Sample form of a stamp with necessary approval is shown below.) MATERIAL REC'D ________ PRICE O.K. ________ EXTENSION O.K. ________ ACCT. TO BE CHGD. ________ EQUIP. TAG NO. ________ O.K. FOR PAYMENT ________
	9) Records accounting classifications on invoice.
	10) Initials stamp on invoice indicating the material has been received and that prices and extensions have been verified.

FIGURE 8.4

	11) Sends invoices to Accounting Supervisor.
Accounting Supervisor	12) Receives approved invoices from the Purchasing department. NOTE: Interjects at this point any approved invoices from Pharmacy or other department and patient refund slips.
	13) Checks invoices, patient refund slips, or other bills for proper accounting classification and initials in "approved for payment" box on invoice.
	14) Forwards invoices to Accounts Payable Clerk.
Accounting Clerk	15) Records due date on accounts payable voucher as follows: a) discounted invoices—10th of the month. b) A-K invoices—15th of the month. c) L-Z vendors—20th of the month. d) any voucher not previously released—25th of the month.
	16) Assigns vendor number to voucher. (See procedure # 010 for assignment of vendor number.) NOTE: For one-time vendors, write check or voucher so that surname is printed prior to given name.
	17) Adds all invoice totals in a batch.
	18) Adds all voucher totals in a batch.
	19) Compares both totals, corrects any differences and writes correct total on transmittal.
	20) Forwards transmittal and vouchers to E.D.P.

FIGURE 8.4 ***(continued)***

January____, 19____

ABC Bank
Financial Avenue
____________, State

Gentlemen:

Our auditors, X, Y, and Z, 100 East Fourth Street, Hometown, State, are making their annual examination of our accounts and records, as of December 31, 19___. In this regard, will you please confirm directly to them the following information, as of December 31, 19___ on our note, which you hold:

Amount owing at December 31, 19___	$ __________
Amount past due, if any	__________
Amount of interest due, if any	__________
Amount of prepaid interest, if any	__________
Security, if any ____________________	
______________________________	
Due date of note	__________

A stamped, pre-addressed envelope to our auditors is enclosed for your convenience.

Sincerely,

____________ Hospital

By: ____________
Administrator

FIGURE 8.5

January_____, 19____

Gentlemen:

In connection with our regular audit, please confirm directly to our auditors, X, Y, and Z, 100 East Fourth Street, Hometown, State, the amount due you as of December 31, 19____.

Amount due you, per our records $____________

Sincerely,

________________ Hospital

By: ____________________
Administrator

The above is correct.

Signed ____________________ Date ____________________

The above is NOT correct. Difference is as follows:

____

____

Signed ____________________ Date ____________________

FIGURE 8.6

9

Auditing Hospital Fund Balances

Definition

The A.I.C.P.A. *Hospital Audit Guide* states, "Funds balances represent the net equity of funds. Unrestricted fund balance includes working capital, net resources invested in plant assets, board-designated funds, and other unrestricted resources. Restricted funds consist of:

1) Specific purpose resources placed with the hospital in a trustee-like arrangement.
2) Plant replacement and expansion resources contributed for additions to property, plant, and equipment. These balances include amounts that are required to be used for property additions, as specified in agreements with third-party payors, and must be distinguished from board-designated, unrestricted funds.
3) Endowment fund resources held for the production of income. Endowment funds terminating after a period of time or upon the happening of a certain event should ordinarily be disclosed separately from other permanent endowment funds."[1]

The emphasis of this chapter will be upon auditing nonprofit (tax-exempt) organizations. Under "Proprietary Hospitals" will be suggestions for auditing their comparable accounts.

REVIEWING THE CONTROLS

Ten Comprehensive Questions

Q. Do permanent records of gifts and bequests show the donor's name, the amount, date received, and whether unrestricted or purpose for which restricted?

---

1. Copyright 1972 by the American Institute of Certified Public Accountants, Inc.

Q. Are documents, such as copies of wills, kept on file to support gifts and bequests?

Q. Do the Board of Trustee minutes report the acceptance of gifts and bequests, and designate a purpose for unrestricted resources?

Q. Are non-cash gifts and bequests recorded at the time of receipt?

Q. Are restricted gifts and bequests treated in accordance with the donor's wishes as to income and principal?

Q. Is restricted fund cash kept separate from unrestricted fund cash?

Q. Are expenditures from restricted funds approved by a responsible person and subject to the regular routines for the payment of vouchers?

Q. Are analyses of fund balance transactions maintained to support the general ledger control accounts?

Q. Are endowment-type funds held in trust by outside parties?

Q. If yes, are the endowment funds controlled by memo account?

Proprietary Hospitals

Q. Does the hospital use an independent registrar or transfer agent?

Q. If no, are unissued certificates and certificate stubs in the custody of a responsible person, who cancels surrendered certificates and controls the documentary stamp?

Q. Does the hospital use an independent dividend paying agent?

Q. If no, is adequate control exercised in preparing and mailing dividends?

Q. Are returned or unclaimed dividend checks promptly redeposited and recorded as liabilities?

THE AUDIT

The Audit Objective

The audit objective is to gather and examine sufficient evidential material to support the purported nature of the fund and its purpose. The auditor must also determine the accuracy of the amount stated and satisfy himself that the hospital is complying with the terms of restricted funds.

The Audit Program (Tax-exempt)

1) Prepare a memorandum explaining the nature and purpose of each fund. Reference should be made to attorneys' letters, Board of Trustee minutes, and other official documents.

2) Obtain an analysis of each fund for the period under review. Reconcile the opening balances with balances shown in the balance sheet at the close of the preceding period.

3) Verify that transfers from endowment or other restricted funds are in accordance with the donor's instructions.

4) Verify that receipt and acknowledgment procedures exist for all gifts and bequests.

5) Ascertain that earnings (losses) on investments of each fund are properly accounted for.

6) Charges to each fund during the period under review should be tested by inspection of invoices or other pertinent data to determine if such charges are within the purpose of the fund.

7) Determine that charges to restricted fund balances involving grants are in accordance with the grant agreement.

The Audit Program (Proprietary)

Capital Stock

1) Determine the number of shares of capital stock issued and outstanding at the balance sheet date.

a) Obtain confirmation from registrar.
b) If the company has no independent registrar, make a listing of stock certificate stubs or stockholders' ledger if stubs are not kept.

NOTE: If a large number of certificates are outstanding, it may be appropriate in subsequent audits to examine only the transfers, and if the total issue has increased too, account for the additional certificates separately without going through all of the old certificates.

2) Prepare an analysis of the entries in the capital stock accounts during the period under review.

a) Inspect the supporting data and explain the nature of the transactions.
b) Trace to the minutes and to amendments to the charter, if appropriate.

3) Review the corporate minutes for information regarding changes during the period under review, as to any stock options, warrants, or reservations, including shares reserved for conversion of debt or preferred stock.

4) Account for certificates of treasury stock by inspection as of the balance sheet date, or by confirmation if held by a custodian.

5) Consider the position of the company with respect to compliance with stock provisions.

6) Read and make excerpts for the permanent files of any amendments to the certificate of incorporation.

Surplus

1) Analyze the surplus accounts for the period under review and reconcile opening balances with balances shown in the balance sheet at the close of the preceding period. Consider the propriety of charges and credits to surplus.

2) Determine restrictions, if any, on surplus of any class under capital stock provisions, loan agreements, indentures, or by reason of treasury stock. Prepare a schedule showing the calculations of the amount restricted at the balance sheet date.

3) Refer to minutes of Trustee meetings to determine if dividends paid were declared and also to determine if all dividends declared have been either paid or included in liabilities.

WORKING PAPERS REQUIRED

Permanent File

1) A copy of the hospital's code of regulations, i.e., articles of incorporation, and by-laws should be a part of the auditor's permanent file.

2) The permanent file should also include excerpts of Board minutes, agreements, contracts, and other documents that describe each fund and indicate the nature of the resources accounted for in the fund.

Current Year File

1) An analysis of each fund for the period, including:
   a) reconciliation of opening balances to previous year statements;
   b) notation that transfers are in accordance with donor's instructions;
   c) verification that each funds' earnings (losses) are properly accounted for; and
   d) notation that ending balance per analysis agrees with general ledger control.

2) A summary of audit work performed and conclusions reached.

Permanent File (Proprietary)

1) A copy of the corporate charter, constitution, and by-laws should be a part of the auditor's permanent audit files.
2) Excerpts of subsequent changes should be a part of the permanent file.

Current Year Files

Capital Stock

1) A trial balance should be included for each class of capital stock (if more than one) showing the following:

a) Stock certificate number
b) Date issued
c) Name of stockholder
d) Name of shares

This schedule may be transferred from one year's working paper to the next, noting on it any subsequent changes.

Surplus

1) A worksheet should be included, showing the balance at the beginning of the year, detail of additions and deductions, and the balance at the end of the year. The transactions in this account are usually few, therefore this schedule may also be transferred from the prior year audit file to the current year file.

2) A summary of audit work performed and conclusions reached should be placed at the front of this working paper section.

FINANCIAL STATEMENT PRESENTATION

A statement of changes in fund balances for tax-exempt hospitals should include all changes in funds and be presented in a form similar to Exhibit C, page 43, of the A.I.C.P.A. *Hospital Audit Guide.* (See Figure 9.1.)

There are a number of acceptable means of reporting the equity section of a proprietary hospital's balance sheet. The following is an example of how to present the capital stock section:

Common Stock, no par value:
authorized—100,000 shares; issued
and outstanding 80,000 shares,
at stated capital amount

The call price and redemption dates and other special features of preferred stock should be considered from the standpoint of disclosing such information. Mandatory redemption dates and any restrictive provisions as to the payment of dividends or other actions by the issuer must be disclosed.

Surplus

The term *surplus* preferably should not be used in the balance sheet presentation of stockholders' equity as recommended in Accounting Terminology Bulletin, No. 1. If, however, the auditor can not make a reasonably accurate classification of all elements in the account, it may have to be shown as one account with an appropriate explanation.

The caption "Earned Surplus" is acceptable if it is the corporation's preference; however, the following are more suitable descriptions:

Retained Earnings
Accumulated Income
Earnings Employed in the Business

Restrictions of retained earnings may be indicated by footnote or parenthetical notation appended to the balance sheet caption.

SAMPLE HOSPITAL[2]

STATEMENT OF CHANGES IN FUND BALANCES

Year Ended December 31, 19___
With Comparative Figures for 19___

	Current Year	Prior Year
Unrestricted Funds		
Balance at beginning of year	$6,918,000	$6,242,000
Excess of revenues over expenses	84,000	114,000
Transferred from plant replacement and expansion funds to finance property, plant, and equipment expenditures	628,000	762,000
Transferred to plant replacement and expansion funds to reflect third-party payor revenue restricted to property, plant, and equipment replacement	(230,000)	(200,000)
Balance at end of year	$7,400,000*	$6,918,000
Restricted Funds		
Specific purpose funds:		
Balance at beginning of year	$ 71,000	$ 50,000
Restricted gifts and bequests	35,000	20,000
Research grants	35,000	45,000
Income from investments	35,260	39,000
Gain on sale of investments	8,000	—
Transferred to:		
Other operating revenue	(100,000)	(80,000)
Allowances and uncollectible accounts	(8,000)	(3,000)
Balance at end of year	$ 76,260	$ 71,000
Plant replacement and expansion funds:		
Balance at beginning of year	$1,100,000	$1,494,000
Restricted gifts and bequests	113,000	150,000
Income from investments	15,000	18,000
Transferred to unrestricted funds (described above)	(628,000)	(762,000)
Transferred from unrestricted funds (described above)	230,000	200,000
Balance at end of year	$ 830,000	$1,100,000
Endowment funds:		
Balance at beginning of year	$3,975,000	$2,875,000
Restricted gifts and bequests	2,000,000	1,000,000
Net gain on sale of investments	175,000	100,000
Balance at end of year	$6,150,000	$3,975,000

See accompanying Notes to Financial Statements.

* Composition of the balance may be shown here, on the balance sheet, or in a footnote.

2. Exhibit C, Page 43 of the A.I.C.P.A. Hospital Audit Guide; copyright 1972.

FIGURE 9.1

10

Auditing the Hospital's Charge Control System

The audit of the patient service revenue system encompasses the admitting department, third-party reimbursement, ancillary departments' charge collection systems, patient billing, and the accounting system. This audit function offers the auditor an opportunity to be both highly visible and very productive to management in terms of "paying his own way." It also presents the risk that the auditor will become stereotyped as "a nit-picking money grubber." The latter can be avoided if the auditor, after completing his examination, has reviewed his recommendations for improving the charge collection system and/or statistical accumulation system with the department managers in the affected areas.

One of the most delicate situations the auditor must face is recommending organizational changes to adequately safeguard the hospital's resources. For example, in most hospitals the ward clerks report to the nursing division. It has been argued that this is a natural relationship inasmuch as the ward clerks are working at the nursing station and are therefore supervised by nurses who assist them in reading patients' medical charts. In reality the ward clerk's primary function may be to see that the prescribed treatment is ordered for the patient. If this is the case, the ward clerk's function is a key element in the patient revenue system. The nursing division is concerned primarily with patient care and secondarily with the recording of patient revenue. The fiscal services division may therefore be the recommended organizational area for the ward clerks.

The internal auditor must remember, in suggesting organizational changes, that it is important not just to have the right idea, but to have the right idea at the right time. Timing is everything!

If the internal auditor is alert during his informal conversations with departmental managers, he will often learn that items thought to be chargeable are not being charged to the patient.

In fact, the materials management department may be issuing charge tickets with items for which charges have not been negotiated with third-party payors. Furthermore, many charge tickets may be rejected by the hospital's data recording system; that is, the NCR posting clerk throws the charges away or the computer rejects such charges and the keypunch operator throws the tickets away.

The internal auditor has rendered a valuable service when he effects the implementation of a protective procedure such as the one outlined in Figure 10.1, which has a high degree of reliability in seeing that chargeable services are in fact being charged to patients.

One Midwest hospital increased its ancillary revenue by approximately $5.00 per patient day by changing its charge control system, implementing strong internal controls, and developing improved management reporting systems. This system, with similar results, could result in an additional $219,000 for a 150 bed hospital with an 80% occupancy. Key elements of this system will be included in this chapter as specific figures.

Following are questions and related thoughts that can serve as a guide in analyzing the hospital's internal controls as they relate to the accumulation of hospital patient service revenue, studying the related statistics, and suggesting improvements to be included in the audit management letter.

Also included is an audit program designed to provide the independent and internal auditors with audit procedures that will identify weaknesses in the revenue accounting and statistical control system of the hospital.

REVIEWING THE REVENUE SYSTEM CONTROLS

Admitting Controls Needed

Q. *Does the admitting department make a list naming all patients admitted either as inpatients, outpatient referrals, or emergency room and clinic patients?*

- Are the admissions numerically controlled and summarized daily.
- Are recurring outpatients properly counted; i.e., each visit recorded as a visit for statistical purposes.
- Is a periodic review made of the total admissions times the routine and customary charges made for such admissions to see if this total approximates the daily revenue recorded.
- Is the medical records or admitting department maintaining a list of all admissions, discharges, and daily patient census in accordance with the record retention requirements of your state.

Q. *Is a patient ledger automatically prepared for each admission by the admitting clerk?*

- Are patients classified, upon admission or immediately thereafter, as charity, insured, private pay, etc.
- Must all patients possess some type of identification to indicate that they have been admitted to the hospital before treatment is rendered.

Q. *Does the admitting department prepare a daily census summary for Administration's review?* (See Figure 10.2.)

- Does the report show it has been checked for mathematical accuracy.

- Are overflow conditions properly identified; i.e., percent of occupancy greater than 100%.
- Does the admitting department maintain at least the previous year's report plus the current year's report.
- Is this report serving the needs of the Administration, or does it need revision.

Q. *Does admitting reconcile its record of inhouse patients to the nursing midnight census?*

- Are corrections to the admitting records reviewed by a responsible person.
- Are the necessary corrections of room charges made to the patient's account.

Q. *Are the admitting personnel properly trained and supervised?*

- Are training manuals and self-instruction study guides used to obtain a high degree of accuracy by the admitting personnel.
- Are the admitting personnel adequately cross-trained in all phases of the admitting functions.
- Is the turnover rate higher in this department than the hospital average, which could indicate a lack of proper supervision.
- Do the members of admitting personnel interviewed by you possess a high degree of self-confidence and understand the importance of their role.

Identifying Weaknesses in the Charge Control System

Q. *Are all patient charges posted daily?*

- Are outpatient charges often left to accumulate for several days before being posted.
- Are all delays in posting charges properly noted in the internal management reports.

Q. *Are charges based on a standard rate list; i.e., the charge compendium?*

- Are such charges approved by a third-party payor before they are included as a part of the charge compendium.
- When was the last time rates were adjusted for changes in financial requirements.
- Are charges cost related so that each department "breaks even" or shows a profit after absorbing its allocation of hospital overhead?
- If the chief financial officer has delegated the responsibility for charge compendium changes, does the designated individual recognize the importance of such responsibility.

Q. *Are rates for identical services the same for all types of patients; i.e., inpatients and outpatients?*

- Are they the same for contractual and non-contractual patients.
- Through proper communication to the medical staff, could the use of contractual adjustments generate additional outpatient business.

Q. If a manual data processing system is used, are pre-posting control totals developed for routine daily service?

- Are they being prepared by a person independent of the accounting department.
- Are they reconciled to posted charges.
- Could similar controls be developed for ancillary services; i.e., home health visits or emergency room treatments.
- Do the daily routine service charges originate from daily census reports.

Q. Are charges recorded as of the same day the service is provided?

- Are the controls over manually prepared charge slips adequate.
- Are there adequate safeguards against understatement of services and revenue through the suppression of charges.
- Are returned drugs and/or other medical supplies supported by adequate data from the pharmacy or central supply; i.e., initialled approval of a supervisor.
- Is the department's daily revenue activity being reconciled to departmental logs by accounting office personnel.
- Does the charging system insure that for each chargeable service a charge document is prepared and forwarded to the accounting department.

Q. Are the charge slips priced at the ancillary departments?

- Are charge slips checked for accuracy by an informed person.
- Are extensions and footings checked by a responsible person.

Q. Are charge slips controlled by the use of prenumbered charge slips and accounted for by numerical sequence?

- Is too much time being expended through the use of this control mechanism.
- Could sufficient control be gained through the use of reconciliations with departmental logs.

Q. Are ancillary charges for services rendered periodically audited by a comparison with nursing notes in the medical record?

- Is the person making the audit independent of the billing functions.
- Is the person independent of the cashiering functions.

Q. Are revenues separately classified in the general ledger departmentally as inpatient and outpatient or other type of patient classification?

- Is the daily revenue collection system flexible enough to allow revenue to be further classified by type of payor; i.e., Medicare, Blue Cross, Welfare, etc.
- Is a monthly management report prepared for Administration, showing admissions, patient days, and revenue by type of patient. (See Figure 10.3.)
- Are these reports used by management in making budget forecast of patient mix and related revenue and contractual allowances.

Q. *Are contractual adjustments computed by the accounting department on a monthly basis?*

- Are these adjustments reviewed and approved by a competent responsible individual.
- Does the computation of such contractual adjustments take into consideration ongoing changes in the reimbursement regulations.
- Where applicable, is there a reconcilement of days of care rendered to third-party agency patients to approved days of care by such agencies.

Questioning the Adequacy of EDP Controls to Process Charges

Q. *Are there sufficient controls relating to the accuracy of the keypunch operators?*

- Are all source documents key verified by another individual.
- Are source documents stamped or initialled so the supervisor can tell who keypunched and key verified the data.

Q. *Are the following controls used in transmitting the charge data:*
1) Sequentially numbered batch control slips, prepared by accounting, showing the department, the number of items attached, and the total dollar value?
2) Reconciled batch control logs in accounting and Electronic Data Processing, showing batch number, number of items, and total dollar value?
3) Machine total of either cards punched and transmitted to the central processing unit (C.P.U.) or dollar value of items, by batch number?
4) Transaction control edit showing the number of cards, by batch, read and accepted, or rejected by the C.P.U.?
5) A written disposition noted in the log of rejected items?

Q. *Is there an E.D.P. listing of inventory supply items that indicates which items are a part of the approved charge compendium?* (See Figure 10.4.)

- Is this list easy to trace into the charge compendium; i.e., are like items identified by like name on both lists.
- Does the director of material management purge the inventory catalog and charge compendium at least annually so that valuable computer file space is not wasted on items no longer used by the hospital.
- Are central sterile supply items reviewed quarterly for increased cost that could be passed on to patients in order to maintain an adequate gross profit percentage.

Q. *Are charges being entered at the nursing station as a by-product of the order-entry system?*

Q. *Does the electronic charging system indicate the time and station from which an order is placed, thereby permitting the supervisors to follow up on training?* (See Figure 10.5.)

Q. Does the electronic charging system produce an audit trail that would permit the review, by patient name, of all charges entered from a nursing station?

Questioning the Accuracy of Patient Service Statistics

Q. Are patient days compiled from daily midnight census reports?

- Is this the basis of the routine service revenue postings.
- Are these patient days reconciled to the medical records statistics.
- Do the patient day counts include one-day stays; i.e., patients admitted and discharged on the same day.

Q. Are patient days classified and summarized as adult, pediatric nursing (babies remaining after mother has been discharged), newborn, and labor room?

- Is there verification of these statistics either through a control mechanism in the report, or by another department.
- Are inpatient aged days (Medicare purposes) being accumulated in a manner that is easily audited.

Q. Are all ancillary departments maintaining occasion of service statistics?

- Are inpatient and outpatient statistics kept separately.
- Are these statistics reconciled with medical records data.
- Can these statistics be used in testing for reasonableness of the departmental revenue recorded by the accounting department.

Q. Is there a comparison of the number of automated laboratory tests, per the invoice from the leasing agency, to the number of automated laboratory tests charged hospital patients?

- Is it possible the physician department manager is "moonlighting" by having his own independent laboratory within the hospital without the knowledge of Administration.
- Is the hospital being charged by the leasor for "quality control" tests.

THE AUDIT

The Audit Objective

The auditor's primary objective in the audit of the hospital's patient service revenue system is to determine that the hospital's statement of income has been prepared in accordance with generally accepted accounting principles applied on a basis consistent with that of the preceding period. The audit scope should also determine satisfactorily the following:

1) That departmental revenue is being summarized in order that third-party cost reports may be readily prepared.
2) That accurate logs are being maintained on a current basis for services rendered beneficiaries of third-party cost plans.

3) That accurate service statistics are being accumulated.
4) That the hospital charging system is accurately reflecting full charges for all chargeable services rendered.

Obtaining an Overview of the Patient Service Revenue System

1) Using the test month previously used for all tests of transactions, compare the individual accounts for the period under audit with those of the same month in the preceding year and with budgeted accounts.

2) Investigate any apparent change in classifications and unusual or new accounts.

3) Determine that the detailed accounts are classified and summarized into the same categories as for the preceding fiscal period.

4) Compare the individual statistical summaries with those of the same month in the preceding year and with the budgeted monthly statistics.

5) Investigate any variations not accounted for by differences in level of activity or the providing of new services.

6) Compare the explanations received for revenue variances with those received for statistical variances. Investigate further those that are not in agreement.

7) a) Obtain a schedule of effective room rates for the year.
   b) Obtain patient day's statistics by major category; i.e., med/surg, pediatrics, labor room.
   c) Compute income using average standard rates and compare to actual booked income and investigate substantial differences (see Figure 10.6).

Testing the Accuracy of Reported Patient Days

1) a) List and total inpatient days for the year, as indicated on the monthly summaries. (See Figure 10.7.)
   b) Relate the monthly totals to monthly revenue summaries and determine that material fluctuations in days between months have a corresponding fluctuation in revenues.

2) Test footing totals of the daily census sheets or equivalent and test add the daily totals to the monthly total for the test month. (See Figure 10.7.)

3) For medical histories used in the following revenue test, trace admission and discharge dates to the applicable business office records and from these records to inclusion in the inpatient day statistical buildups. This should cover a sampling of both Medicare and non-Medicare patients.

4) a) If the statistical accumulation above is performed in the business office (usually as a by-product of the revenue posting) by persons *not* maintaining medical record data, obtain from the medical records department its patient day accumulation. If this accumulation is on the basis of patients "in the house," it should agree with the business office data. If the accumulation is based only on discharged patients, make a general comparison, giving consideration to a difference in census at the beginning and end of the period.
   b) If there is not a separate accumulation, expand the test by reference to nurses'

floor counts of patients "in the house" and similar census data prepared by non-business office personnel.

Testing the Accuracy of Reported Patient Revenue

1) Obtain the revenue journal for the test month.

a) Verify footings of the monthly recap.
b) Trace postings to the general ledger.
c) Foot and crossfoot daily totals for four days within the test month and trace totals to the monthly summary.

2) Select a sample of patients incurring charges during the period, using random sampling with the population, including the following:

a) Patients inhouse at the beginning of the test period. (Obtain from the accounts receivable detail.)
b) Inpatients incurring charges and admitted during the test period. (Obtain from the patient register.)
c) Outpatients incurring charges during the test period. (Obtain from the patient register.)

NOTE: If a numerical sequence is kept on all patients, consider testing a block of these patients instead of using the steps *a, b,* and *c* above.

3) For the first patient selected, use the first day as the test day. For the second, use the second, and so on through five days. If the patient was released prior to this test and incurred no charges on the selected test day, use the day of admission as the test day.

4) For patients and test days selected, do the following:

a) Trace the patient name to the daily census report.
b) Trace detailed charge slips for test day to posting record (usually some form of bookkeeping machine listing or data processing printout).
c) Trace patient charges to the daily charge register or other record used for the accumulation of charges and determine whether the charges were properly segregated between departments, if appropriate, and between Medicare and non-Medicare categories.
d) Obtain patient medical record file and determine that all charges (by type) for test day appear as charges on patient accounts receivable ledger.
e) Test check the pricing on charge tickets with the standard pricing sheets; i.e., compendium.
f) Trace the services rendered to the ancillary departmental logs.
g) Determine that the patient was charged for a room for all days in the hospital, except the day of discharge.
h) Determine that all types of patients are being charged consistent and comparable charges for comparable services.

5) Calculate the gross profit percentage for pharmacy and central supply. Investigate and document the explanation of variances with prior year's gross profit percentages. Bring substantial unfavorable variances to the attention of Administration.

Special Audit Consideration for Medicare Patients Included in Revenue Test

1) For all Medicare patients selected, refer to the Report of Eligibility and determine whether the patient had benefits available for the full period of occupancy.

2) a) Refer to the Report of Eligibility and determine whether the proper deductible and co-insurance amounts were charged to the patient. (These amounts and the non-covered charges are the only items that can be billed to the Medicare patient.)

b) Trace these items to the provider's accumulation of deductibles and co-insurance and test footings.

3) If the patient's benefits were exhausted prior to the date shown in the Report of Eligibility, determine that charges were properly segregated between the Medicare and non-Medicare categories in the recording of revenue.

4) Determine whether required physician's certifications and recertifications were on file. If care was deemed no longer necessary by the physician or the provider's utilization review committee, determine whether subsequent provider charges were categorized as "non-Medicare" in the revenue accounts.

General Audit Tests of the Charge Control System

1) Trace from the records of each ancillary service department to the daily charge register or other record used for the accumulation of charges, ____ to ____ charges for service (including both inpatient and outpatient, and Medicare non-Medicare).

a) Determine that charges are properly segregated and distributed in the register or other record.

b) Review amounts charged for services as to consistency and comparability.

2) Prepare a summary of revenue by month and department.

a) The detail should be classified as in the following example:

Radiology

Inpatients—
  Medicare covered
  Non-Medicare

Outpatients—
  Medicare
    Part A
    Part B
  Non-Medicare

b) Foot the individual categories and trace totals to the general ledger.

c) Compare totals between months and explain unusual variances.

d) Relate this information to the similar analysis of inpatient and outpatient statistics (i.e., number of patient days or occasions of service times average of rate structure).

3) Test compare x-ray and laboratory and other physician service revenue with amounts used to compute commissions paid under contract with the physician. If the amounts are not the same determine why, and note in the management letter that the situation needs to be corrected.

WORKING PAPERS REQUIRED

The audit working papers for the patient service revenue section should evidence that the auditor has made sufficient tests of the revenue system to satisfy himself that the hospital's system of internal control and accounting procedures is, or is not, comprehensive.

Patient Days

A schedule should be included that lists the total patient days by month, the daily patient days for the test month, and the detail patient days, per the nursing floor counts, for at least one day in the test month. Figure 10.7 is an example of an adequate working paper.

A summary of audit work performed should be written by the auditor indicating that monthly patient day totals were compared to the monthly gross revenue and explained (or not explained) satisfactorily. Notation should be made of the explanation for subsequent review. The summary should also explain how the hospital segregates its statistics by patient type.

Patient Service Revenue

A memorandum should be prepared noting that the auditor compared the individual accounts and their balance with those of the preceding year. Explanations of the substantial differences should be included in the memorandum. The memorandum should also note the extent to which statistical summaries for the current year were compared to the preceding year. The memorandum should conclude by stating whether or not the monthly fluctuations in the service statistics were (or were not) satisfactorily explained.

A schedule should be included that tests the reasonableness of the recorded routine service revenue, nursery revenue, emergency room revenue, or other type of revenue where a standard rate times the recorded units of service should produce a close approximation of the recorded revenue. Figure 10.6 is an example of such a working paper.

A working paper schedule, or copies of the patient ledgers, should be included, showing the extent of testing the charges for service to patients. The test should include a sampling of inpatients, outpatients, and other types of patients serviced by the hospital.

Working papers should be prepared that show the gross profit percentage for pharmacy and central supply as compared to that of previous years. Substantial variances should be adequately explained.

A schedule should be prepared tracing a sample of the services rendered, per departmental logs, to the charge for such services indicated on the patient ledger.

Revenue per general ledger for departments operated by physicians who are compensated on a gross revenue basis should be scheduled and compared to the hospital's calculation of professional compensation.

A summary of audit work performed and conclusions reached (see Figure 10.8) should be prepared and placed in the front of the audit working papers for this section.

FINANCIAL STATEMENT PRESENTATION

Patient service revenue generated from all services is usually reported as a single figure captioned "Patient Service Revenue." In the supplemental information, the hospital may choose to show the departmentalization of such revenue, segregated between inpatient and outpatient, on a comparative basis with that of the preceding year.

_________________ HOSPITAL

CHARGE CONTROL SYSTEM

RESPONSIBILITY	ACTION
Ward Clerk	1. Prepares prenumbered requisition for service (charge tickets).
	2. Forwards original to ancillary department.
	3. Forwards one copy to billing department.
	4. Retains final copy at work station for accounting control.
Accounting Clerk	10. Obtains ward clerk's copies of charge ticket at end of second shift.
	11. Batches charge tickets by department.
	12. Logs last used number by department.
	13. Runs adding machine tape of charges by department.
	14. Logs total charges by department and number of charge tickets in batch.
Accounting Supervisor	18. Compares accounting control log of charges and tickets processed to posting totals for the previous day.
	19. Assigns accounting clerk to sort, in numerical sequence, the charge tickets for any department that shows a material difference between departmental charges posted and departmental charges per the control copy of charge tickets.
Accounting Clerk	20. Sorts and compares posting and control copies of charge tickets.
	21. Lists missing charge tickets for accounting supervisor's review.
Accounting Supervisor	22. Investigates reason for missing charge tickets.
	23. Leaves instruction for posting clerk to add late charges per control copy of charge tickets, if ancillary charge copy can not be located.

FIGURE 10.1

DAILY CENSUS SUMMARY
MIDNIGHT ____________

	Beds Available	Occupied	Unoccupied	% of Occupancy
1st Floor–I.C.U.	8	4	4	50.0
3rd Floor–C.C.I. Phase I	8	8	0	100.0
3rd Floor–C.C.U. Phase II	13	11	2	84.6
Total I.C.U. and C.C.U.	29	23	6	79.3
3rd Floor–Medical and Surgical	66	56	10	84.8
4th Floor–Medical and Surgical	88	81	7	92.0
5th Floor–Medical and Surgical	88	81	7	92.0
6th Floor–Medical and Surgical	88	84	4	95.5
Total Medical and Surgical	330	302	28	91.5
Total Hospital	359	325	34	90.5

Admitted from Emergency Room	13	Emergency Room Visits	90
Emergency Admissions	7	Waiting for S.P. Beds	19
Scheduled Admissions	27	Unoccupied Medical &	
		Surgical Beds - Female	1
Total Admissions	47	Male	2
Total Discharges	(32)	Comp.	0
Net Change to Census	15		

Scheduled Admissions
Month, Day, Year – 15
Month, Day, Year – 23
Month, Day, Year – 18
Month, Day, Year – 8
Month, Day, Year – 1
Month, Day, Year – 27
Month, Day, Year – 22

PERCENTAGE OF OCCUPANCY

	Available Bed Basis	This Day	Month To Date	Anticipated Occupancy
Med. & Surg.	330	91.5	88.8	83.76
I.C.U.	8	50.0	68.8	63.30
C.C.U. Phase I	8	100.0	93.8	73.39
C.C.U. Phase II	13	84.6	88.5	71.71
Total Basis	359	90.5	88.4	82.64

FIGURE 10.2

__________ HOSPITAL
WEEKLY MANAGEMENT REPORT WEEK ENDING __________

	THIS WEEK		MO. TO DATE		
	ACTUAL	BUDGET	ACTUAL	BUDGET	%
STATISTICS:					
Admissions	275	280	807	800	100.9%
Patient Days	2,407	2,198	6,686	6,280	106.5%
E.R. Visits	785	588	2,050	1,680	122.0%
GROSS REVENUE:					
Inpatient	$403,213.71	$374,024.91	$1,136,756.28	$1,068,642.60	106.4%
E.R.	9,303.51	7,238.70	24,335.28	20,682.00	117.7%
Outpatient	20,683.94	26,586.00	69,094.01	75,960.00	91.0%
Total	$433,201,16	$407,849.61	$1,230,185.57	$1,165,284.60	105.6%

NO. OF ACCOUNTS	BILLING BACKLOG REPORT	THIS WEEK	VARIANCE LAST WEEK	VARIANCE LAST MONTH
133	Needing Medical Information	$237.324	$ 1,973	$ 30,215
131	Needing Approvals and Forms	81,480	8,009	3,967
11	To Be Billed or Corrected	7,269	(952)	5,265
275	Total	$326,073	$ 9,030	$ 39,447

ANCILLARY INPATIENT REVENUE:

	MO. TO DATE			MO. TO DATE	
	ACTUAL	BUDGET		ACTUAL	BUDGET
Operating Room/Hour	129.44	140.65	E.M.G./Pt. Day	.24	.20
Recovery Room/Surgery Pt.	9.64	10.38	Radiology/Pt. Day	7.53	8.44
Sale of M/S Sup./Pt. Day	11.60	10.04	Nuclear Medicine/Pt. Day	3.42	3.19
I.V. Therapy/Pt. Day	5.26	4.51	Pharmacy/Pt. Day	8.31	9.12
Clin. Lab. & Path./Pt. Day	18.35	19.27	Anes./Surgical Pts.	41.25	47.06
Blood Bank/Pt. Day	2.86	2.62	Inh. Ther. & Pul./Pt. Day	7.05	6.60
E.K.G./Pt. Day	2.28	2.50	Physical Therapy/Pt. Day	.66	.82
E.E.G./Pt. Day	.29	.26			

FIGURE 10.3

CATALOGUE LISTING BY CATALOGUE NUMBER 7/12/

CATALOGUE NO.	CATALOGUE DESCRIPTION	SERVICE CODE	SERVICE CODE DESCRIPTION
18192641	TUBE-LEVIN-DISP 12 FR	27781905	TUBE-LEVIN-DISP
18192898	TUBE-LEVIN-DISP 14 FR	27781905	TUBE-LEVIN-DISP
18198663	TUBE-LEVIN-DISP 16 FR	27781905	TUBE-LEVIN-DISP
18204685	TUBE-LEVIN-DISP 18 FR	27781905	TBUE-LEVIN-DISP
18222752	TUBE-LUKI-ASPIRATING	27782002	TUBE-LUKI-ASPIRATING
18319061	TUBE-PENROSE ¼X12	27782101	TUBE-PENROSE ¼X12
18343228	TUBE-PENROSE-DRAIN ¾X1	27782101	TUBE-PENROSE
18343319	TUBE-PENROSE-DRAIN 1X18	27782101	TUBE-PENROSE
18379180	TUBE-PENROSE-DRAIN ½X1	27782101	TUBE-PENROSE
18548024	TUBE-RECTAL DISP 24 FR	27782200	TUBE-RECTAL DISP 24 FR
18617019	TUBE-SALEM SUMP 18 FR	27711407	TUBE-SALEM SUMP 18 FR
18620047	TUBE - T 8 FR	27782309	TUBE - T
18620062	TUBES - T 10 FR	27782309	TUBE - T
18626085	TUBES - T 12 FR	27782309	TUBE - T
18632109	TUBES - T 14 FR	27782309	TUBE - T
18638122	TUBES - T 16 FR	27782309	TUBE - T
18644146	TUBES - T 18 FR	27782309	TUBE - T
18650309	TUBES - T-DRAINS 22 FR	27782309	TUBE - T
18788851	TUBE-TRACHEOSTOMY SZ 6-3	27782705	TUBE-TRACHEOSTOMY-DISP
18788919	TUBE TRACH SZ 8-36	27782705	TUBE-TRACHEOSTOMY-DISP
18836809	TUBES TRACH 30 FG	27782705	TUBE-TRACHEOSTOMY-DISP
18836825	TUBES TRACHEOSTOMY 36 FG	27782705	TUBE-TRACHEOSTOMY-DISP
18836833	TUBES TRACHEOSTOMY 33 FG	27782705	TUBE-TRACHEOSTOMY-DISP
18836866	TUBES TRACHEOSTOMY 39 FG	27782705	TUBE-TRACHEOSTOMY-DISP
18837013	TUBE TRACHEOSTOMY SZ 4-26	27782705	TUBE-TRACHEOSTOMY-DISP
18837039	TUBE TRACHEOSTOMY 6FR DP	27782705	TUBE-TRACHEOSTOMY-DISP
18837120	TUBE TRACHEOSTOMY SZ 10	27782705	TUBE-TRACHEOSTOMY-DISP
18837153	TUBE TRACH W/CUFF SZ4-26	27782705	TUBE-TRACHEOSTOMY-DISP
18837161	TUBE TRACH W/CUFF S10-39	27782705	TUBE-TRACHEOSTOMY-DISP
18837252	TUBE TRACH W/CUFF S6-30	27782705	TUBE-TRACHEOSTOMY-DISP
18837286	TUBE TRACH W/CUFF S8-36	27782705	TUBE-TRACHEOSTOMY-DISP
18994103	TUBING FOAMCATH POLY	27781806	TUBEING FOAMCATH POLY
31109671	DISINFECTANT PHISOHEX	27706704	DISINFECTANT PHISOHEX
32361081	TISSUE-FACIAL 50-SHEET 8	27708502	TISSUE-FACIAL
42099606	KETO-DIASTIX #2882	27704659	KETO-DIASTIX #2882
50077320	PENS SURGICAL MARKING	27707603	PENS SURGICAL MARKING

FIGURE 10.4

CHARGE ORDER AT ANCILLARY TERMINAL

U-URINALYSIS, ROUTINE			QUAN	0001
DOE, JOHN			EDP #	614
DAY/TIME	217	1323	CHARGE ID	3255**
CHG #2755			RTB ICU-03	
DR. QUE, X.				

CHARGE COPY AT REQUISITIONING TERMINAL

U-URINALYSIS, ROUTINE		D/T	217	1323
DOE, JOHN		EDP #		614
ROOM/BD	ICU-03	DOB		11-25-11

** Denotes terminal station from which order was placed.

FIGURE 10.5

_____________ HOSPITAL
ROUTINE SERVICE REVENUE TEST FOR
THE YEAR ENDED ____________, 19___

	INITIALS	DATE
PREPARED BY	JLD	1-15
APPROVED BY	BH	1/20

	(1) JAN. 1 TO JUNE 30	(2) JULY 1 TO DEC. 30	(3) TOTAL	(4) DIFFERENCE
MEDICAL/SURGICAL:				
Private Beds	100	100		
Rate	$ 85	$ 97.50		
	8500	9750		
# Days	181	184		
	1538500	1794000		
Avg. Occupancy	85%	87%		
	1307725	1560780	$2868505.00	
per general ledger			2868212.50	
				$ 292.50
SEMI-PRIVATE BEDS	50	50		
Rate	$ 75.50	$ 85		
	3775	4250		
# Days	181	184		
	683275	782000		
Avg. Occupancy	88%	90%		
	601282	703800	1305082	
per general ledger			1305337	<255>
ICU/CCU BEDS	8	8		
Rate	$ 120	$ 140		
	960	1120		
# Days	181	184		
	173760	206080		
Avg. Occupancy	62%	59%		
	107731.20	121587.20	229318.40	
per general ledger			229580 —	<261.60>
				$ <224.10>

NOTE:
Based upon revenue calculations using average occupancy levels for the period, the revenue per books appears reasonable. Also, it appears the hospital is adequately controlling room and board charges.

FIGURE 10.6

______________ HOSPITAL

INPATIENT DAY TEST FOR THE

YEAR ENDED ______________, 19___

	INITIALS	DATE
PREPARED BY	JLD	1-15
APPROVED BY	B.H.	1/20

FORM P-554-2 (GREEN) P-554-B2 (BUFF) Rool-Rite SYSTEMS CELINA, OHIO · DALLAS · LOS ANGELES LITHO IN U.S.A.

LINE No			(1) PER MONTHLY SUMMARY	(2) PER DAILY SUMMARY	(3) PER NURSING SUMMARY	(4)	LINE No
1			8479	284	35		1
2			8477	285	37		2
3			8225	254	35		3
4			8341	280	38		4
5			8370	284	33		5
6	*	(test period)	8163 *	281 *	34		6
7			8374	268	36		7
8			8118	253	37		8
9			7425	240	285		9
10			8390	258	<281>		10
11			7695	282	4 F ч		11
12			8467	288			12
13				289			13
14			98524 F	283			14
15				280			15
16				256			16
17	ч	hospital has not accounted		255			17
18		for patients admitted		284			18
19		and discharged the same		280			19
20		day; i.e., one day stays.		277			20
21		Total patient days must be		275			21
22		adjusted upward to reflect		277			22
23		an estimate of these days.		270			23
24				267			24
25				287			25
26				291			26
27				285			27
28	NOTE:			268			28
29		Rather than listing the data		247			29
30		it is permissable to attach		235			30
31		a properly identified		8163 F			31
32		adding machine tape of the					32
33		days to a working paper.					33
34							34
35							35
36							36
37							37
38							38
39							39
40							40
			1	2	3	4	

FIGURE 10.7

_______ HOSPITAL

SUMMARY OF AUDIT WORK PERFORMED—REVENUE

_______ , 19 ___

Twelve patients were selected from the hospital's records: four from the admissions register, four from medical records, and four from the Medicare log. All patients selected were admitted during the test month of _______ , 19 ___ . Two days' charges for each patient were tested, and the room charge for the total stay verified.

The objective of the audit tests was to determine that all patients were charged for all services performed; that all services performed were ordered by a physician; and that all patients were charged the same charge for the same service.

Supporting source documents examined were medical records, nurses' notes, physicians' orders, patient accounts, physician certifications and recertifications, and the hospital's approved charge schedule.

The departmentalization of charges and the segregation between covered and non-covered charges for certain third-party payors were determined to be adequate.

Two long-term stay patients were included in the test. It was determined that after the expiration of their Medicare benefits, their days and charges were included in the non-Medicare days and charges.

During the test, it was noted that both Medicare and non-Medicare patients had charges made for services not ordered and conversely some items of service were rendered for which the hospital failed to charge. The effect of such charging errors was not deemed material, and in my opinion the hospital's statement of patient service revenue is fairly presented and prepared in accordance with generally accepted accounting principles applied on a basis consistent with that of the preceding period.

_______________ Auditor   _______________ Date

FIGURE 10.8

11

Auditing the Hospital's Other Revenues and Deductions from Revenue

In addition to revenue from patient services, hospitals obtain revenue for sources and activities that are indirectly related to patient care. These "other" revenues may be classified as other operating revenue, which is a result of the day-to-day operations or non-operating revenue.

Other operating revenue could include such items as revenue from educational programs, research, and other specific purpose grants, fees charged for reproduction of records, cafeteria sales, revenue from gift shops, and other service facilities operated by the hospital.

Non-operating revenue includes grants, gifts, and donations not restricted by the donor, regardless of the ultimate purpose later designated by the Board of Trustees. Also included in this classification is income earned on investments of endowment funds that have no restrictions on income.

As was noted in Chapter 4, hospitals do not receive full charges for all their services; therefore, hospitals must recognize such deductions from revenue as charity allowances, courtesy allowances, and contractual adjustments. The audit procedures for revenue deductions will closely parallel those used in auditing revenue and are usually performed in conjunction with the examination of accounts receivable.

Even though the Medicare program has been in existence for years, many hospitals still fail to properly compute the contractual allowance and the related deduction from revenue and are consequently surprised at year-end to learn the actual results of operations. The reasonableness of these accounts can be tested by completing the blanks in an informative paragraph, which the financial officer may want to make a part of the interim financial statements. (See Figure 11.1.)

Also provided are internal control questions and audit procedures that can be adapted to determine if the hospital's policies are being followed in accounting for "other" revenue and deductions from revenue.

REVIEWING THE CONTROLS

Determining If the Hospital Is Receiving and Properly Recording Other Income

Q. *Are educational program revenues reconciled with student registration records?*

- Is the reconciliation prepared by someone separate from the cashiering function.
- How is the school's refund policy reflected in such reconciliations.
- Are prenumbered receipts used in recording the receipt of student tuitions.

Q. *Are there separate revenue accounts for:*

a) nonpatient drug and supply sales,
b) property and equipment sales,
c) cafeteria sales,
d) snack bar, vending machines, etc.,
e) scrap and salvage,
f) interest,
g) dividends,
h) rent,
i) telephones, and
j) televisions?

- Does the analysis of miscellaneous income indicate that certain major items of a recurring nature should be accounted for separately, and some of the lesser items previously mentioned should be recorded as "miscellaneous income."
- During that last audit did you find miscellaneous non-patient revenue being posted to reduce expense accounts. If so, has this been corrected.

Q. *Are there adequate safeguards over the sale of scrap and salvage of equipment to insure that the hospital receives the income?*

- Are "mini-audits" made to verify the existence of major movable equipment per the property records.
- Are checks made payable to the hospital for the sale of placentas, x-ray silver, and used paper products.

Questioning the Application of Deduction from Revenue Policies

Q. *Are credit and collection policies written?*

- Have such policies been approved by the Board of Trustees.
- Are the policies in compliance with Federal, State, and municipal guidelines; i.e., Hill-Burton Charity Regulations, State Medicaid Regulations, or requirements for the issuance of tax-exempt municipal bonds.

- Are such policies consistent with community practices.
- Are patients classified, upon admission or immediately thereafter, as charity, insured, private pay, etc.

Q. *Are credit and collection procedures written?*

- Have such procedures been approved by the chief financial officer.
- Are the procedures written in a clear and concise manner.

Q. *Does the hospital record, on a monthly basis, bad debt write-offs and other non-contractual write-offs; i.e., charity and administrative adjustments?*

- Does a responsible individual approve such write-offs.
- Are the write-offs consistent with the hospital policy.
- Is there adequate documentation of bad debt, charity, and administrative write-offs.
- Are policy discounts and administrative adjustments accounted for separately.

Q. *Are bad debt ledgers governed by a control account?*

- Is the total of such accounts reflected in memorandum form in the interim financial statements.
- Are the written-off accounts kept on file in accordance with the record retention guidelines, as suggested by the Hospital Financial Management Association.

Q. *Are accounts placed with an outside collection agency also governed by a control account?*

- Is the total of these accounts also reflected in memorandum form in the interim financial statements.
- Does it appear that the collection agency is "creaming" the accounts (i.e., making only the easy collections).
- Has consideration been given to utilizing the services of two collection agencies to generate competition between the agencies.
- Does the number of recoveries of uncollectible accounts indicate that the hospital policies are too weak and the accounts are being given to the collection agency without an adequate collection effort being made by the hospital.

Q. *Are third-party contractual adjustments cleared from patient ledgers monthly?*

- Are such amounts for inhouse patients adequately reflected in the interim financial statements, so as not to result in a overstatement of income and accounts receivable.
- Have contractual write-offs been inadverently billed to Medicare program patients.

Q. *Are detailed lists maintained for bad debts reimbursed under the Medicare/Medicaid programs?*

- Is the amount recorded overstated by the inclusion of non-covered charges such as personal comfort items.

- Is responsibility fixed for the maintenance of the list of Medicare bad debts.

THE AUDIT

The Audit Objective

The primary objective in performing the audit of other revenue is to determine that the revenue has been recorded in accordance with generally accepted accounting principles on a basis consistent with that of the preceding year. The auditor should also verify:

1) That the accounting treatment of other income items maximizes third-party reimbursement.
2) That internal controls are adequate to safeguard the receipt of other income items such as rebates, telephone, and television rentals. (See Figure 11.2.)
3) That internal controls are adequate to reasonably insure the receipt and recording of income from the infrequent sales of scrap, salvage, and other such miscellaneous items.
4) That management reports will highlight the omission of substantial other income items either through budget variances or monthly listings of other income items.

The primary objective in performing the audit of deductions from revenue is to see that such deductions have been recorded in accordance with generally accepted accounting principles on a basis consistent with that of the preceding year.

Secondly, the auditor should satisfactorily assure himself that the hospital-approved policies and procedures are consistently applied in determining deductions from revenue.

Performing the Audit

Tuition Income

1) Obtain a list of participating students.
2) Through conversations with the students and teachers, determine if any students have "dropped out."
3) For students who have dropped the program, review correspondence and cancelled checks to see that the appropriate refund, in compliance with the school's tuition refund policy, was given.
4) Multiply the number of students in the program times the tuition rate and compare amount with gross revenue recorded. Reconcile any differences.

Audit Procedures—Other Revenue

1) Determine the reason for substantial monthly and annual variances in the other revenue accounts.
2) Verify the receipt of vending machine income by machine, if possible.
3) a) Review correspondence relating to grants and gifts and determine that ap-

propriate mention of their receipt is made in the minutes of the Board of Trustees.

b) Analyze large donations and determine if for a specific purpose.

c) If the donation is restricted, verify that the hospital is complying with the terms of the restriction.

4) a) Test check numerical sequence of credit memoranda.

b) Test a representative number of credit memoranda.

c) Check credits appearing in selected patient accounts receivable to approved credit memoranda.

5) Analyze interest income by fund and source.

6) Review large and/or recurrent credits to expense accounts. Substantiate their propriety.

Auditing Policy Write-Offs

1) Obtain a copy of the hospital's credit and collection policies and procedures.

2) Note that the policies have been approved by the Board of Trustees and the procedures have been approved by an appropriate Administrative Staff member.

3) Carefully review the policies and procedures for inconsistencies.

4) Take a random sample of the patients' files placed with the collection agencies, approved for charity, or written off administratively within the last year.

5) Review the sample of patient files to see that the following is clearly indicated:

a) balance of account;
b) date and type of collection effort; i.e., phone calls, collection letters, visits, etc.;
c) notes as to the patient's financial resources;
d) reasons for suggested disposition of account balance; i.e., charity, administrative write-off, or placed with collection agency;
e) approval of disposition of account balance by appropriate individual; and
f) approved policy and procedures were followed.

6) Trace the properly approved account disposition to transmittal documents to verify that the approved amount is the amount recorded for accounting purposes.

7) Verify that the monthly totals of such transmittal documents agree with the postings of general ledger control accounts.

8) Test trace the collection on accounts to individual postings to the patient records.

9) Trace the amount remitted by the collection agency to postings in the cash receipts journal. If the net amount, after deduction of the collection fee, is remitted, note that the gross amount collected is posted to the patient record and a proper recording of the collection fee is made in the accounting records.

10) Investigate, through correspondence with other hospitals and professional organizations, the reasonableness of the hospital's percentage of deductions from revenue, by category, to gross charges. Also determine the effectiveness of the collection agency through similar correspondence, being careful to see that the items included for comparison purposes are similar.

11) Review the hospital's pre-admission procedures to see if sufficient information is obtained to allow the hospital to classify the financial or payment status of the patient at the time of admission.

12) Observe and interview the admitting personnel in the course of performing their duties to verify that the pre-admission procedures are being followed.

13) Check to see that the notices required by Federal, State and local governments regarding the availability of financial assistance or treatment and admission of patients are properly posted in the admitting or cashiering offices.

Audit Procedures—Contractual Allowances

1) Review contracts with third-party payors to determine the basis of reimbursement.
2) Review the hospital's monthly calculation of third-party contractual allowances to determine that proper consideration has been given to inhouse patients. (See Figure 11.1.)
3) Examine a sample of discharged Medicare/Medicaid patient ledgers to see that the appropriate contractual allowance is being recorded at the time of discharge, or shortly thereafter.
4) Trace the non-payment of Medicare deductibles and co-insurance to the appropriate log.

WORKING PAPERS REQUIRED

Other Income

A schedule should be prepared comparing account balances with those of the preceding period. Notation should be made explaining such variances.

Copies of correspondence relating to gifts, grants, and donations should be included in the working papers. The auditor should comment in the working papers if the restrictions placed on the donations are being met.

Policy Write-Offs

The working papers should contain a copy of the hospital's policy and procedures regarding charity, courtesy allowances, and uncollectible accounts.

Sufficient tests should be performed and noted in the working papers to verify that the policies and procedures have been consistently applied.

The collection agency transmittal document remitted during the test month should be copied and made a part of the working papers, with notations keyed on the document to indicate the proper accounting treatment and posting to patient ledgers, and traced to the cash receipt journal for the month.

A summary of audit work performed should be prepared, including the conclusion reached by the auditor. The memo should also include a statement regarding the adequacy of the admitting procedures and collection agencies as they relate to the containing of policy write-offs and bad debts.

Contractual Allowances

The auditor should prepare a calculation of third-party contractual allowance (see Figure 4.6), if cost reports are not available until after the auditor completes his examination.

A list of discharged Medicare/Medicaid patients who were selected for verification of the posting of contractual allowances, covered charges, and the payment or non-payment of deductibles and co-insurance, should also be included in the audit working papers.

FINANCIAL STATEMENT PRESENTATION

The various deductions from revenue are usually combined in one total captioned "Allowances and Uncollectible Accounts," which is shown as a deduction from patient service revenue. The net result is captioned "Net Patient Service Revenue." Significant deductions from revenue may be indicated by footnote disclosure.

The components of "Other Income" should be separated and reported as other operating revenue and non-operating revenue. Other operating revenue is usually reported after the deduction of allowances and before reaching the total of operating revenue. Non-operating revenue would be reported after the net income or (loss) from operations.

INFORMATION CONCERNING MEDICARE CHARGES

Medicare-covered charges, per patient day, this month are ________ and ________ year-to-date compared to ________ for the same period last year.

Medicare allowable cost, per patient day, this month is ______ and ______ year-to-date compared to ______ for the same period last year. The allowable cost is estimated by using a short factor method, which has been reviewed and found to be satisfactory by our auditors.

Our Medicare interim reimbursement rate is $____ per covered day as compared to $____ per day last year.

Medicare patient days this month are ______ and ______ year-to-date compared to ______ for the same period last year.

We can review the reasonableness of the amount due (to) or from the Medicare Intermediary by multiplying Medicare patient days for the period ______ by the difference ______ in the Medicare interim reimbursement rate and Medicare allowable cost. This gives a product of $______ as compared to the recorded (liability)/receivable of $______ .

The reasonableness of the Medicare contractual allowance can be determined by multiplying Medicare patient days of ______ by the difference ______ between Medicare-covered charges and Medicare allowable cost per day. This calculation suggests that we should have a contractual allowance of $______; however, this amount must be reduced by $______, which represents prior year's Medicare charges settled in this accounting period and adjustments by Medicare on paid-out accounts to reflect an increase of $______ in the per diem.

FIGURE 11.1

_______________ HOSPITAL

PROTECTIVE PROCEDURE

SUBJECT: Collection of Telephone and Television Rental

RESPONSIBILITY	ACTION
Admitting Clerk	1. Informs guarantor of rental fees and prepayment policy.
	2. Notes on "Inpatient Payment" card the proper amount to be collected and indicates by the following code what is being rented: T–Telephone V–Television Ŧ–Television and Telephone
	3. Directs guarantor to the cashier window.
Cashier	4. Collects amount due.
	5. Prepares receipt in triplicate.
	6. Distributes receipts as follows: original–guarantor 1st copy–admitting 2nd copy–accounting
	7. Balances receipts and cash collected at the end of the shift and prepares deposit slip for separate account from the general fund.
	8. Lists patient room and bed number on the "Maintenance Request" list for those patients who have paid for a television.
Cashier	9. Tubes list to Maintenance twice a day at the scheduled times.
Maintenance	10. Checks "Maintenance Request" list twice a day for rooms renting televisions.
	11. Goes to room and activates the television control.
Admitting	12. Determines from payment receipt copy if a telephone was rented.
	13. Writes an asterisk after the room number on the Patient Information Desk card.
	14. Delivers card to PBX.
PBX	15. Activates telephone for patient room and bed number indicated.

NOTE: When the rental payment is made on a date after admission, the cashier will write an asterisk on the receipt after the patient's name and notify PBX to turn on the telephone.

FIGURE 11.2

12

Performing an Audit of the Hospital Payroll and Personnel Functions

Payroll constitutes from 50 to 65% of the total cost of most hospitals. The independent certified public accountant usually spends one to three man days auditing this category of expense. The independent certified public accountant reviews the payroll accounting methods and the expense accounts to the point where he becomes satisfied that such records, as they relate to the Statement of Income, have been prepared in accordance with generally accepted accounting principles applied on a basis consistent with that of the preceding period.

The hospital-based internal auditor should review the administrative controls in the payroll personnel department while maintaining his primary interest in accounting controls as they affect the financial records.

While the internal auditor is not expected to be an expert in the area of employee relations and wage administration, he should be alert for certain administrative deficiencies in the payroll system. He should raise questions that may at first appear to be naive. For example, why shouldn't full-time registered nurses, who are professionals, be classified as "exempt" employees? Why should shift differential be paid for non-productive hours; i.e., vacation, holiday, and sick pay? Why is shift differential higher for nursing and other professional personnel than for housekeepers, maintenance, and clerical employees? Isn't the purpose of the shift differential to recognize the inconvenience of working second and third shifts? Are the salary administration programs and employee applications discriminatory? Do management information reports, such as hours analysis reports and payroll distribution reports, reflect properly all the paid hours that the hospital has paid during the period of the report; i.e., if an employee is terminated from the payroll register, are his hours also deleted?

Both independent and internal auditors are interested in detecting fraudulent abuses of the payroll system. The following are effective and adaptable methods which both auditors should be made aware of.

Twelve Ways the Hospital Payroll System Can Be Corrupted

1) Reimbursement of payroll cash account for amounts greater than the total payroll.
2) Padding the payroll; that is, payments made to fictitious names or former employees, but mailed to the embezzler's home address.
3) Failure to deduct absent time of employees in figuring total payroll and withholding the excess or having the excess added to the embezzler's time.
4) Increasing rate or hours for particular employees.
5) Falsifying payroll totals.
6) Recording payment for fictitious casual labor.
7) Duplicating payroll payments through payroll and petty cash.
8) One employee punching two or more time cards.
9) Payroll amounts shown in excess of time card amounts.
10) Reimbursement for payroll advances charged to accrued payroll.
11) Holding out amounts refunded for overpayments of payroll.
12) Withholding unclaimed payroll checks.

Protective Procedure

As previously stated, where there is collusion between two or more employees, as there was in one Midwest hospital of 2,000 employees, fraud is extremely difficult to detect. In the Midwest hospital, examples number 4 and 8 (on the preceding list) were used to embezzle over $100,000 before being detected. To protect the hospital from such practices, or at least result in early detection, the hospital Administration should require an independent manual distribution of checks, or pay stubs if a "checkless" system is used. Also, routine comparisons of hours worked, by department, should be made of the time cards and payroll records. This comparison should also be made by someone independent of the payroll function. Administration should require department managers to routinely pull the time cards for a particular day to verify that the employees "punched in" are working. This practice will often result in detecting such payroll abuses as a buddy punching in for a friend who is late, or who left early.

Included in this chapter are extensive internal control questions and "thoughts" which the auditor may further develop for his management letter, an audit program, and sample personnel forms.

REVIEWING THE CONTROLS

How to Review the Hospital Employee Personnel File

Q. Is there an adequate investigation into an employment candidate's background before he is considered for employment?

- Are formal forms used to correspond with former employers.
- Are unfavorable responses regarding the employment candidate's background followed up by the personnel director or department manager and so noted in the file.

- Has the local police department been contacted as to the background of the candidate who applies for a position in pharmacy, supply, processing and distribution (S.P.D.), cashiering, accounting, or other areas of the hospital that would allow the employee to handle valuable, tangible assets.

Q. *Are personnel files maintained on a current basis for each employee?*

- Does the application bank contain a condition of employment that is properly dated and signed by the employee. (See Figure 12.1.)
- Is the current rate of pay, as indicated by the personnel file and approved by the appropriate responsible individual, the same as the rate of pay used by the payroll department.
- Are there properly signed and dated authorization cards for payroll deductions.
- Have payroll deduction authorization cards that are expired been stamped in such a fashion as to indicate their expiration.

Q. *Are personnel files permitted to be removed from the personnel office?*

- If so, is there a sign-out system to ensure the return of such records.
- Could an area in the personnel department be utilized for the review of personnel files, thus eliminating the need for personnel records to leave the area.

Q. *Do employee files document the date of employment, position, rate of pay, and termination?*

- Are initial rates of pay and subsequent changes properly authorized.
- Are additions, transfers, and terminations to payroll properly authorized.
- Does the director of employee relations sign all requests for wage or salary changes. (See Figure 12.2.)

Challenging the Hospital Payroll System of Controls

Q. *Is a time clock system or other method of recording time used for hourly employees?*

- Are Hospital security officers near the time clocks during the most common clock in/out times to help "keep the employees honest"; i.e., deter their punching other employees' time cards.
- Are there sufficient time clocks in the proper location to insure a smooth flow of employees clocking in or out during peak hours. In other words, are people incurring overtime because of long lines at the clock.

Q. *How is vacation, holiday, and sick pay recorded and monitored by the department managers or Administrative Staff members for the "exempt" employees?*

- Is the system employed a one-over-one system whereby the employee does not prepare and approve his own time card regardless of his status within the organization, with the exception of the administrator.
- Are such records of vacation, holiday, and sick pay forwarded on a timely basis to the confidential executive secretary, who prepares the confidential payroll.

Q. *Are time cards, or equivalent records, prepared by the payroll department or data processing department?*

- Are such records completed by the employees on a timely basis.
- Do employees sign their time cards before they are submitted to the supervisor.
- Are the attendance records approved by a supervisor and/or department manager who has no other duties in connection with payroll.
- Must overtime be approved in advance by the supervisor.

Q. *Are payrolls prepared so that checks, registers, and earnings records are prepared simultaneously?*

- Are all copies legible.
- If corrections are made, is the transaction marked "Void."
- Are all corrections initialled by an appropriate supervisor.
- Are the payrolls independently checked as to names, hours worked, rates of pay, extensions, and footings.

Q. *Does payroll preparation require more than one person?*

- Are payrolls prepared by persons who do not have access to cash.
- Are the duties of the persons preparing the payrolls rotated.
- If there is only one payroll clerk, is that person required to take vacations, at which time payroll is prepared by someone with non-related duties.

Q. *Are all hospital employees paid by check?*

- Are disbursements made from a separate bank account.
- If so, is the account on an imprest basis.
- Are all payroll checks prenumbered.
- Are payroll checks accounted for by numerical sequence during the process of reconciliation.
- Does the hospital maintain adequate control over the payroll advances to employees.
- Is consideration given to payroll advances at the time the payroll checks are prepared.

Q. *Are payroll checks signed, either manually or in facsimile, by an employee who does not participate in the preparation of the payroll or have access to cash or maintenance of accounting records?*

- Who performs this duty while the primary individual is on vacation, on holiday, or sick.
- Is the person performing such duty bonded.
- Is there a log maintained of all checks signed that indicates the beginning and ending check number.
- Does the log indicate the number of signatures produced by the facsimile check signer, the number of checks voided during the process, and the check number of the voided check.

- Are the keys and facsimile plates properly safeguarded when not in use.

Q. Are the payroll checks or envelopes distributed by someone other than the person who prepares the payroll or upon whose authority they are based?

- Does the hospital have paymasters who function independently of the payroll department.
- Are paymasters rotated from time to time.
- Are signed pay receipts obtained from all employees paid in cash.
- Are such pay receipts cancelled promoptly after proof against disbursements to prevent their reuse.
- Are unclaimed wages and salaries controlled to prevent abstraction.
- Is there a hospital policy against mailing an employee's pay check to his home.

How to Question the Hospital Payroll Accounting System

Q. Are reconciliations of the hospital payroll bank accounts made by employees whose duties are unrelated to the payroll system?

- Is the reconciliation reviewed critically each month by a member of the hospital administration or other qualified, responsible individual.
- Does the reconciliation procedure include comparing pay checks with the payroll register.
- Are random checks made comparing the endorsements with the employee's signature on file in the personnel office.
- Does the reconciliation procedure include accounting for the check number sequence.

Q. Are payrolls checked for hours, rates, deductions, extensions, and footings?

- Is there a periodic review of deductions made from the employee's pay against the authorizations for such deductions.
- Are rates of pay ever given retroactively, and if so, are they approved by a responsible Administrative Staff member.

Q. Is a comparison made between payroll periods of the payrolls by departments, jobs, or other significant classifications?

- Are significant variances reviewed with a responsible member of the hospital's Administrative Staff.

Q. Does each employee actually work in only one department or cost center?

- If no, is the payroll expense distributed between departments.
- Is the basis used for making this distribution a reasonable and equitable basis.
- In determining a proper basis for allocation, is proper consideration given for third-party reimbursement purposes.
- How do the personnel and payroll departments know when an employee has changed his status in regard to working in multiple departments.

Q. *Are payroll tax returns filed only after preparation by a responsible person, reviewed by another responsible person, and reconciled to the general ledger payroll expense accounts?*

- Do the individuals involved initial and date their particular performance; i.e., preparation, review, or reconciliation.
- Are reconciling items adequately explained.

Questioning the Payroll System for Nonpaid Workers and Hospital-Based Physicians

Q. *Are nonpaid workers' services used?*

- If so, is there a contract with the nonpaid worker organization.
- Are the values of services for nonpaid workers adjusted at least annually.
- Are such values based on comparable compensation paid employees within the hospital.
- Are such values recorded in the general ledger.
- If nonpaid workers such as volunteers are utilized by the hospital, are they in violation of the Department of Labor Regulations. Volunteers who are not paid may not be used in the performance of duties that are necessary for the operation of the hospital and that therefore would require the use of paid employees.

Q. *Are hospital-based physicians' services used in the departments of pathology, radiology, electrocardiology, electroencephalogy, electromyography, emergency room, or other departments?*

- If so, are written physician agreements in effect.
- Have such contracts been forwarded to the Medicare Intermediary, and the proper professional components calculated and reflected in the patient billing system.
- Before the contracts have been signed, have they been reviewed by the hospital's attorney and certified public accountants in order to minimize hospital losses due to third-party reimbursement peculiarities.
- Have the professional component calculations been reviewed at least annually to determine if any changes have been made in the administrative or professional duties of the physician.

Q. *Is the physician's reimbursement computed by a responsible person?*

- Is the calculation also reviewed by a responsible person.
- Has the expense been charged to a separate general ledger account.
- Is the pathologist being paid a professional component for services sent to outside laboratories, for which he should not receive compensation.
- Is the radiology department receiving the charges for certain laboratory tests that are designated as isotope tests, such as T3s and T4s, because of improper coding in the charge collection system.

- Are gross charges, as recorded by the accounting department, reconciled to departmental logs kept in the ancillary departments.
- Is there a proper accounting of late credits and/or charges given in these departments so that the physician compensation is properly adjusted.

Questioning the Payroll/Personnel Relationships

Q. *Are new hires and terminations reported by the personnel department in writing to the payroll department?*

- Are such reports timely.
- Are payroll rates verified against the personnel records by a responsible person.
- Does a responsible person authorize, in writing, all wage rates not fixed under bargaining agreements.

Q. *Is there a written hospital policy authorizing payments for vacation, sick leave, holidays, overtime, and on-call time?*

- Are such policies being compiled by all departments and reviewed by the payroll department.
- Are such policies being misinterpreted with the result that shift differential is being authorized on hours not worked.
- Are there adequate controls to prevent the payment for items listed above in excess of the amounts authorized by policy.

Q. *Do the policies and procedures comply with the Fair Labor Standards Act current provisions for minimum wages, overtime pay determination, and wage discrimination?*

- Have any deductions been made from an employee's wage for breakage, cash shortages, or other types of deductions that brought the employee's wages below the legal minimum wage.
- Does it appear that only selected individuals are permitted to work overtime within certain departments; i.e., on the basis of longevity or on the basis of preferential treatment by the department manager.

Questioning the Operations of the Personnel Department

Q. *Do the hospital's department managers know the extent and limits of the personnel department's authority and responsibility?*

- Has the personnel department been specific about which personnel policies are subject to interpretation by the department managers and which are not.
- Do personnel policies fluctuate from department to department; i.e., do the personnel policies in departments managed by hospital-based physicians differ from those in other departments.
- Do employees and the department managers try to resolve their own problems without consulting the personnel department.

Q. Do the personnel department and the accounting department communicate with each other in forecasting manpower needs for budgetary purposes?

- Are good planning techniques utilized to minimize the need for "crash" recruiting programs.
- Is emergency hiring kept to a minimum.
- Does the hospital invest in people, as well as equipment, when offering a new or expanded service to the public.
- Is the use of "temporary help" adequately reviewed by Administration with the personnel department before agreements are signed.

Q. Is a merit-performance evaluation system used to evaluate employees? (See Figure 12.3.)

- Are supervisors and department managers adequately trained to eliminate personnel biases, halo effects, and the error of central tendency.
- During the performance evaluation, is there an exchange of information, or does the supervisor dominate the conversation.
- Is there an alphabetic or numeric "grading" system used which will later be a part of determining the amount of the employee's salary increase.
- Does the personnel department review the performance evaluations to see if the department managers may have inadvertently included personal connotations.
- Is the personnel department adequately staffed and properly utilized to provide timely assistance to Administration and the department managers.
- Has the personnel department adequately explained in a cover letter the negative effects of disregarding the proper techniques to be used in completing the performance evaluation.

Q. Are personnel development programs in effect?

- Are such programs confined only to nursing services personnel.
- Has the hospital ever documented and catalogued the various capabilities of all of its employees; i.e., an inventory of its human resources.
- Does the training for management personnel involve film strips and outside personnel in order that the hospital management may be exposed to different successful management styles.

Q. Are requests for additional manpower adequately reviewed in terms other than budget; i.e., need?

- Does the personnel department submit to every employment requisition it receives or do they refer seemingly unjustified requisitions to Administration.
- Does the personnel department review the budget assumptions, which may have resulted in the position being budgeted, to see if they have been met or are still valid assumptions for additional personnel.
- Does the hospital use a "task force" comprised of department managers to review and comment upon requests for additional W.H.L. employees.

Q. Are job descriptions maintained?

- If so, do they meet the Fair Labor Standards Act requirements.
- Are job descriptions maintained on a current basis and used by the personnel department in screening applicants.
- Are job descriptions used by the industrial engineering department or personnel department in evaluating the employee's position and where it should fall within the wage administration program.
- Are the job descriptions reviewed by the department manager.
- Does the department manager know what aspects of the position the personnel department should discuss with the applicant and what aspects he should cover.
- During interviews with applicants, is there a good, balanced exchange of information between representatives of the hospital and the applicant.

Q. Are personnel applications adequate?

- Does the completed application give the interviewer sufficient information regarding the applicant and his work experience.
- Does the application contain questions prohibited by law; i.e., age, race, creed, national origin.
- Are all questions relevant to the job and not superfluous; i.e., mother's name.
- Has Administration blindly accepted the personnel department's explanation that alternate wordings and formats are not used because they may be illegal.

Q. Does the personnel department use tests and physician examinations to evaluate applicants before hiring?

- Are the tests relevant to the job the applicant would be performing.
- Are applicants "categorized" by labels that may be accurate, but an inadequate reason to declare them ineligible for the position.
- Is it necessary to require a physical exam for positions that are strictly clerical in nature.

Q. Does the personnel department adequately investigate all references, including previous employers, before the applicant is sent to the department manager for an interview?

- Are the persons performing reference checks adequately trained and supervised.
- Are the techniques and manners used by the hospital employee checking references professional and courteous.
- Is an applicant considered further for employment when his statements regarding his abilities and training differ greatly from those obtained as a result of the reference check.

Q. Is a formal salary and benefits administration program in effect?

- Has the salary administration program been reviewed and approved by the Board of Trustees.

- When was the last major revision to salaries and benefits.
- Does the turnover rate in certain departments indicate that the personnel there may be misclassified within the existing payroll system; i.e., entry levels, salaries and steps too low to retain qualified and competent personnel.

Q. Are exit interviews conducted by the personnel department for employees who may resign their positions?

- Does the interview elicit comments from the employee regarding what he feels the hospital should look for in his successor.
- Is the employee asked how the hospital could improve its services.
- Is the department manager permitted to attend the exit interview.
- At the exit interview is an attempt made to dispose of any resentfulness or bitterness the employee may have toward the hospital.

Q. Are all employees provided with a personnel handbook?

- Are revisions given to each employee.
- Are original drafts of the personnel handbook prepared by the personnel department with the public relations department assisting only with the style.
- Are department managers told in advance of changes in personnel policy and other contents of the personnel handbook.
- Are the department managers given adequate information to answer questions from the employees regarding such changes.
- Does the announcement of the change cover the effective date, who is affected, if the change is temporary, permanent, on a test basis, etc., and exactly what the change entails.

Q. Does the hospital have an effective grievance procedure?

- Is the employee presented an opportunity to present his grievance, without his supervisor being present.
- Is there an appropriate appeal mechanism whereby the employee may present his grievance to his supervisor's department manager.
- Do the employees feel protected if they use the grievance procedure.
- Does the grievance procedure merely "rubber stamp" the actions of the supervisor or are corrective actions taken when appropriate.
- Is there a specific time table in which grievances must be filed, heard, and answered.

Q. Does the hospital publish a house organ?

- What is its purpose.
- Does it meet the purpose.
- Is it geared toward the hospital's employees and what they are doing or is it a sounding board for management.
- Have the employees ever been asked what they would like to see in the house organ.
- Do the employees take an interest in the paper or would no one notice if it were discontinued.

THE AUDIT

The Audit Objective

The auditor's primary objective in the audit of the payroll and personnel functions is to determine that the expenditure for hours worked and nonproductive hours is in compliance with existing personnel policies for legitimate employees of the hospital, and is reported in accordance with generally accepted accounting principles applied on a basis consistent with that of the preceding period. In addition the auditor should be concerned that these costs are recorded in the proper cost centers and that the procedures for transfers of employees are adequate to develop reasonable records of cost data.

Testing the Hospital Payroll Transactions

1) On a test basis, compare the names appearing on the payroll with the personnel records or other satisfactory evidence of employment.
2) Test check the payroll hours with time cards or other supporting data of hours worked.
3) Compare rates of pay with authorization forms, union scale books, or other data.
4) Test the computation of gross pay and net pay.
5) Substantiate the deductions by computation or reference to proper authorization.
6) Test the payroll extensions and footings.
7) Test the distribution of the payroll, per voucher, to the accounts.
8) Examine checks for proper payee, proper amount of net pay, and proper endorsement of checks.
9) Check personnel records to ascertain if persons being paid were employees during the pay period being tested.
10) Check for proper initials on the payroll journals, etc., indicating review and approval by a responsible individual.
11) Ascertain if the hospital is complying with Federal Wage and Hour Laws as they relate to minimum pay.
12) Test the calculation of overtime and call pay for technicians.
13) Note the type of payroll and pay dates.
14) Investigate the method of handling unclaimed pay checks.
15) Be present to observe actual paying of employees, or make a surprise pay-off.
16) Trace payroll test to summaries.
17) Trace postings of summary totals to general ledger and subsidiary ledgers.
18) Check propriety of distribution.
19) Compare total of payroll tested with recorded disbursement from general bank account for such payroll.
20) Reconcile payroll bank account.

NOTE: In testing the compensation of key personnel, trace the computation to terms of the employment contract.

WORKING PAPERS REQUIRED

The preparation of a payroll summary permits the auditor to check quickly the accrual of the various payroll tax accounts and the accrued payroll expense.

The auditor should prepare a reconciliation of the payroll bank account for the test month, including a summary of work performed.

A summary of the quarterly payroll expense per the quarterly payroll tax returns should be prepared and reconciled to the payroll expense for the period.

Copies of employment contracts, including those with physicians, should be included in the permanent file. Calculations of the applicable compensation should be included in the current year working papers.

Excerpts from the personnel policies and employee handbooks that relate to the calculation of pay should be included in each year working papers.

The auditor's test of payroll transactions, with a complete summary of audit work performed, is an integral part of the audit working papers.

FINANCIAL STATEMENT PRESENTATION

The operating expenses of the hospital are usually shown in total by area of responsibility; i.e., nursing service, other professional services, etc. In such instances payroll expense is included with the other operating expenses for each division.

The supplemental financial information will include schedules that detail the expenses, on a comparative basis, by expense category. In this detail, payroll expense will be the first expense category listed.

Hospitals who choose not to follow the recommended reporting format will list their expenses by natural expense category as developed by the American Hospital Association in its Chart of Accounts. This form of reporting will reflect payroll expense as the first item under the category "Operating Expenses."

Acknowledgments by Applicant

1. Any information which is falsely given on the application blank may disqualify you from being hired for employment or, once hired, may be cause for termination.
2. You must submit a medical examination just prior to or shortly after your date of hire, as scheduled by the Hospital. Also, once employed, examination by a doctor of the Hospital's choosing may be required on a yearly basis or at other times when it becomes necessary to insure the health and welfare of an individual, patients, or fellow employees.
3. The Hospital, in making its determination of an applicant's qualifications for employment, is authorized to make third party references concerning your prior work history and personal characteristics. In making reference checks, the Hospital may make only those necessary for determining your suitability for work. Where disclosures are required by law, you will be notified of the findings.
4. HOSPITAL is an equal opportunity employer and does not discriminate on the basis of race, color, creed, sex, age or, national origin. However, the completion of an application blank does not in any way obligate the Hospital to provide work.
5. Your application blank will be kept in active review for a period of three months. Should you have any questions about your status during the three-month period after filing an application, feel free to contact the Personnel Office. If, after a three-month period, you have not been contacted and are still interested in seeking employment with Hospital, you should refile a new application.
6. In the event this application results in employment with Hospital, you will be expected to comply with the rules and regulations established from time to time by the Hospital for the general operations of the Hospital, and to further comply with the rules and regulations established in the department to which you are assigned.

SIGNATURE OF APPLICANT________________________DATE______________

FIGURE 12.1

______________ HOSPITAL

REQUEST FOR WAGE
OR
SALARY CHANGE

INSTRUCTIONS TO REQUESTOR:

1. Complete all pertinent portions: improperly completed requests *will not be approved* and may result in a delay (allow 4 to 6 weeks for processing normal salary changes).
2. Wage and salary increases exceeding 10% will not generally be approved—except for promotions or where exceptional merit can be demonstrated. (Increases exceeding 10% require special review!)

EMPLOYEE'S NAME: ______________________ DATE OF HIRE: ____________

TITLE: ________________ TIME IN PRESENT POSITION: _____ YEAR _____ MONTH

REQUESTOR'S NAME: ____

EMPLOYEE'S IMMEDIATE SUPERVISOR? ( ) NO ( ) YES

REQUEST BASED ON DIRECT OBSERVATION OF EMPLOYEE? ( ) NO ( ) YES

IF "NO," PLEASE EXPLAIN; ______________________________________

____

DAYS ABSENT LAST 3 MONTHS (other than vacation, holidays or maternity leave) ______

COMMENTS ON ABSENTEEISM: ____

____

____

CHANGE IN EDUCATIONAL OR PROFESSIONAL STATUS SINCE LAST INCREASE (i.e., degrees, appointments, memberships, etc.)? ATTACH APPLICABLE DOCUMENTATION:

____

____

____

CHANGES IN TYPE, DEGREE, OR NUMBER OF RESPONSIBILITIES.
EXPLAIN OTHER REASONS FOR REQUEST: ______________________________

____

____

____

____

____
Signature of Requestor

(COMPLETE BOTH SIDES)

FIGURE 12.2

ANALYSIS OF CHANGE

CHANGE CODE		INCREASED	DECREASED
A	Reclassification:	______%	______%
B	Merit (Productivity):	______%	______%
C	Transfer:	______%	______%
D	Demotion:	______%	______%
E	Promotion:	______%	______%
F	Wage Adjustment:	______%	______%
G	D.M.R.:	______%	______%
H	Probationary:	______%	______%
I	Other: ______	______%	______%
	TOTAL:	______%	______%

PERCENT CHANGE: ______%

* * * RECOMMENDATIONS * * *

	PRESENT		PROPOSED	
DEPARTMENT				
TITLE				
RANK	___/___ SCORE: ______			
RATE				
LEVEL				
EXEMPT	( ) YES	( ) NO	( ) YES	( ) NO

* * * PREVIOUS PAY RATE HISTORY * * *

	RATE 1	RATE 2	RATE 3	RATE 4
DATE:				
RATE:				
CHANGE CODES:				

DO NOT WRITE BELOW THIS LINE

APPROVALS:

______ Department Head ______ Administrative Member ______ Director of Employee Relations

APPROVED CHANGE: ______/ HOUR RETROACTIVE TO: __/__/__ Month Day Year

APPROVED EFFECTIVE DATE:

(COMPLETE BOTH SIDES)

FIGURE 12.2 ***(continued)***

EMPLOYEE EVALUATION

* * * SUMMARY * * *

EMPLOYEE NAME ______________________________

JOB TITLE ______________ DEPARTMENT ______________

SERVICE IN DEPARTMENT: YRS. __________ MONTHS __________

ATTRIBUTE	SCORE	DESCRIPTIVE RATING (or Rank)
I. Job Knowledge		
II. Housekeeping		
III. Dependability		
IV. Inventiveness		
V. Quantity of Work		
VI. Adaptability		
VII. Quality of Work		
VIII. Personal Relationships		
IX. Initiative		
X.		

TOTAL SCORE: __________

AVERAGE SCORE: __________ GENERAL RANK __________
OF __________

* * * SUPERVISOR'S COMMENTS * * *

AREA OF CONCENTRATION: ______________________________

STRENGTHS: ______________________________

COUNSELOR __________ TITLE __________ DATE __________

EMPLOYEE'S COMMENTS: ______________________________

EMPLOYEE'S SIGNATURE __________ DATE __________

FIGURE 12.3

13

Auditing Third-Party Reimbursement, Cost Finding, and Budgeting to Maximize Reimbursement

The major portion of this chapter deals with an area unique to the health care industry—third-party reimbursement. Budgeting and cost finding will be covered, but slanted toward their relationship to third-party reimbursement.

This chapter is not a primer on third-party reimbursement for the uninitiated, but will be a guide in examining the major areas of concern with a view toward maximizing third-party reimbursement.

Cost finding and the accumulation of statistics are extremely important in maximizing the hospital's reimbursement, regardless of the reimbursement system. Pricing strategies based upon reliable statistical and cost data can yield good profits that result in the financial viability of the hospital. Remember, there is a substantial difference between being tax exempt and being non-profit. Hospitals, as a rule, are tax exempt under Section 501(c) (3) of the Internal Revenue Service Codes.

This chapter will not delve into the intricacies of sophisticated costing systems, but will offer points of consideration by the hospital management.

Advanced budgeting techniques, such as flexible budgeting and the development of sophisticated forecasting models, are still uncommon in the majority of hospitals. Unfortunately, most third-party reimbursement systems do not encourage the development of such tools. Most third-party reimbursement programs dictate either that the hospital be reimbursed on a "defined" cost basis, or that it establish prospective rates on a "per patient day" basis. Creativity on the part of the hospital to accurately forecast the results of operations is viewed in a hostile arena. Many times the hospital must yield to political realities in forecasting by using methods that will be acceptable to third-party payors. This does not mean, however, that we must give up the struggle to utilize advanced industrial methods in preparing budgets.

This chapter will suggest budget techniques for consideration. Certainly the auditor must yield to the desires of Administration in their implementation, but he has a responsibility to bring suggestions for improvements to the attention of Administration.

REVIEWING THE FUNCTIONS

Questioning the Hospital's Third-Party Reimbursement Data

Q. *How many third party reimbursement contracts are in effect with the hospital to furnish services to their participants?*

- Does the contract contain a clause whereby the hospital must furnish services even though the third party may not be able to pay for such services. (See Figure 13.1.)
- Does the contract require the hospital to share in any losses incurred by the third-party payor.
- Does the contract require the hospital to comply with certain other Federal, State, or municipal regulations as a condition of participation. (See Figure 13.2.)

Q. *Does a qualified person prepare third-party reimbursement cost reports?*

- If cost reports are prepared by an independent firm, what is the depth of its experience; i.e., how extensive is its hospital practice. If cost reports are prepared internally, are they reviewed by an experienced independent firm.
- Are the types of adjustments to the cost reports due to:
  1) Clerical or bookkeeping errors.
  2) Attempts to legitimately maximize reimbursement.

Q. *How are third-party reimbursement contractual settlements controlled?*

- Is there a separate balance sheet account for prior years' settlements.
- Are the cost reports filed on a timely basis.
- Are the agency adjustments to the cost reports challenged.

Q. *How is third-party reimbursement program data accumulated?*

- Manual logs from billing records.
- Data processing logs from the revenue system.
- As a part of the general ledger system.

Q. *What corrections to the program data are made by the hospital?*

- Exclusion of non-covered days.
- Rejection of program coverage.
- Revision of deductible and co-insurance amounts due from beneficiary.
- Changes in interim reimbursement rates.

Q. *Are period-end split billings prepared for inhouse contractual third-party reimbursement patients?*

- If no, is the method used accurate and does it result in maximum reimbursement.
- Are split billings prepared for only those patients for whom the hospital has received acknowledgment of program liability.

Q. Are sufficient departmental categories maintained in the general ledger to identify all service areas?

- If the hospital has a delegated Professional Standards Review Organization (PSRO) program, is the hospital receiving full reimbursement.
- Are patient accounting areas properly identified, and is approval obtained from Intermediaries to maximize reimbursement.

Questioning the Adequacy of the Hospital's Cost Finding

Q. Do the reported departmental expenses conform with the actual responsibility centers?

- Are appropriate changes in comparative data made to reflect organizational realignments.
- Is there a cost center for each revenue center.

Q. Is one of the American Hospital Association's (A.H.A.) recommended cost-finding methods used consistently between current and prior reporting periods?

- Method number 2 (step down).
- Method number 3 (double apportionment).
- If another method, such as computerized algebraic method, is used, could it also be used for third-party reimbursement purposes.
- If no, why.
- Is the cost finding performed under the direction of a qualified person.

Q. Is the clerical accuracy of the cost finding verified?

- If yes, how is it noted; i.e., initialled and dated.
- Are there written instructions for checking the clerical accuracy.

Q. Is sufficient attention paid to the collection of cost-finding statistics?

- Is one person assigned the responsibility of accumulating the cost-finding statistics.
- Are there written procedures to the departmental managers describing the method and frequency of collecting cost-finding statistics.
- Are the cost-finding statistics reviewed periodically to avoid maintaining useless or irrelevant data.
- Are ledgers, journals, or their equivalent used to summarize cost-finding statistics.

Q. Does the hospital have any special or unique cost centers?

- Clinics.
- Schools.
  1) medical,
  2) nursing,
  3) lab technicians or

4) x-ray students.

- Nursing home or extended care facility.
- Non-patient cost centers.
  1) gift shop,
  2) public parking lots,
  3) non-employee cafeteria, or
  4) rental property.
- If yes, are their full costs segregated.

Q. Does the hospital utilize the services of nonpaid workers?

- Are room, board, or other personal living costs provided.
- If yes, is the "analysis method" used to determine these costs.

Questioning the Hospital's Budgeting Process for Acceptance and Utility

Q. Is there a hospital budget committee?

- Are there physician representatives.
- Are there community representatives.
- Are formal minutes of their meetings maintained.

Q. Are budget manuals and calendars prepared and distributed:

1) to the Finance Committee of the Board of Trustees,
2) to the hospital budget committee, and
3) to the Administrative Staff members and departmental managers?

Q. Is an orientation program conducted each year for the benefit of the departmental managers?

- Is attendance mandatory.
- Are the instruction material and examples concise and clear.
- Is the instruction well received.
- If no, why.

Q. Do most department managers feel the budget is a useful tool?

- Does the budget manager provide assistance to the department managers, or does the budget manager actually prepare some departmental budgets.
- Are administrative and/or trustee changes to the departmental budgets communicated to the managers.
- Are department managers required to explain actual vs. budget variances.
- Are monthly actual vs. budget reports distributed to management on a timely basis.

Q. Are regulatory requirements for budgeting followed?

- Three-year capital budget.
- Prospective operations budget.

Q. Are improvements in the budgeting process made each year?

- Use of unit of service statistics.
- Identification of fixed, semi-variable, and variable cost.
- Identification of changes in categories of cost at varying levels of service.
  1) supervision,
  2) equipment,
  3) space allocation, and
  4) maintenance.
- Use of property records to identify future capital equipment replacements.
- Noting effect of regulatory changes in third-party reimbursement.
- Proper consideration of contractual allowances. (See Figure 13.3.)

Q. Is exception reporting used to highlight those categories of revenue and cost that vary by a predetermined percentage of budget?

- Are written explanations required of the departmental managers.
- Are the explanations tested for validity by the accounting office.
- Are causes for budget variances noted by the budget office and efforts taken to correct the situations causing such variances in subsequent years.

Q. Are reasonableness tests performed in analyzing actual vs. budget results?

- Percent of expense to gross operating revenue.
- Comparison of increase in productive hours to increase in units of service, patient mix, or patient days.
- Is consideration given to rate increase and intensity of service when testing the validity of the results of operations.

THE AUDIT

Third-Party Reimbursement

Much has been written on the subject of third-party reimbursement and rate setting; i.e., cost finding and budgeting. Certainly an entire book could be devoted to this subject, in which maximization techniques and their justification or rationale could be discussed.

Reimbursement under the Medicare Program relates primarily to the reasonable cost of a given item or service related to patient care. Guidelines and policies used in implementing the cost principles are contained in the Provider Reimbursement Manual, HIM-15. The "Introduction" to HIM-15 states:

> Under generally accepted accounting principles, or under the "Principles of Reimbursement for Provider Costs," there may be more than one method for handling a particular cost item; in such case the method elected by the provider must be consistently followed in subsequent reporting periods. A change of method must be approved by the Intermediary (or SSA for providers dealing direct) on a prospective and not retrospective basis. Where the manual sets a time limit for requesting such change, or limits the number of changes, the provider and Intermediary will be guided by the manual instructions.

The "Introduction" also notes that in instances where its provisions do not speak to a particular cost situation, generally accepted accounting principles (GAAP) should be applied.

In addition, the American Institute of Certified Public Accountants (A.I.C.P.A.), in its publication "Hospital Audit Guide," specifically relates GAAP to hospitals.

The point is, when you encounter a transaction that may have been handled in questionable fashion for "reimbursement" purposes, stop and challenge its accounting treatment if not applied in accordance with GAAP.

> The provider has the right and the obligation to arrange its transactions in a manner which will "maximize" third-party reimbursement, but transactions which are instigated solely to create reimbursable cost are likely to cause more controversy than net return.[1]

The auditor, in advising Administration, should point out that the hospital that consistently claims reimbursement for costs that are well known to be non-allowable will lose its credibility with the Intermediary. The hospital may, therefore, subject itself to annual full audits and the disallowance of "grey area" costs.

In your investigation of third-party reimbursement, you should determine if the hospital's long-range planning committee includes an employee or retains a consultant with a thorough knowledge of third-party reimbursement. With proper planning, potential risks of third-party disallowances will be disclosed and Administration may make its decision based on the probable affect of planning decisions on the financial statements.

Your audit should reveal if the Administration, in planning its transactions, always accomplishes the following:

1) Preparation of adequate documentation for financial transactions.
2) Avoidance of transactions with no independent business justification.

Even the hospital that has accomplished the above and properly reported the applicable cost may still find the allowability of certain items challenged by the Intermediary.

The Audit Program

1) Compare and reconcile expense *accounts* on the year-end adjusted trial balance with those on the cost statements.
2) Reconcile, and obtain explanations, for any differences between total *expenses* on the trial balance and cost statement with the hospital's annual independent audit report.
3) Review reconciling items for the prior period for comparability.
4) Review and analyze any new expense accounts, i.e., any new service, to determine appropriateness and applicability to third-party reimbursement.
5) In analyzing the various expense account classifications, the following should be given special emphasis to determine the nature of the charges to the account; i.e., capital item or unallowable expense:

1. Jack C. Wood, *Medicare Reimbursement*, 58. (Topics in Health Care Financing, Vol. 1, No. 3, 1975; Aspen Systems Corporation.)

a) Miscellaneous or sundry expense.
b) Repair and maintenance.
c) Operation of plant (utilities and/or supplies).
d) Professional fees, other than medical.
e) Administrative and general supplies.
f) Laboratory supplies and expenses.
g) X-ray supplies and expenses.
h) Pharmacy supplies and expenses.
i) Dietary supplies and expenses.
j) Operating room supplies and expenses.

The scope and detail of these expense analyses should be evaluated by reference to the materiality of the total amount charged to the account and the nature of the individual items included in the account. The scope established should be indicated on the appropriate schedule. (See Figure 13.4.)

6) Rent expense/other purchased services:
   a) Rent expense should be analyzed for the year and supported by reference to lease agreements and correspondence.
   b) If the expense is incurred between related parties, see that it is reflected in the cost statement in accordance with HIM-15, Principle 1-10.
   c) Review lease agreements to determine if there are substantial differences between normal depreciation and the lease payment. If so, this should be commented upon in your management letter, noting the probable effect on reimbursement.
   d) Sale and lease-back arrangements should also be reviewed and commented upon.
7) Education and research:
   a) Review HIM-15, Principle 1-4, "Cost of Educational Activity."
      1) Review the license or other documents indicating approval for the operation of the educational program.
      2) Review the direct expenses of the educational activity, for reasonableness and applicability to these activities (salaries, supplies, maintenance, etc.).
      3) Determine that all related income has been properly offset against expenses of the educational activities.
   b) Review HIM-15, Principle 1-5, "Research Cost."
      1) Review correspondence relating to the method of financing.
      2) Review correspondence relating to the purpose and relationship to patient care.
      3) Observe the research activities and consult with the personnel to determine compliance with the intended purpose of the research.
8) Value of voluntary services:
   a) Review HIM-15, Principle 1-7, "Value of Services of Non-Paid Workers."
   b) Review written contracts establishing a legal obligation for payment of the services.
   c) Obtain a schedule showing the value of service and other allowances by occupation and the department to which the related amounts are charged.
   d) Review the schedule and see that the hospital has increased the amounts by similar increments granted others for similar services.

e) Determine that maintenance cost for religious personnel has not been included in the allowable cost.
f) Determine that the methods used to establish the maintenance cost are reasonable and provide maximum benefit to the hospital; i.e., use of separate meters for utilities.

9) Non-patient related cost:
a) Review the cost recovery items on the previous year cost report to determine if cost could be determined in those instances where revenue was used as an offset.
b) Question Administration regarding changes in the utilization of certain areas such as convents, gift shops, etc., to less costly areas.
c) Consider claiming unfinished areas as stand-by cost, storage areas, or archive space.

Maximizing third-party cost reimbursement is never easy, but with sufficient planning of transactions and a knowledge of how the system works the hospital can receive full allowable cost reimbursement.

The change in utilization of space, use of industrial engineering studies, and the practice of defensive accounting will certainly minimize losses.

Included in this portion of the chapter is a statistical checklist (see Figure 13.5), comments on reclassifying certain revenue/expense items, and suggested allocation bases for your consideration in maximizing third-party reimbursement.

The Audit Objective—Cost Finding

The auditor's objective is to verify the accuracy of the statistics for the general service departments and the special service departments (where such statistics are used as the basis of cost allocation) against the basic records of original entry.

In addition, the auditor should review the expense and revenue reclassifications, the cost sequence, and allocation bases for reasonableness, with a view towards their effect on third-party reimbursement.

The Audit Program

1) Using a checklist like the one in Figure 13.5, note the basis for the various statistical accumulations used by the hospital, the frequency with which such statistics are gathered, and the date of the most recent study or sampling.

2) Note whether the basis used in these allocations was consistent with that used in prior periods. If the effects of such changes are not noted on the cost reports used for management purposes, comment upon their affect in your report to Administration and recommend that such notation be made on subsequent reports.

3) Review for reasonableness those bases of allocation used for management cost that do not conform to those used in filing third-party cost reports.

4) As a detail test of the reasonableness of the statistical bases, the following tests should be made of the allocation bases chosen for examination:

a) Obtain and review the hospital's worksheets supporting the allocation bases.
b) Discuss the allocation bases with *operating* personnel as to reasonableness and current status.

c) Check the clerical accuracy of the computations and footings.
d) On a test-check basis, recompute the bases of allocation; i.e., remeasure square footings departmentally, test the number of meals served for short period, verify the location of major items of equipment, etc., and test the arithmetic accuracy of the detail.

5) Write a memorandum as to the reliability and adequacy of the statistics used in cost finding.

Reclassification Entries That Maximize Reimbursement

Listed in alphabetical order are reclassification items to be considered before beginning the cost allocation procedure. These items usually result in additional third-party cost reimbursement and are generally recognized as more accurate and sophisticated methods of classifying the hospital expenses for costing purposes.

ADMITTING OFFICE

Most hospital admitting offices deal only with inpatients; however, the cost is usually accumulated under Administration and General. If the cost is left in Administration and General, it will be distributed based on accumulated costs, which produce inequitable results. Therefore, the cost should be reclassified to inpatients and maternity, based on admissions.

BABY FORMULA

Frequently, this cost may be charged to Medical Supplies or Pharmacy. In this case, the transfer should be made to nursery.

BILLING OFFICE

A study of functions performed by the personnel involved in the billing department should be performed. This study should result in costs for inpatient, outpatient, emergency room, and private ambulatory being identified and segregated.

BLOOD BANK

When the payroll cost of the blood bank is not separately allocated, the salaries should be transferred from the departments charged, usually laboratory and/or intravenous therapy. Where blood bank supplies have been charged to laboratory, they also should be transferred.

COMPENSATION INSURANCE

The premiums on compensation insurance are computed on a salary base. Accordingly, they can be distributed departmentally on that base.

DATA PROCESSING COSTS

The cost of payroll preparation can be allocated based on time studies of transactions processed. Additional functions performed such as accounts receivable, billing, and other services for departments can be distributed on the basis of statistical studies and transaction counts, as well as time.

DEPRECIATION

Allocation of depreciation on total square feet does not always produce the proper result. For example, if buildings have been constructed at different times, they would have a different cost per square foot. Accordingly, they should be treated separately. The square feet for each building should be obtained and the depreciation on that building allocated among the departments using it. Furthermore, fixed equipment, such as built-in counters, shelving (if identifiable), and other items should be identified and the depreciation transferred to the appropriate department.

DISABILITY BENEFITS

Premiums for many policies are based on the number of employees. Therefore, these costs should be transferred directly to each department on this basis. Otherwise, gross salaries used as the basis for distribution will be inequitable.

EMPLOYEE HEALTH INSURANCE

This can also be identified by numbers of employees and allocated on that basis.

EMPLOYEE HEALTH SERVICE

Health services rendered to employees can be recorded in a log, noting the employee's department. This log can then be analyzed and the department cost allocated to the various departments.

F.I.C.A.

This expense should be allocated based on taxable wages in each department, which are readily determinable from any payroll system. The increasing significance of this item in dollars and the variations in pay scale make this allocation imperative. If gross salaries are used, departments having highly paid technicians, physicians, and administrative personnel would receive an inequitable share of the cost which would eventually wind up in outpatient and non-covered areas.

FIRE INSURANCE

Information can be obtained from the carrier on the computation of the premiums. Buildings and contents can be allocated using this data. Since many property ledger updates give the insurable value, allocation can also be made on this basis.

HOME CARE PROGRAMS

Where these programs are in effect, a computation of salaries applicable to discharge planning can be made and transferred directly to inpatients.

INTEREST

Where the proceeds of a capital loan were used for specific construction, the interest on that loan may be charged to that area.

LAUNDRY AND LINEN

An analysis of linen and bedding use should be made to determine the amount used for inpatient and maternity areas and the cost allocated to them. If this is not done, cost of bed, linen, and comparable items could be distributed to ancillary services and through them to outpatient centers.

LIFE INSURANCE

This premium cost is determined by employee and can be distributed departmentally.

MALPRACTICE INSURANCE

The premiums on this insurance are computed on the basis of beds and outpatient visits. These can be analyzed so that the cost may be distributed to the proper service. Care should be taken in hospitals having large outpatient departments that an excessive amount of this cost is not charged to this area.

NURSING SERVICE

If direct charges are not made to each service, an analysis of payroll must be made, and nursing service reclassified to nursing administration, intensive care, inpatient, maternity, and other, as may be applicable. Hours of service would otherwise be a basis for distribution that would provide less equitable results.

PACEMAKERS

Where the hospital is on the departmental basis, pacemakers can be set up as a separate special service department allocating costs from medical supplies and operating and recovery rooms. Since experience has shown that more patients over 65 use pacemakers, the cost of these should be handled separately to more equitably distribute the costs.

PENSION EXPENSE

Premiums paid or amounts funded are computed actuarially on an employee base and can therefore be distributed on that base. Direct pension payments should be charged to the department involved.

PERSONNEL OFFICE

This office serves hospital personnel and can therefore be allocated to departments, based on employees in the department during the year.

PREPARATION OF PAYROLL

Where the hospital uses a service bureau or has an in-house computer, the number of checks per department can be counted as a by-product of the payroll and the cost of preparing the payroll can be allocated departmentally. In lieu of this statistic, the number of employees can be used, or even W-2s. Cost to be distributed should include outside service bureau charges, internal computer costs, and personnel identifiable with the preparation of the payroll. If available, supplies specifically used for payroll can be allocated also.

PROFESSIONAL FEES

Special professional studies can frequently be identified and allocated to the areas or departments involved. Assistance in allocation can be obtained from the firm performing the study.

RADIOLOGY—THERAPEUTIC

Usually, radiology personnel work on both diagnostic and therapeutic patients. Since a higher percentage of therapeutic radiology will be allocated to outpatients, the salaries should be transferred to this cost center, based on periodic time studies.

SECURITY

Where a separate security department or outside service is used, assignments to specific areas are usually determinable and the cost can be allocated directly to the area.

UNEMPLOYMENT INSURANCE

If the hospital has elected to use the state program, the same principles apply as to the FICA taxable salary base. If the hospital elects to pay claims, the payment should be allocated directly to the department in which the employee worked.

This is particularly important because the departments having the most turnovers are usually those that are heavily involved in inpatient areas.

Reviewing the Bases of Allocating Service Department Cost

To help you understand the allocation bases generally utilized by the Medicare Program, the following description of their recommended bases and suggested alternative bases has been provided.

BUILDING DEPRECIATION

The recommended bases for allocating this cost element to departments are either gross or net square feet of the building(s). "Gross square feet" includes common areas such as halls and corridors, whereas "net square feet" excludes these areas. Also, in cases of multiple buildings housing various departments, it may be appropriate to analyze the cost element and departments housed to determine if direct reclassification may not be a more appropriate means of allocation. For example, the depreciation applicable to a building housing personnel may result in a higher reimbursement if reclassified directly to the maintenance of personnel department, as opposed to being included with total depreciation expense and allocated based on total hospital square feet.

ADMINISTRATION AND GENERAL

This cost element is allocated based on accumulated costs of specialized service areas; however, it may be more appropriate to analyze the cost elements included and make direct reclassification or allocation based on areas or patients serviced. Examples of cost elements to be reviewed are the admitting office, data processing, communications, credit and collection costs, insurance costs, purchasing department, etc.

EMPLOYEE, HEALTH, AND WELFARE

The recommended bases for allocating this cost element are gross salaries of all personnel; however, it may be more appropriate to allocate components of this cost element directly to other areas due to differences that may exist in personnel coverages or maximum limitations. Examples of cost elements to be reviewed are FICA and unemployment taxes, disability and workman's compensation insurances, pensions, etc.

OPERATION AND MAINTENANCE OF PLANT

The recommended bases for allocating this cost element are total square feet of the institution; however, it may be more appropriate to allocate components of this cost element directly to other areas based on usage. For example, security service may be allocated on areas patrolled. Light, heat, and power may be allocated on cubic or metered consumption of an area. Repairs may be allocated by specific job orders performed in an area.

NURSING SERVICE AND NURSING ADMINISTRATION

Since this cost element is generally the largest in the hospital operation, particular emphasis should be placed on reviewing staffing patterns to insure that payroll costs allocated to a nursing service coincide with the staffing patterns for the service. Similarly, nursing administration costs should only be allocated to nursing stations serviced.

OTHER COST ELEMENTS

Salaries and expenses of escort personnel, i.e., tray girls, x-ray attendants, should be analyzed to determine that the proper department is charged in terms of allocating the cost by the type of patient served.

Bases of Allocating Service Department Cost

The listing on the facing page identifies the various types of service cost centers and the Medicare accepted and alternative statistical bases which could be utilized.

The Hospital Budget—Fact or Fiction

For fiscal years beginning after March, 1973, as a condition of participation in the Medicare Program a hospital must have a written overall annual operating budget and a three-year capital expenditure plan. The annual operating budget is to include all anticipated income and expense as determined under generally accepted accounting principles. The capital expenditure plan must cover at least a three-year period, including the year to which the annual operating budget applies.

The auditor should have a working knowledge of the three main budgeting methods; i.e., appropriation, fixed, and flexible.

APPROPRIATION BUDGET

This method may apply to the capital or plant and equipment budget. Expenditures are determined and become the maximum spending level for which appropriations are then made. Procedures should exist for a formal request and authorization for supplemental appropriations of funds in excess of the original appropriation. This method anticipates a specific level of spending for a single level of activity.

FIXED BUDGET

This method is applicable to both the operational budget and the capital or plant and

COST CENTER	RECOMMENDED BASES	ALTERNATIVE BASES
Depreciation–building and fixed equipment	Square feet	Depreciation cost by specific building
Depreciation–movable equipment	Dollar value or square feet	Actual department depreciation
Employee health and welfare	Gross salaries	See section on reclassification entries
Administration and General	Accumulated costs	See section on reclassification entries
Maintenance of plant	Square feet	Hours of service rendered to each area
Operation of plant	Square feet	Square feet weighted amount of extra service provided (i.e., extra kilowatts of electricity to certain cost centers.)
Laundry/linen service	Pounds of laundry	Pieces of laundry processed
Housekeeping	Hours of service	Square feet
Dietary	Meals served	Meals served weighted by relative difference in meal costs by various consumption centers
Cafeteria	Meals served	Number of employees or sales value of meals
Maintenance of Personnel	Number of employees housed classified by department where employed	
Nursing administration	Hours of service	Days of service
Central supply	Dollar value of processed requisitions	Units used in each area
Pharmacy	Costed requisitions	
Medical Records	Percent of time spent	
Social Service	Percent of time spent	
Nursing school	Assigned time	Number of students enrolled or hours of education
Approved intern and resident service program	Assigned time	

equipment budget. Revenue and expense estimates are based on a planned level of activity by month and remain in effect throughout the year. The value of this method is diminished for control purposes if the actual level of activity deviates to any significant extent from the planned level.

FLEXIBLE BUDGET

This is the most effective method for operational budgets. It requires refined statistics and data classification in the collection and processing procedures. Expenses are separated into categories of fixed, semi-fixed, semi-variable, and variable, as related to the volume of activity. Revenues are classified according to payor category and the type of reimbursement associated with each. The flexible expense portion is reflected at dollar amount per unit of output while the fixed portion is reflected in the total amount.

The flexible budget consists of a regular line item budget and a control budget. The control budget is earned based on the level of service rendered and measured against the actual dollars spent in achieving that service.

The Audit Objective—Budgeting

1) Determine that accounting considerations were given in the development of the budget to properly reflect the estimated or budgeted year-end balances in accordance with consistently applied accounting principles.
2) Verify the accuracy of the statistics and economic assumptions used in preparing the budget.
3) Review the requested price increases to determine that proper consideration was given to their affect upon third-party cost reimbursement.

The Audit Procedure

1) Review the budget workpapers to see that proper accruals have been reflected in the budget for:
   a) salaries and wages, including vacation and holiday pay,
   b) employee fringe benefits, including pension costs,
   c) audit and legal fees,
   d) depreciation and interest expense, and
   e) insurance expense, especially malpractice.
2) Review the previous year and current year budget reports to determine those areas that appear to pose the greatest budget problems; i.e., budget variance.
   a) Note the explanation given for each of the material variances; i.e., change in patient mix, decrease in length of stay, economic factors, etc.
   b) After noting such explanations, review the items in the aggregate to determine if any two or group of explanations are contradictory; i.e., treated more patients, yet total patient visits down. Investigate further those explanations to arrive at probable causes of budget variance.
3) a) Review the budget for the subsequent year to determine that proper consideration has been given those areas posing the greatest problems in previous years.
   b) Using a procedure similar to that shown in Figure 13.3, test the accuracy of the budgeted Medicare/Medicaid contractual allowances.

c) Review the current year file of budget variances for items that should be reported in the subsequent year budget.
d) Review the correspondence, articles, and notes supporting the economic assumptions for:
 1) salary and wage adjustments,
 2) fringe benefits (by category),
 3) pharmacy and I.V. solution costs,
 4) medical/surgical supply costs,
 5) printing and office supply costs,
 6) food; i.e., meat, canned goods, and vegetables,
 7) utilities (by category),
 8) insurance (by category),
 9) radiographic film,
 10) lease agreements, including maintenance,
 11) professional fees (contract terms), and
 12) housekeeping and laundry supplies, including replacement linen.

NOTE: If adequate documentation is missing for any of these areas, excluding salary and wages, send confirmation request to major vendors asking for estimate of inflation factor for their product during the subsequent budget year.

e) Review the budget workpapers for the inclusion of items that should be capitalized.

NOTE: Be familiar with the hospital's election for the treatment of minor equipment for Medicare reimbursement purposes.

f) Note that *all* manually prepared budget workpapers and the budget reports include a dated initial of the preparer and the verifier.
 1) Test the footing and cross footings, including selected items on computer prepared reports.
 2) Trace the salary total to the departmental summary.
 3) Test check selected departmental salaries to the departmental prepared budget work sheets.
 4) Verify the mathematical accuracy of the selected departmental budgets.
 5) Trace other major expense items to budget summaries.
g) Review the prospective budget data in the form of pro-forma revenue and expense summaries.
 1) Adjust the expense categories for changes in utilization; i.e., patient days, etc. Investigate why the adjusted expense total, as a percentage of current year projected actual, is materially more, or less, than the inflation factors used in the budget assumptions.
 2) Compare each expense category as a percentage of gross patient revenue, to the current year projected percentages. Investigate material variances.
 3) Compare budgeted increases in revenue and expense per patient day to the increases used in the budget assumptions.
h) Using total paid hours for all employees, calculate the average straight time hourly rate (ASTHR) for the projected year. Compare to the budgeted ASHTR. Reconcile increase by category; i.e., new positions, promotions, merit increases, scale adjustments, etc.

i) Review a comparison of previous year, adjusted projected current year, and budget year statistics for discrepancies.
j) Review the budget working papers and cost-finding data to determine that the following have been considered before requesting specific rate changes:
   1) Hospital charges departmentally exceed cost.
   2) Routine service costs do not exceed Medicare allowable cost ceiling. If such costs are in excess, can the hospital reconcile and justify differences in costs?
   3) Has experimentation been made to estimate which rates for services should be increased in order to maximize third-party cost reimbursement based on the ratio of beneficiary covered charges to total covered charges. (See Figure 13.6.)

WORKING PAPERS REQUIRED

Third-Party Reimbursement

1) The permanent file should contain copies of the third-party reimbursement contracts that are in effect.
2) The current working paper files should contain a summary of work performed to substantiate the hospital's compliance with Title VI of the Civil Rights Act of 1968.
3) A memorandum of new accounts for the year under audit, their content, the reason for any differences between total expense per the audited financial statements, and the third-party cost reports should be included in the current year working paper files.
4) Analysis of new accounts and certain key activity accounts should be prepared and notations made as to their appropriateness and applicability to third-party reimbursement.

Cost Finding

1) A checklist such as shown in Figure 13.5 should be completed and included in the current year working papers. Notations should be made as to the consistency and effect of such bases on reimbursement.
2) Copies of the working papers used in preparing the allocation bases should be obtained and the extent of the auditor's test of their accuracy should be noted on the copies.
3) Copies of all reclassification entries should be obtained and examined for reasonableness and acceptability for third-party reimbursement.

Budgeting

1) The current year working papers should include a copy of the budget calendar and budget manual.
2) Working papers should be prepared (or copied, showing the extent of the auditor's test of accruals, budget assumptions, and problem areas.
3) The working papers should include a test of the Medicare/Medicaid budget contractual allowances. (See Figure 13.3.)

4) A memorandum should be prepared that indicates the extent of the auditor's test of the budget for the inclusion in the operating budget of such items that should be capitalized.
5) A summary of work performed should be prepared, listing the budget working papers tested, the extent of mathematical test, and the type and extent of reasonableness test used.

NOTE: If space does not present a problem, copies of the actual working papers tested should be included in the current year working paper files.

6) A schedule should be prepared showing the calculation of the ASTHR and detailing the increases in the payroll; i.e., new positions, merit increases, etc.
7) A memorandum should then be prepared summarizing the audit work performed and conclusions reached.

EXCERPT FROM A STATE'S BLUE CROSS AGREEMENT

"We agree that if at the end of any accounting period you are financially unable to pay the full cost of subscriber's benefits, we will accept a pro-rata share of your funds available in full settlement of same, and that there will be no further liability on your part or the patient's. It is understood, however, that any deficit occasioned by such pro-rata payment shall be carried as a memorandum account on your books, and that you will reimburse us whenever you are able financially to do so."

FIGURE 13.1

CONDITION OF PARTICIPATION

Regulation No. 5, Subpart F, paragraph 405.602 states:

> "A hospital, skilled nursing facility, or home health agency which meets the conditions of participation (see Subparts J, K, and L of this part) will be qualified to participate in the health insurance program and shall be eligible for payments if it is found to be in compliance with the provisions of title VI of the Civil Rights Act of 1964 (78 Stat. 252; P.L. 88-352) and if it submits to the Secretary a duly executed agreement to participate and such agreement is accepted for filing by the Secretary."

HIM-10, Chapter 1, paragraph 102, further elaborates:

> ". . . Under the provisions of that Act a participating hospital is prohibited from making a distinction on the ground of race, color, or national origin in the admission and treatment of patients; the accommodations provided; the use of the equipment and other facilities; and the assignment of personnel to provide services.
>
> Title VI prohibits discrimination on the ground of race, color, or national origin in the selection by the hospital of physicians, surgeons, dentists, or other practitioners seeking the privilege of practicing in the hospital, as well as of consultants, advisers, volunteers, and observers.
>
> The Department of Health, Education, and Welfare is responsible for investigating complaints of noncompliance."

FIGURE 13.2

INSTRUCTIONS FOR CALCULATING FOR BUDGETED MEDICARE CONTRACTUAL ALLOWANCE

I. Deduct Non-contractual Deductions from Revenue from Gross Patient Revenue to arrive at Net Patient Revenue.

Total Patient Revenue
Less: Non-contractual Deductions
Net Patient Revenue

II. Since most of "Other Income" will be offset against Operating Expense, it should be deducted from Total Controllable and Unassigned Expense to arrive at Net Reimbursable Expense.

Total Expense (Controllable and Unassigned)
Less: Other Income
Net Reimbursable Expense

III. Deduct Net Reimbursable Expense from Net Patient Revenue to arrive at Net Gain or (Loss) from Operations.

Net Patient Revenue
Less: Net Reimbursable Expense
Gain or (Loss) from Operations

IV. If Step III results in a (Loss) from Operations, no Contractual Allowance exists. If Step III results in a Gain from Operations, divide this gain by the total Budgeted Patient Days to arrive at a gain per Patient Day.

$$\frac{\text{Gain from Operations}}{\text{Total Budgeted Patient Days}} = \text{Gain per Patient Day}$$

V. Multiply the Gain per Patient Day by the Budgeted Medicare Patient Days to arrive at the Medicare Contractual Allowance.

Gain per Patient Day
Times: Budgeted Medicare Patient Days
Medicare Contractual Allowance

If the Net Gain from Operations is to be a specific percentage of Total Patient Revenue, the calculation must be amended and to a large extent becomes a "trial and error" process to achieve the precise percentage desired. After completion of Step III, the following steps must be substituted:

IV. Apply the desired percentage of Gain from Operations to the existing Total Patient Revenue to ascertain the proper dollars of Gain to be obtained.

Total Patient Revenue
Times: Desired % of Gain
Desired Gain on Operations

FIGURE 13.3

V. Deduct the Gain or (Loss) from Operations obtained in Step III from the Desired Gain on Operations in IV above to obtain additional Gain required. (Note: If a gain, although not the desired gain, exists in Step III, then the Medicare Contractual Allowance arising from that gain must be calculated and deducted from the Gain on Operation prior to performing this step.)

Desired Gain on Operations
Less: Gain on Operations
Additional Gain Required

VI. Divide the Additional Gain Required by the *Non*-Medicare Patient days to obtain additional Gain to be derived from each Non-Medicare Patient Day.

$$\frac{\text{Additional Gain Required}}{\text{Non-Medicare Patient Day}} = \text{Additional Gain per Non-Medicare Day}$$

VII. Multiply the Additional Gain per Non-Medicare Patient Day by the Total Budgeted Patient Days to obtain Additional Revenue Required to produce the Desired Gain on Operations.

Additional Gain per Non-Medicare Patient Day
Times: Total Budgeted Patient Days
Additional Revenue Required

VIII. Add this Additional Revenue Required to the existing Total Patient Revenue to arrive at the New Total Revenue.

Total Patient Revenue
Plus: Additional Revenue Required
New Total Revenue

IX. Repeat the original Steps I through V to obtain the Medicare Contractual Allowance.

X. This will not produce the *Precise* percentage of Gain from Operations desired, but will be extremely close. If the *precise* percentage is required, it becomes a matter of gradually increasing revenues and recalculating the original Steps I through V.

FIGURE 13.3 *(continued)*

_______________ HOSPITAL
936.81 REPAIR & MAINTENANCE - E.D.P.
_______________, 19___

	INITIALS	DATE
PREPARED BY	JLD	1/10
APPROVED BY	PH	1/15

FORM P-554-2 (GREEN) P-554-B2 (BUFF) Post-Rite SYSTEMS CELINA, OHIO - DALLAS - LOS ANGELES LITHO IN U.S.A.

	(1)	(2)	(3)	(4)
February	J.E. 129		$ 363 4	
July	J.E. 783		1050 4	
August	CK# 1064		200 ✓	
			1613	
Balance at 12/31/XX			2024	
Amounts not analyzed			$ 411 F	

4 - examined maintenance work orders, invoices, and cost allocations supporting proper charge for repair and maintenance.

✓ - examined invoice, purchase order, and cancelled check to XYZ Co., for the installation of cable to new using department. Amount should be capitalized - see proposed adjustment number 22.

NOTE: All postings to the account for amounts in excess of $149 were examined for propriety.

FIGURE 13.4

Suggested Cost-Finding Checklist and Workpaper Summary

Workpaper Index

A-1 Inpatient statistics—all patients:

	Beds at End of Year	In-Patient Days	Admissions	Discharges (including deaths)
Adults	______	______	______	______
Pediatrics	______	______	______	______
Total	______	______	______	______
Newborn	______	______	______	______

Labor room days included in above inpatient days ______

A-2 Inpatient statistics—Health Care Program

	TITLE V	TITLE XVIII	TITLE XIX
Adults and Pediatric Inpatient Days	______	______	______
Admissions	______	______	______
Discharges (including deaths)	______	______	______
Newborn Days	______	______	______

A-3 Nursing Service Salary Cost Differential Statistics

______ Aged Days

______ Maternity Days

______ Pediatric Days

A-4 Outpatient statistics—all patients

Occasions of Service	______
Emergency Room	______
Clinic	______
Private referred	______
Total	______

A-5 Average number of employees (full-time equivalent)

Seculars	______
Sisters	______

FIGURE 13.5

B-1 Department Statistics—area

_______ Same as prior year—note year of survey_______

_______ Specific department changes

_______ New area survey

B-2 Personnel productive hours

_______ Full year

_______ Partial survey

_______ Not available

B-3 Operation of plant

_______ Survey of usage

_______ Area from B-1

_______ Equated area

_______ Same as prior year—note year of survey_______

B-4 Repairs and maintenance

_______ Survey of time and material

_______ Area from C-1

_______ Equated area

_______ Same as prior year—note year of survey _______

B-5 Meals served

_______ Patients

_______ Cafeteria

_______ Sisters

Other _______

Total _______

_______ Not available (meals estimated)

B-6 Housekeeping

_______ Survey of hours

_______ Survey of work schedules

_______ Area from B-1

_______ Equated area

_______ Same as prior year of survey _______

B-7 Laundry and Linen

_______ Pounds distributed

_______ Equated distribution (weight or dollar value)

_______ Same as prior year—note year of survey_______

FIGURE 13.5 ***(continued)***

B-8 Central service and supply

_______ Survey of time

_______ Survey of time and material

_______ Same as prior year—note year of survey _______

_______ Not applicable

B-9 Nursing education

_______ Equated value of services

_______ Hours of service

_______ Not applicable

B-10 Medical education

_______ Hours of service

_______ Rotation schedules

_______ Not applicable

B-11 Medical records

_______ Hours of service

_______ Equated patient days

B-12 Social Service

_______ Hours of service

_______ Number of referrals

_______ Not applicable

B-13 Patient Accounting

_______ Gross revenues from services to patients

_______ Number of admissions

B-14 Departmental equipment

_______ Direct charges

_______ Area

C-1 Special Service Statistics (if available)

_______ Operations

_______ Deliveries

_______ X-ray examinations

_______ Laboratory tests

_______ Physical therapy treatments

_______ Inhalation therapy treatments

_______ Cardiology readings

_______ Pharmacy prescriptions

_______ Emergency room visits

FIGURE 13.5 ***(continued)***

ANALYSIS OF X-RAY DEPARTMENT CHARGES

Assumed Facts for a hospital serving a high percentage of Medicare patients:

—Overall inpatient Medicare utilization of department based on statistics is 52%.

—Overall inpatient Medicare utilization of department using relative values of examinations is 51%.

—Medicare utilizations by type of examination are:

Gall Bladder	40%
Abdomen	48%
Chest	52%
G.I. Series	57%*
Skull	63%*
Hip	87%*

Consideration should be given to increasing primarily the asterisked items of service because of their impact on the reimbursement ratios.

FIGURE 13.6

14

Evaluating the Hospital's System of Electronic Data Processing

The auditor must be concerned with electronic data processing (E.D.P.) planning and control.

Segregation of duties is just as important in electronic data processing system as it is in a conventional accounting system. In fact, greater care must be taken in auditing this area since a greater concentration of responsibility for data processing is lodged in this department than in any other single unit in the hospital. During your audit, if you find an absence of written instructions, manuals and/or the prevalence of oral instructions, you should regard such findings as an extreme weakness in the E.D.P. system of internal control and advise management to correct this situation as soon as possible.

The internal auditor should become familiar with the nature, scope, and capabilities of the E.D.P. system used by his hospital. This knowledge may be obtained by a review of flow charts, input and output formats, observation of computer operations, discussion with computer manufacturer representatives, and a review of the computer operations manuals.

Computer Problems Are Usually People Problems

Often times, those non-members of the E.D.P. mystique make the invalid assumption that all weaknesses in internal control and systems will be solved by merely putting "it" on the computer—"it" meaning whatever application the hospital is experiencing difficulty with.

For example, a group of hospitals had been using a shared hospital accounting system for approximately three years when one of the hospitals hired a new controller. The new controller installed what was considered to be an elaborate system to account for and control the debits and credits to the accounts receivable file.

At the end of the first complete month after initiating the controls, the controller saw that the total accounts receivable, per his manual controls, differed from the accounts receivable control total as generated by the computer. After wrestling with this problem for two months, the controller had the director of the shared computer center spend a day at the hospital reviewing and analyzing the problem. The day concluded with no significant findings. This unusual occurrence continued for several months up to and including the month when the auditors came to perform their annual examination.

Finally, the controller assigned a clerk to run an adding machine tape of the year-end detailed aged trial balance of accounts receivable. The aged trial balance showed the total accounts receivable as well as a breakdown of the balance between patient pay and any one of four types of insurance plans. To everyone's surprise the total of the accounts receivable per the computer-prepared aged trial balance was greater than the computer-prepared total of the same report. The $45,000 difference was the total amount of the insurance balances shown to be due from the fourth type of insurance plan.

Protective Procedure

This weakness had not been detected for over three years in a shared group comprised of ten hospitals with an average capacity of 350+ beds. There were several ways this weakness could have been determined earlier:

1) A closer review of the computer programs to determine how the computer arrived at the grand total of accounts receivable. This would have revealed that the instructions did not call for the computer to pick up the total of the fourth insurance proration plan.
2) The use of separately prepared batch totals for all changes made to the accounts receivable file, then using the batch control totals to reconcile, at month end, the balance of accounts receivable rather than depending completely upon data processing reports.
3) The use of adequately trained and supervised staff to use the reports generated by the computer. Such individuals would have known how to use the data to reconcile the accounts receivable—not just "juggle figures" until they arrived at two comparable totals.

Those who have had little experience with computer operations will readily appreciate the value of an objective basis from which to begin your audit of this segment of hospital operations. The internal control checklist will serve as an invaluable aid in this regard. The reader is reminded again that the use of the internal control check list does not negate the need for judgment on the part of the auditor. The list merely provides a framework around which an informed decision may be reached regarding the adequacy of the system of internal control.

REVIEWING THE CONTROLS

The auditor should have a mastery of computer jargon in order to do an adequate evaluation of the E.D.P. system. As is true in all areas of the hospital that you audit, it is incumbent upon you to enter discussions as well informed as possible. In preparing this checklist, it is assumed that the reader has a reasonable understanding of computer terminology. The internal control checklist for this segment has been divided into logical segments to assist you in developing an orderly approach to the evaluation of the strengths and weaknesses of the E.D.P. system and procedures. The sections and sub-sections are:

I. ORGANIZATION CONTROLS
- a) Segregation of duties
- b) Systems development
- c) Operations
- d) Back-up procedures

II. APPLICATION CONTROLS
- a) Input controls
- b) Output controls
- c) Processing controls
- d) File controls and record retention
- e) System implementation

Reviewing for Adequate Segregation of Duties

Q. Is the E.D.P. department independent of all operating units for which it processes data?

- If the data processing department is not included in the fiscal services division, what problems are being encountered that could lead to increases in accounts receivable, delays in posting charges, and delays in preparing financial statements.
- Does the department manager of the data processing area have other department responsibilities. Does the performance of these other duties interfere with the performance of his primary responsibilities.

Q. Are future applications for E.D.P. the decision of one person or is there a steering committee?

- Does the steering committee approve the E.D.P. policies.
- To whom does the individual or steering committee report.
- Does the individual or steering committee have a formal definition of authority and responsibilities.
- Does the individual or steering committee hold regular meetings.
- Are formal meeting minutes prepared and available for review.
- Does the individual or steering committee issue progress reports to the individuals who have received copies of the overall plan of future applications.
- Are there regular communications from the individual or steering committee for future applications to the Administrative Staff and department managers to keep the users informed and interested in electronic data processing.

Q. Are E.D.P. employees prohibited from having authority, responsibility, or duties in any other department?

- Are data processing employees called upon to relieve, because of their familiarity with the projects, in the payroll department or other areas that relate to the processing of accounting data.
- Do any E.D.P. employees:
  1) initiate data,

2) initiate master file changes, or
3) have final approval of results.

- Are the duties of the operating staff periodically rotated and all personnel required to take vacations.
- Are E.D.P. employees covered by fidelity insurance.

Q. *If the hospital uses an outside service bureau, how is data protected?*

- If a batch system is used, can data in transit be readily reconstructed if lost in an accident.
- How does the service bureau protect against the commingling of data.

Reviewing Systems Development, Documentation and Maintenance

Q. *Is there a written overall plan of future applications?*

- To whom has the plan been communicated.
- Is there a good mixture of professional backgrounds to give a variety of input into the plan development.

Q. *Are approvals of future applications supported by feasibility studies?*

- Are the feasibility studies prepared by inhouse personnel who may be prejudiced in their recommendations.
- If independent personnel are not being used in developing feasibility studies, has anyone requested that these independent sources submit cost estimates or are such studies routinely dismissed as being "too costly."

Q. *Is there a steering committee or an individual who approves all future applications?*

- Does this person or committee also review implementation schedules.
- Is this same approval required for modifications to the application.

Q. *Do user departments review and approve:*

a) systems specifications,
b) program specifications,
c) error rejection criteria,
d) data for testing programs,
e) results of program testing,
f) results of parallel test, and
g) systems documentation?

- Does this advance review and approval include an appraisal of internal controls by the user department, the internal auditors, and/or the independent auditor.
- Is this same approval required for modifications.

Q. *Is there a standard format that is used in the assembling of new programs for the program file?*

- Have new employees deviated from this format, which will lead to later conflicts.
- Are the block diagram symbols and procedures standardized.

Q. Are program techniques standardized for table look-up or search methods, program switches, tape record blocking, and other routines?

- Are such techniques posted.
- Are all standardized procedures compiled in a manual that is kept current.
- Are symbolic programming labels or tags standardized and included in the programming manual.

Q. Are all addresses standardized as to core location and use?

Q. Are program-testing procedures established?

- Are programmers prohibited from operating on live data.
- If yes, do they use previously processed data, error test data, or valid test data.
- Are the results of this testing reviewed by the using departments.
- Is testing done during hours when the fewest transactions are processed by the hospital.

Q. Before an application has been implemented are the following reviews conducted by qualified individuals?

a) initial file creation
b) training programs
c) program and systems test
d) parallel test run results
e) results of initial processing
f) program and system documentation

- How is it evident that these reviews have been conducted.
- Is such documentation retained for a reasonable length of time.

Q. Does the current documentation for each computer program contain:

a) narrative description of the system and program,
b) system flow charts and program block diagrams,
c) specifications for input data, output reports, and files,
d) program listings,
e) operator's manual,
f) written procedures for testing new program before use,
g) file retention, and
h) backup procedures?

- Are program changes cleared through persons of authority other than the programmers directly involved in the preparation of the programs.
- Are program changes documented as to the reason for change and the effect of change.
- Are there written notes as to the agreement of what source data is to be ready for processing and what output is required; i.e., format, etc.
- Does the documentation specify when the reports are due and how various transactions and exceptions are to be handled.

Q. Does the operator's manual contain:

a) setup instructions,
b) description of input layouts

c) description of output layouts,
d) operating messages (errors, halts, and required action),
e) procedures for labeling and disposition of input, and
f) procedures for labeling and disposition of output?

- Are the operating instructions so clear and simple that no oral instructions are required to operate the programs.
- Do the instructions identify the tape units or disks on which various input and output files will be mounted.
- Do they specify console switch settings.

Q. *Are there written procedures for program maintenance that provide for a written request for a program change?*

- Is the reason for change stated.
- Is the effect of the change stated.
- Does the request contain an approval by a responsible individual.
- Does the request state that a test of the change is needed prior to acceptance.

Auditing the Computer Operations Controls

Q. *Is there a schedule of daily computer operations?*

- Is the schedule of computer operations prepared in advance and compared with a summary of actual use.
- Does the summary indicate at least the following detail:
  a) normal production
  b) re-run time
  c) program development
  d) program testing
  e) system software maintenance
  f) hardware maintenance
  g) down time
  h) idle time
- Are substantial schedule deviations followed up by a supervisor.
- How are unscheduled computer runs authorized.
- What exceptions are required for night shift operations.

Q. *Is there a control unit responsible for recording and expediting all data processing reports, including the number issued?*

- Do they also monitor the due dates of the reports to see that reports are issued on a timely basis.
- Is a daily report of the jobs processed reviewed by a responsible person.

Q. *What procedures are followed to control data files?*

- Does the hospital employ a full-time librarian with exclusive storage control.
- What exceptions to library or testing procedures are made for night shift operations.
- Do the library procedures require that all files be catalogued and a record be made of all files issued and returned to the library.
- Are adequate precautions taken to protect live data files during program testing; i.e., label checking by program or system.

Q. *Are there adequate controls maintained over operating programs?*

- Does the hospital employ a full-time librarian with exclusive storage control.
- Are program version numbers or change levels printed out when used.
- Are operating programs periodically matched with a duplicate copy.

Q. *Is there a current operating manual for the department?*

- Are operators' manuals detailed enough to enable computer operators to run programs without referring to program listings.
- Are operators' manuals detailed enough to enable computer operators to run programs without referring to the programmers.

Q. *Are current organizational charts and flow charts available?*

- After the flow charts are prepared, does a responsible person review and approve such flow charts.
- Are the flow charts prepared in such a manner that they are easily understood.

Q. *Does the general housekeeping of the area indicate that the employees are conscientious in the performance of their duties or does it indicate a possible sloppy and lackadaisical attitude?*

- Could a bad appearance be attributable to a lack of adequate working and storage space.

Q. *Has management established a policy regarding visitors, neatness, smoking, etc., in the computer center?*

- Is this policy posted in a conspicuous place.
- Is this policy adhered to.

Q. *Are the manufacturer's recommendations followed?*

- Cleaning.
- Temperature and humidity requirements.
- Storage of magnetic tape reels or disks.
- Hardware service by qualified engineers on a regular basis.

How to Review the Adequacy of Backup, Reconstruction Procedures, and Sundry Items

Q. *What controls are used to prevent damage to the computer equipment and the need for backup facilities?*

- Is the computer room located where it is secure and not readily found by outsiders.
- Is it adequately protected from fire and flood.
- Is the computer equipment separated from the file storage and data preparation area.
- Is preventive maintenance of equipment scheduled.

Q. *Does the hospital have a formal agreement for standby equipment?*

- Is the hospital informed of changes in the backup facilities computer system configuration.

- Is the location visited periodically for familiarization.
- Are the hospital's programs run on a test basis.

Q. *Are duplicate copies of either the source decks, object decks, or program listings maintained away from the E.D.P. premises as a protection against loss?*

- How often are these materials updated.
- By whom and how evidenced.

Q. *Are backup copies of data files maintained and available for file reconstruction?*

- How often is the status of this backup checked.
- By whom and how evidenced.

Q. *Is the following insurance coverage maintained for data processing?*

a) physical damage to the equipment
b) loss of data files
c) business interruption
d) employee fidelity bonds

Q. *Does the hospital keep a record of machine maintenance?*

- Is preventive maintenance always performed on schedule.
- Are adequate facilities available for storage and use of maintenance materials and supplies.

Q. *Are personnel adequately screened before being assigned duties in sensitive areas of data processing?*

- Does the hospital use psychological testing.
- Did the background investigation confirm the education of the applicant.
- Was there confirmation of prior employment experience.

Q. *If the hospital uses a service bureau, is there a written contract between the parties?*

- Does the contract provide for
  a) cancellation.
  b) penalties where the service bureau's performance is unsatisfactory.
  c) the service bureau to provide full systems documentation to the hospital.
- Is the basis for the service bureau's charge for its services specified in the contract.
- Does the contract require adequate insurance coverage to protect the hospital.

APPLICATION CONTROLS

Auditing the Hospital's Data Input Controls

Q. *Are predetermined control totals established independently of the E.D.P. department?*

- Are these control totals reviewed and reconciled daily by someone in the user department before submission.
- Are differences in control totals reconciled on a timely basis.

- Can the control established by the user department be identified as:
  a) document count
  b) batch numbering
  c) sequential numbering
  d) financial control totals
  e) hash control totals

Q. *Are input documents prenumbered?*

- Are numbered documents accounted for by the control clerk.
- Is it feasible to continue controlling data to be processed by sequentially numbered batches.

Q. *Are there adequate controls over the conversion of data to machine readable form?*

- Is the input data reviewed for acceptability before giving for keypunching.
- Is a self-check digit employed on patient numbers, chart of account numbers, employee numbers, and charge compendium items.
- Are keypunching and key-verifying instructions documented.

Q. *Are the following controls recorded and maintained by the user department as well as E.D.P.?*

a) batch register
b) input suspense file
c) sequence number register

- Are these controls checked and action taken on differences.
- To whom are differences reported and how is it indicated that appropriate action was taken.

Q. *Are internal header labels prepared for all transactions?*

- Is all data processed in sequentially numbered batches.
- Are all source documents identified with batch number and cancelled to prevent reprocessing.

Q. *Are internal header labels tested by program instructions to determine if the proper input data is being used?*

Q. *Are internal trailer labels containing control totals generated for all magnetic tapes or disks?*

- Does the control unit use a document register or other positive method of comparing machine run totals with control totals.
- Is the responsibility fixed and adequate procedures in effect for tracing and correcting input errors.

Q. *Are internal trailer labels tested by program instructions to determine whether all records were processed?*

Q. *Are corrections identified and recorded in such a manner that duplicate correction will not occur?*

- Are all instructions to keypunch operators or other personnel involved written in clear and concise form.
- Is there a procedural manual that can be followed by new employees.

Q. If date of transmission is used, what other procedures are used to determine that the receiving station receives all of the data correctly and the sending station receives an acknowledgment of transmission accuracy?

Q. Are the following individual data items reported by the computer program?

a) all data
b) accepted data
c) warnings on accepted data
d) rejected data

Q. What controls are maintained to determine that all transmissions are received and are complete and accurate?

- Message count.
- Sequentially numbered transmissions.
- Computer response to sendor.
- Dual transmissions.
- Character or bit count.

Q. Does control exist over rejected input to ensure that all items are corrected and reintroduced without undue delay?

- Who reviews the rejects and how are they checked.
- How is this evidenced.

Q. What controls are maintained to prevent unauthorized access by terminals?

- Passwords.
- User codes.
- Terminal codes.
- Physical security.
- Badges.
- Terminal locks.
- Are these controls checked.
- By whom and how evidenced.

Reviewing the Hospital Computer's Controls

Processing in this chapter includes all functions performed from the point at which the computer receives data in machine language to the final report. The auditor should be familiar with how data is processed, with what form, and with what results. This information may be obtained from flow charts and block diagrams.

Q. Is a record of error halt or error messages retained for review by someone independent of the operating staff?

Q. Is the supervision of console operators sufficient to prevent unauthorized program changes or entry of data through the console?

- Are the situations whereby data may be exerted or extracted by the use of the console set forth in writing and limited to circumstances that can not be handled through the stored program.
- Are console printouts controlled and reviewed by responsible individuals other than the operators who are familiar with the activity being performed.

- Are console printouts labeled so as to be reasonably intelligible.

Q. *Do programs test for valid codes in input data?*

- Through the use of programmed double calculation.
- By using validity checks.
- Through limit or reasonableness checks.

Q. *Are changes in program rate tables and other constants initiated in writing by persons authorized to do so?*

- Are all such changes recorded and retained for audit.
- Are operators cautious not to accept oral instructions.
- Are operators instructed to contact programmers directly when errors are detected.
- Is there a positive follow-up to determine if corrections are made on errors found by the machine.
- Is the use of external switches held to a minimum and are the instructions for their use set forth in writing.

Reviewing the E.D.P. Output Controls

Q. *Are checkpoints provided in lengthy processing runs and/or programmed or external restart instructions provided in case a checkpoint fails to balance?*

Q. *Is output reviewed for completeness by a responsible person?*

- Is a report distribution file maintained.
- Are output control totals balanced against the predetermined input totals by the department being serviced.

Q. *What controls are maintained over forms such as invoices and refund vouchers that require special control?*

- Prenumbering.
- Storage in locked cabinets.
- Batch list.
- Number or count reconciliation.

Q. *Is there a report available for use in tracing transactions through the system?*

- How often is the report prepared.
- Is there sufficient reference information on the report to permit tracing to source documents.
- Is there sufficient reference information on both the report and source documents to permit tracing all input data and totals through to a final output or total.
- Is there sufficient reference on the report and source documents to permit tracing totals on the report to detail items on the report or detail source documents.

How to Question the E.D.P. Record Retention and File Controls

Q. *Is there a written plan for retaining original source documents?*

- What provisions are made for backup and reconstruction of master files.
  a) retention of input media to update or re-create
  b) duplicate records, including manual records
  c) regular dump of files (random files)
  d) sequential files
- Are at least two previous generations of files maintained in order to reconstruct the records if necessary; i.e., grandfather, father, son routines (sequential files).
- Is at least one generation maintained in a location away from the storage area.

Q. *Do existing controls reasonably ensure that the latest version of significant files is used for processing?*

- Is a library maintained under the supervision of a librarian.
- Do external tape labels contain such information as reel or disk number, serial number, number of reels or disks in the file, program identification number, date created, retention date, density, and drive number.
- What controls are maintained over the file by the E.D.P. department:
  a) financial totals,
  b) hash totals,
  c) record counts,
  d) file label contents.
- Do the programs test for header and trailer labels each time a new tape is accessed or the end of the tape is sensed.
- Do header labels have the following data:
  a) program identification number,
  b) reel number,
  c) date created, and
  d) date obsolete.
- Do tailer labels have the following data:
  a) block count,
  b) record count,
  c) hash totals, and
  d) end of reel or end of file designation.
- Are there physical controls to prevent the inadvertent erasure of tapes.

Q. *Has a policy been established for the retirement of tape reels or disks that have extensive read or write errors?*

Q. *What controls are maintained over masterfile changes?*

- Is this material ever issued to persons outside of the data processing area.
- If yes, is it issued only after the issuance of a written request and receipt of written authorization.
- Are masterfile changes checked by the user department.
- Does the user department review the detail items processed.
- In the event of an unmatched or invalid masterfile change, does:
  a) the entire transaction reject,
  b) the entire transaction go to a suspense file,
  c) only the invalid portion of the transaction reject, or
  d) a listing prints.

- Are masterfile contents periodically checked by:
  a) a full listing printed and reviewed, or
  b) periodic tests against detail items; i.e., physical count.
- By whom and how evidenced.

Q. Do the record keeping and retention procedures provide audit trails for external audit purposes as well as internal audit purposes?

Reviewing System Implementation Controls

Q. Is there adequate segregation of duties independent from users?

- Are the user department and data processing responsibilities segregated.
- Is there no overlap of duties in the data processing functions.
- Are the duties in the data processing group periodically rotated and all personnel required to take vacations.

Q. Do existing procedures ensure proper controls over the development and maintenance of and provide sufficient documentation for system applications?

- Before development, is the application approved by a steering committee.
- Before testing, is it reviewed by the user department.
- Have the independent auditors recommended control features for the new application.
- Is the sufficient testing done with valid test data.
- Is a pre-implementation review made by the user department, internal auditor, and E.D.P. department.
- Is the documentation complete and reviewed by a responsible person.

Q. Do the procedures ensure effective control over the computer operations and access to data files and programs for the applications?

- Are runs scheduled.
- Are unscheduled runs reported to management.
- Is access to the computer limited to authorized personnel only.
- Is a librarian utilized to limit access to data files and operational programs.

Q. Do the backup and reconstruction procedures provide for reasonable continuity of processing this application in the event of a disaster?

- Have the programs been tested on the standby facilities.
- Are duplicate copies of the programs stored in a remote location.
- Are backup copies of the data files maintained.

THE AUDIT

The Audit Objective

The primary objective in the audit of the hospital's system of electronic data processing is to verify that duties are properly segregated and that adequate controls are present to ensure the security of the computer, programs, and files. You should also be concerned with the flexibility of the systems and the ability of the department to meet the growing demands of the future.

To ensure that a computer application is under control, there are general controls that apply to all applications as well as additional audit techniques peculiar to the specific application under consideration. The general controls relate to documentation, record, security, and operational security. Specific controls must be discussed on an application-by-application basis.

The minimum documentation required for any application is whatever is necessary for the system to be completely understood by all affected groups. Each system must be so documented as to provide for changes without risking undetected errors. Finally, operating instructions should be so complete that the computer may be operated properly, yet appropriately restricted to avoid unauthorized console intervention. The required documentation must therefore be at four levels of detail.

Auditing the Documentation

1) Obtain a copy of and review the general flow charts that explain the entire operation from the creation of a master file to the development of all related outputs.

> NOTE: This type of generalized flow chart should include a simple explanation of the overall flow of data and should be supported by complete, detailed operating procedures.

2) Secondly, review the flow charts that show the logic of the computer processing.

> NOTE: These charts are essentially blowups of the charts mentioned in step one, except that they should highlight all control points structured into the procedure.

3) In auditing the third level of documentation, review the program listings that detail the computer instructions. Make this review to determine if changes have been made since this program was last run.

> NOTE: This level of documentation is critical in determining the use and role of test checks.

4) Review the operating instructions to determine if the instructions are specific enough, yet limited in scope or explanation to minimize the possibility of deliberate manipulation of the programs.

> NOTE: This fourth level of documentation should require that the operators and other computer room personnel function as mechanics following instructions set forth in mechanical terms.

Auditing the E.D.P. Security

1) Review the storage of the magnetically stored records to see if the current status of records could be reconstructed with minimum effort; i.e., off-site storage of master files and transaction documents or files.

2) Examine the magnetic records (tapes or disks) for external, visual labels to ensure the proper use of records.

> NOTE: The files should also have internal labels.

3) Review the computer programs to see if meaningful control totals are collected so that in the event of a computer malfunction, a "flag" will be raised before the computer proceeds to the next phase of processing.

4) Examine the computer log to determine that the following data is being recorded:

a) description of job or transaction,
b) operator,
c) elapsed time, and
d) description of difficulties.

5) Review the "run book" at the computer console to determine that a rotation program is in effect to prevent one person from having complete control of a specific application.

When these general requirements as to documentation, record security, and operational security are met, and a controlled situation exists, the audit of a specific computer application is relatively simple. Each individual application must be so controlled that all data is processed accurately and consistently throughout the input, processing, and output phases of the procedure. An auditor must therefore evaluate each application for its own specific and peculiar requirements for controls and for special techniques or programs.

Beyond these controls, each application or system must be evaluated as to its susceptibility to error or fraud. Every system involves people, and over the years people have demonstrated an amazing ability to devise new ways of beating any system.

The auditor therefore must use imagination to develop special audit programs aimed at closing suspected loopholes in the control techniques. For example, in auditing the computerized accounts payable system, the auditor may request that a specialized program be written for his sole use, which would compare last month's outstanding invoices against the current month's cash disbursements. Any item not on the last month's list, and not a current bill, would be printed out and investigated by the auditor. This technique, therefore, would surface a situation where an employee was creating a revolving credit account by lapping payments to vendors.

The day when auditors could successfully audit around the computer is rapidly disappearing. This should challenge the auditor, for this situation affords the creative auditor an opportunity to render greater service to the hospital.

WORKING PAPERS REQUIRED

The minimum audit working papers would consist of a copy of the flow chart depicting the entire operation of the overall system, notes regarding the adequacy of the logic of the computer program control points, and notes regarding the extent of the auditor's examination of the computer instructions and operator instructions. The working papers should also include a summary of work performed, detailing the steps followed by the auditor to satisfy himself with the adequacy of the E.D.P. security measures.

Then, depending upon the complexity of the computer operation, the auditor would maintain in the current year files such items as test decks, special audit program routines, and detailed flow charts of application. Should storage space present a problem for the auditor, a detailed analysis of such items as test decks and audit program routines could be prepared and attached to the results of such tests.

This hospital function, and in fact the industry, provides an interesting and challenging opportunity for the independent and internal auditors.

Index

S

T

U

V

W